HOUSES are DESIGNED by GENIUSES and BUILT by GORILLAS

An Insider's Guide to Designing and Building a Home

by Bob Johnson

D1435758

ADDAX
PUBLISHING
G R O U P

Published by Addax Publishing Group

Design and Typography by Anita Stumbo
Cover Design by Jerry Hirt
Edited by John Dodderidge
Cartoons by Brad Kirkland

Addax Publishing Group
8643 Hauser Drive · Suite 235
Lenexa, KS 66215

ISBN: 1-886110-48-4

Distributed to the trade by:
Andrews McMeel Publishing
4520 Main Street
Kansas City, MO 64111

Printed in the United States of America

1 3 5 7 9 10 8 6 4 2

Library of Congress Cataloging-in-Publication Data

Johnson, Bob, 1952–
    Houses are designed by geniuses and built by gorillas: An insider's guide to designing and building
a home/by Bob Johnson. p. cm. Includes index.
    ISBN 1-886110-48-4 (alk.paper)
    1. House construction—Amateurs' manuals. I. Title.
    TH4817.3.J646   1998   97-49009
    690'.837—dc21   CIP

This book is dedicated to the memory of my father,
Colonel Harvey W. Johnson

Acknowledgments

I would like to acknowledge the following people:

My brother rat Roland Lazenby for helping me get this book published. Thanks BR.

My mentor Ken Perkins, of Hendersonville, NC, who helped me learn the skill of home design.

My friend Hans Baker, of Mooreseville, NC, who helped me learn the skill of home building.

My Aunt Priscilla, who provided encouragement, guidance and inspiration.

*My wife Pamela and three sons Martin, Jeremiah, and Spencer,
for being the wonderful people that they are—I am blessed.*

Contents

Introduction

Bob Vila is working for Sears now. Norm Abram has his own TV show. So does Roy Underhill and Dean Johnson. These guys aren't going to build your house. They never were. Your house is going to be built in the real world with real carpenters, plumbers, masons, and carpet layers. While your house design might be real genius, it is going to be built by gorillas.

This is not to say that all builders are gorillas. In fact, most are highly skilled and fully capable of translating your dream home into reality. And not all design is genius. The world is full of poorly designed homes. These often home grown disasters leak, rot and function so poorly that they are sometimes closed down as uninhabitable. Even the most capable builder cannot save a poorly designed home.

With a workforce full of gorillas and home design relying on genius to function, how can you avoid the pitfalls of building in America today? The answers are found in this book. They are subtle, simple and methodical. This book will bridge the gap between the genius of your design and the reality of building in America today. It will show you the time tested basics of designing and building a house. Along the way, you will obtain a better understanding of the industry. This knowledge will help you more successfully manage the process and keep you out of trouble.

Starting with a discussion of design and architecture, this book covers all aspects of the creation of a home. Using an actual house, you will see how ideas are transformed into blueprints. It continues with code issues, permits, laws and regulations. This is followed by a review of the many building options available to you. Determining budgets and specifications are discussed. Hiring and managing subs as well as scheduling the work rounds out the review. It ends with the completion of a home and discusses common new home problems. Along the way, this book uses dozens of "war stories" that relate actual problems encountered in the building of numerous homes around the country. More importantly, these war stories tell you how these problems were solved.

No matter what your interest in the designing and building of your home, you will find this book invaluable. If you've hired professionals to do all the work, you still will be required be make dozens of important decisions about your home. This book will guide your choices and put your mind at rest. If you want a more active role, it will show you the shortcuts and the pitfalls. This knowledge will result in a better designed, more properly functioning home that will be built closer to schedule and on budget.

Nevertheless, this book will not make you a design genius or a master carpenter. It covers just the basics and points out the common hazards. It shows you the reality of the work force and what to expect. Building a house is a complicated undertaking that is not for the fainthearted. You will meet frustration and see waste and error.

While your house design might be real genius, it is going to be built by gorillas.

There is a saying in the industry that "there is no such thing as a perfect house." There are excellent homes and beautiful homes, but no perfect homes.

One of the goals of this book is get that message across. Following the basics and the methods of this book will get you closer to that mythical *perfect* home. You will have a much more pleasurable trip if you build your home in the real world rather than a dream world. The gorillas are there, they show up every day. You cannot ignore them and they are not going away. However, they can be tamed and you can still have your dream home. You just need to learn how to get along with them.

This book was written from notes I made for the many seminars and college courses I taught to people interested in designing and building their own home. The seminars I presented were to help people design custom homes using building systems (kits) that I sold. In working for some of the biggest "kit" home manufacturers in the country, it was in our best interest that our homes were well designed in both function and appearance. Beyond that, we hoped that these homes were built within a prescribed budget, on schedule and within acceptable quality levels. A common aspect of building systems is that they were finished by the owner or local contractors. However, our building system formed the core of the home as well as the catalyst for undertaking the project. We were still held accountable for the entire process.

My seminars were intended to ensure that process went smoothly and that the customers were happy with their homes. I found that knowing what to expect usually resulted in a happy customer and a better house. I also found that most people wanted quick answers and did not want to get bogged down in detail. Therefore, my seminars were kept simple, to the fact, yet were presented in an entertaining manner. I've carried this style over to this book.

The college classes I taught were more generic. I had a rare distinction of having a broad background in many different aspects of building. This ranged from actually being a gorilla on a framing crew to being a superintendent for a national production builder. Later experience included being a manager in a number of different building system companies. There I designed hundreds of homes as well as taught other builders throughout the country how to build with these systems. I had to ensure that our homes complied to regional building codes and became an expert in many of the technical aspects of building systems, especially energy efficiency. I even had the experience of selling new subdivision homes from models as well as being a land developer. This experience included a thorough knowledge of mortgage financing.

About 10 years ago, I took all this knowledge and experience, combined it with my seminar notes and created a college course. The course filled up the very first day it was offered and had a waiting list. I was amazed at the interest people had in designing and building their own homes. Their hunger for knowledge was contagious and became fun for me as well. As my career took me to other regions in the country, I took my course with me. While making adjustments for local codes and building conditions, I found a universal interest in building homes. This book shares that interest and enthusiasm.

In conclusion, this book is intended to give you an insider's view of the building of a house. It presents the genius of how it should be done as well as the gorilla of how it often is done. Hopefully your home will have more evidence of genius than gorilla. Good luck! ∎

The gorillas are there, they show up every day. You cannot ignore them and they are not going away. However, they can be tamed and you can still have your dream home. You just need to learn how to get along with them.

1

Why Does Everyone Want to Design and Build Their Own Home?

The Joys of Home Ownership

Nothing beats owning your own home. It is truly the American dream. And uniquely American, as no other country in the world has the home ownership rate (about 60%) that America has nor a system of government that requires it for its success. If you've never owned a home before, you don't know what you're missing. It's like tasting butter after a lifetime of margarine. It's your biggest investment and the core of your net worth. It will make you richer or break your heart. It's one of the few things that gets better and more valuable with age. Any improvement to your home will almost surely increase its value. You can almost never go wrong owning a house. Almost.

Beyond this, owning a house lets you express who you are and how you live. Home ownership, however, is full of voodoo, witchcraft and mysticism. You have to live in the *right* house, in the *right* neighborhood, built by the *right* builder, on the *right* side of town. Your house, like your car, tells the world how they should think about you. You can show your wealth or be so wealthy that you don't need to show it. Your lifestyle is reflected in your house. Grand up-scale living for entertaining and showing off or warm and inviting for the home-body in you. Slick, sterile and stainless steel or an English cottage with heavy timber. A cabin in the woods or a showcase on Main Street. It's all there waiting for you.

If you own your home now (after renting), you know how pleasant it is to not have to deal with a landlord. Damage deposits, fights upon checking out, huge sums of money at both ends of the lease. And leases that need to be broken and are so hard to break. Yes, renting is a hassle, and makes home ownership such a dream. On the other side, when you own it, it's your baby. If something goes wrong, you have to fix it. You also have to cut the grass, repaint and fix the broken doors. Yet, this usually is not a bad trade off.

In This Chapter . . .

▲ Should you own or rent?

▲ Who loves you when you own?

▲ Should you design your own house?

> 66 *The strength of a nation lies in the homes of its people."*
>
> —ABRAHAM LINCOLN

Probably the best thing about owning your own home is that it is the last great government handout. They've taken away most all of the other good deals. IRAs and tax credits went away when too many people saw the good deal they were (at the same time the government saw the loss of revenue). The mortgage tax credit is the last and most sacred of the government cows. It's not going to be gored on anyone's watch. Now you probably think that's because of the building industry's huge lobby. Yes, it is large and powerful and arguably the largest in the country. Construction is big business. But so is banking, AT&T and the airlines. They certainly got skewered and not necessarily to everyone's benefit. I'm not sure my lower phone bills are worth the barrage of sales calls (switch to MCI, Sprint, LCI, ALTELL, my uncle's new phone company) I get at work or while I'm trying to eat my supper. The 32 numbers I have to punch in to use a calling card on someone else's network has brought me close to murder.

The real reason housing is supported so fully by the government is because homeowners make better citizens. Remember when you were renting? Did you really care about zoning, land use regulations, school districting, etc.? Probably not. When you own the property, however, then you care about everything, from property values to zoning to stopping all the growth (right after you move in). Homeowners have a stake in the country and our democracy works best when people are interested in their communities. If you own a house, you're going to pay attention to the issues at home and not so much about the rain forest as in your renting days. Home ownership is going to make you not only a better citizen, but a better parent, a better consumer and a better taxpayer.

The High Costs of Home Ownership

Well, if home ownership is so wonderful, why doesn't everyone own a house? Beyond the main reason that the cost to get in the game can be quite high, it's not always the best deal going. Owning a home is like having kids. Like it or not, they are yours forever. You own that puppy and it needs to be fed every month. It also has many mouths to feed, some you didn't know about as a renter, like property taxes, insurance premiums and monthly payments that your new landlord (the bank) isn't going to be as understanding about being late on. Your house is not maintenance free, either. There are things that need to be done on almost a monthly basis. Left undone, it can get real expensive later on. Deferred maintenance takes on a whole new meaning when it's your house.

Another reason you might not want to own a house right now is that they are expensive to sell and sometimes can take all you put into them (and more) to get rid of. The going rate is 6% of the selling price which goes away from your column at closing and into someone else's. While there is some accounting magic (depreciation expense, tax credits, etc.) that is really helpful when you sell, if you didn't live in your home long enough for it to appreciate (which it should), you could be in a world of hurt. Also, if your local nuclear power station had a recent meltdown or the Serb nation just moved in next door, you've got some property valuation problems. It also doesn't help if you're living in boom/bust markets like California and the Northeast, which has made just as many people poor as it has rich.

Your best bet on buying a home is that you plan to be in it at least three years and that prices have been fairly steady for the past six months to a year. It also helps to be working for a stable, forward looking company and your marriage looks secure. If "boom town" is used as a headline in a local newspaper story more than once a month, be careful. It's hard to look at housing statistics and get a real sense of this. Besides, the guys who are reading and reporting on these figures are wrong over half the time. Sometimes, it's just a gut call.

The high costs of the game vary around the country and are constantly changing. The cheapest out of pocket way into a house is through a large building company that knows how to package a mortgage. Since you're looking to build your own home, you might not be able to benefit from the big builder's mortgage game. However, if the banks in your town are familiar with these games, maybe they can help you. The best mortgage you will see is probably a 90–95% loan. This deal is usually combined with a buy down on a mortgage rate with the builder paying some of the closing costs. What this means is that you can get into a house for a couple of thousand bucks down. Not a bad deal in a growing market and you with a steady job and loving spouse.

The other side of the coin is less attractive. Let's say you live 100 miles away from Metropolis and the local bankers make Mr. Potter in *It's a Wonderful Life* look like Donald Trump. These guys will be talking about 60–80% loans, with huge up-front money before you even get to see a monthly payment. Forget about buy downs and closing cost giveaways. It's their money and you're not going to get any if they can help. At least not if you're building your own house on the lower forty you just bought from cousin Wilbur. We'll talk about how to get around these guys later, but they can try your patience and are high on the list of people trying to keep you away from your dream.

Creative Genius in Us All

So now we know why it might be a good idea to own a new home, what about designing one? Don't most people just pick a plan? Well, yes, sort of. Except there hasn't been a plan made that didn't need a push here, a tug there and a charming touch just to make it yours. There are roughly 35 plan book magazines published every month. Each with an average of 200 plans. Month after month, year after year. Do you know how many of these plans get built exactly as they are drawn each year? The number "0" comes to mind. Nobody builds the plans exactly as they are drawn, often for very good reason, like how they fit the land or the budget. "Great plan, but too expensive, cut out two feet here." Or "Wonderful plan, but I need three more feet in the master bedroom." It just doesn't happen.

And then there is the other reason. Not only do people want their house to be theirs alone, but it also has to be a monument to them and their very particular and exciting lifestyle. If they have enough money (and ego), they're going to start *a cappella.* Frank Lloyd Wright reborn. It's their baby, their masterpiece.

WHEN SHOULD YOU BUY A HOUSE

▲ You have a stable job

▲ You plan to live in the area at least three years

▲ You have a loving spouse

▲ The builders are competitive

▲ Growing but not "boom" town

▲ Progressive financing is available

Damn the codes, the appraisers, the resale market. In fact, damn everyone living there except themselves. This is a life's work and the creative juices are going to flow. It's here where many of the home built disasters begin, usually resulting in a house that can't be built (or won't stay up), doesn't function properly, is unsafe or unhealthy, rots away, or can never be resold. Not to mention a budget that has no chance of being met. The joys go out the window. ■

2

Who Says You Can Do It and What Can You Save?

What Does the Government Say About it?

Housing is a cottage industry. While there are giant builders in giant cities, most houses are built in small cities and towns all over the country. The top 100 builders do not even build ten percent of the houses built in America. Therefore, chances are you're going to be one of the few dozen or so houses built in your county this year. Every place is different, so you have to find out how your state and county deals with owner-built housing. Call your local housing office, which is found in the county/city section of your phone book. You might have to call several numbers before you get the right office, as each area calls their office by a different name.

The range you will find is incredible, especially in this world of big government interference in our lives. Believe it or not, there are still counties in America where there are no building officials. No permits, no checking up on your schemes. You must also believe that there are counties that build less than ten homes a year. With that volume, there is no need for a code enforcement office. More typical is a health office, with a sanitary section for septic tank and well approval. Since there is little building in those communities, there are most likely no public sewers. Waste is handled by septic systems. Since there are sick people everywhere, there is most probably a health department and someone in that office is probably wearing a dual hat for approving septic tanks and wells. Go find that person.

The next level ranges up to bona fide building inspectors and a one to 1,000-man office (Los Angeles's building department covers one city block). These are the folks who will tell you if you can build a house and how many hoops you have to jump through. The rubber meets the road when you plan to build in a county where permits (permission) are required. When there is someone to tell you what to do in their county, they are also there to tell you what your state or

In This Chapter . . .

▲ How much can you expect to save?

▲ Who's going to help you?

▲ Who doesn't want to help you at all!?

region wants you to do. The law flows from these guys and they hold your fate in their hands.

In general, the rules are that you can build your own home provided you intend to live in it and not sell it anytime soon. There will most likely be a number of things you cannot do, like wiring and plumbing. Many areas, while allowing you to do the work, make it virtually impossible to do because of hidden requirements, tricks and the general bad attitudes of building officials. You'll need to get a gut check of how your local office feels about you building your own home. Some places might have a test you have to take. Some might require a supervising builder. The bottom line is to find out what the requirements are and go from there. Make that phone call and visit that office.

What Does the Bank Say About It?

The other element of building your own home is how you are going to pay for it. If it's all out of pocket, more power to you. You're home free, even though your accountant will probably want to kill you (remember the last great deal the government gives you—the mortgage tax credit? If you don't borrow the money, you don't get the tax break). If that's no big deal or it's your third or fourth house, don't worry about it. It will be a whole lot easier to build your own home if there are no bankers involved. A whole lot easier.

Bankers act like they hate to lend money. It is the heart of their business. It is how they make money. They just act like they are doing you a favor by lending you money. They truly don't hate you unless you're asking to borrow money to build your own home. Yes, they will hate you for that and they will take it personally. Don't expect glad tyding and good cheer when you go in and explain your needs and plans. Trust me. As an experiment, go to your favorite bank and ask to speak to your *personal* banker about buying a new home. Don't let them know that you are planning to "build it" yourself. Just play the game until you get to the point where you have to confess about building it yourself. Look for facial expressions, arms crossing, pins dropping. They don't want to do it. No way, José.

The reason is experience. If any loan in a bank's portfolio is going to go sour, it's a owner-built loan. They've got files of them. More banking careers are lost on bad home loans than fraud. Statistics (numbers) are against you and numbers are the essence of banking. The chances are pretty good that you're going to screw up the house and they're going to own that disaster in a couple months. And take a bath and bankers hate to bathe. Is all lost? Not at all. Just realize that you're going into the first (or second, if you met resistance at the building permit office) fight to build your own home.

There are three basic solutions to this inherent problem to building your own home. First, the bank will want you to put a huge amount of money down. They could ask for as much as *40 percent down*. What they are telling you is that they really, truly, honestly don't want to lend you the money. This will break your heart and shock you, especially if you're familiar with the 90 and 95 percent loans so common in the big boom towns. The 60 percent guy is asking you to leave. Don't let the door hit you in the butt when it slams. They figure if you're too stupid to leave, at least when (if) the deal goes sour, they can bulldoze the site and still keep enough of your 40 percent down to show a small profit.

So what is real? Probably the best you're going to do is an 80 percent loan in normal banking channels. If you can deal in those terms, you can probably find a bank. However, it will not be many banks and you'll be hunting for a while. There are those *very hungry* banks that will also specialize or allow a few high risk owner-built loans. While many banks might allow this, they have a quota and might be over their quota when you show up. Don't be discouraged. Keep looking.

Realize, too, that while you might get an 80 percent loan, you won't be looking at tremendous rates or buy downs. The rates are going to be stiff. Interest rates are made up of two things. The cost of money (what the bank has to pay to get the money versus opportunity cost) and *risk*. When you come into the bank asking for a owner-built loan, there is an invisible light that shines on your forehead. It says "Beware–Danger–Risk!" You might hear a computer click on in the background, figuring out the cost of your risk to the bank. For you, G.I., special rate.

The third choice is companies that specialize in owner-built home loans. These companies are far and few between and go in and out of business. They're hard to find and you might need to call a state banking or mortgage company to find out who these guys are and if they will lend you money. Along with these guys are some of building systems (kit) companies that might be dabbling in some homeowner assistance. The problem of this last category is that it is risky all the away around and you're paying for that risk at its highest level. You have to be totally committed and desperate.

The good news is that you can most likely get the loan you want by shopping around and finding the bank with a quota of money available for you. You won't get the very best rate or get in for the least amount of money, but you'll get your loan and you can get on with the project. Hang in there, know what you'll be facing and keep your spirits up. Realize, too, that if everything goes okay, you can refinance your loan several years in the future and get a better mortgage that is based on the true value of your finished home rather than on the risk that you brought to the bank on a piece of paper.

WHAT'S THE MOST YOU CAN SAVE?	
Schematic design	10%
Realtor's fee	6%
Builder's discount on materials	4%
Careful building/better supervision	5%
Self labor	9%
Builder's markup	20%
	44%

How Much Do You Think Builders Make?

Just what do you think builders make? Rich guys, right? Some of them are. Many go broke. What kind of money are they trying to make on you? You'd be surprised. Round figures say ten percent, with a chance to lose every bit of it. If you ask them candidly at a cocktail party, they might even say 15 to 20 percent. It's kind of like fishing. Every once in a while, you do catch the big one. However, in a lifetime of fishing, it's usually the small stuff that feeds your family.

So, why do it? Well, first of all, it's ten percent (or eight or twelve) of a pretty big number. And there is always the chance that you can save more and that things won't go wrong.

The upside is that you can get lucky and that you can, by putting a lot more effort than your builder would, save even more money. Careful shopping for materials. Preventing waste, damage and theft. Good economical design. Efficient land purchase. Sweat equity and doing the relatively simple, but dirty jobs yourself. There is money to be saved and more. Do you feel lucky?

Is it Worth it?

There is little more satisfying in life than building your own home, your homestead . . . your hearth and home.

Is it worth it? It depends on what you're trying to do by building your own home. If the goal is just to save money, it still costs. It's a life without weekends, evenings and free time. It could go on for years. Every penny you have, every vacation you've earned will be going into that house. However, there is little more satisfying in life than building your own home, your homestead. Your hearth and home.

It is not for the faint of heart. If you're a perfectionist and think everyone else is a idiot, you're in for a tough time. Home building is not rocket science and people don't drop out of Harvard to go into banging nails. You have to go with the flow, do the best you can and hope for the best. The frustration level is extremely high for those in the profession. Why would you think it would be any different for you? The pros have a hard time with it, so will you. When you're standing up to your knees in mud while $200 of gravel washes into the stream, you have to dream about the nights ten months in the future when you're sitting in front of your fireplace of the home you built by your own two hands. If you can keep that thought through the entire process, you should be building your own home. Yes, it is worth it. ■

3

Pitfalls and Other Disasters

What Can Go Wrong?

Usually everything can go wrong. It's tough to build a house in the rain. Dishonesty abounds in this world. People cheat and try to steal your hard-earned possessions. Mathematical errors can ruin a house, as can miscommunications, late deliveries, subs not showing up, wrong orders, short orders, back orders. Building a house is like conducting an orchestra. All the pieces have got to be there at the right moment and in the right amount. The bassoons can't play until the violins finish. It's tough and in hundreds of years it's never been easy nor is it going to get easy.

One of the first things to go wrong is in planning home design. If it doesn't work on paper, it's not going to work on the ground. Draftsmen make mistakes all the time. Even CAD (Computer Assisted Design) isn't foolproof. On a recent set of plans I had drawn on CAD, the windows didn't match the floor plan. The draftsman said he had to draw the windows on the outside view or *elevation* separately from the floor plan. He just made a mistake. I asked him if the computer could have caught this. He said, "Sure, but my program isn't hooked up to do that." So much for technology. Never assume that just because it *can* be done that it *is* being done. You still have to check plans, regardless of how they are drawn.

There is still a pretty good chance that your plans will be drawn correctly. However, they also have to be read and interpreted correctly. Plans are not easy to read. There are a lot of numbers and very fine print. While there are many drawings of the same thing (to show it from different angles and perspectives so that it is better understood) it still takes skill to interpret plans. A clarification of a particular part of a plan might be well detailed but put in an obscure part of the plans. The kitchen cabinet layout might be on the roof plan. A foundation *detail* might share a page with a nailing *schedule*. This hodgepodge of locations for

In This Chapter . . .

▲ Mistakes you can make

▲ Mistakes you can avoid

▲ Mistakes that are probably going to happen anyway

WHAT CAN GO WRONG?

▲ Government interference

▲ Cost overruns

▲ Theft

▲ Damage

▲ Miscalculations

▲ Mistakes

details often comes as the result of trying to save paper and use all the white space. It's economical but difficult to keep track of. The result of a missed detail is often a mistake because the plans were not followed properly.

Let's assume you're ready to go and have done everything else properly. You're ready to move some dirt! What could go wrong here? Not much, except serious bodily harm or even death, hitting water, sewer or power lines. You can also go seriously over budget in your first day of building through a series of mistakes and screw-ups. To avoid hitting underground lines, you have to call the utilities in your area, usually 48 hours in advance, so that they can locate these underground lines. If you break the line, it's your baby—you just bought it. Well, almost. If you did everything right, called it in, acted responsibly, notified whoever that you did cut it, you might be able to weasel your way out of trouble. The utilities make mistakes too and are more willing to own up to one if you did your part right.

The next thing that can go wrong in clearing the lot is dealing with the mess you're making. This phase of construction is where you really learn to appreciate the purpose and function of grass. Grass keeps the soil from washing away and you just removed the grass. When it rains, the soil is going to wash. The problem isn't only that you now have a sloppy site, but you also have an erosion problem. The government is big on erosion. They are experts and have big federal agencies (like TVA and EPA) that care very much about erosion. Dirt (they like to call it silt) has a tendency to escape from your lot. There are two places it likes to go, both real bad. First is into streams, where it clogs them up and kills the fish. If there is a lake nearby, it won't be clear for long. The silt from your lot will cloud it up, making those that like to look at clear lakes unhappy. If a lot of building is going on around a shared lake, your future neighbors have probably already put the government's erosion control department's phone number on their speed dial. They'll turn you in a New York minute.

The second place dirt likes to go is on the road. Big clods of ugly, sticky dirt, commonly known as mud. It is usually illegal to track mud onto a public highway. Plus, your neighbors will hate you for messing up their nice streets. The government is standing by, waiting for the call about *your* mud.

The first thing the government will do is shut your job down. No more work until you clean up the mud and prevent the silt from going into the stream, road, or lake. Then they will probably issue a summons and possibly a fine. It depends on how their day is going and your attitude. This isn't the time to discuss constitutional government (and getting it off your back.)

The third thing they will do is schedule a return visit to ensure you've done the right thing. Your job can stay shut down until it is reinspected. Not only will this cause delays, it will cost you extra money to clean up the road (a bobcat at $35 an hour for a minimum of four hours), plus silt fences (at $2.50 a linear foot, installed, times 125 feet), plus the very real possibility that those big machines you waited so long to get are going to another job where they can make some money. You've got government problems, big government problems, and the government operates real slow and can be real mean.

Now you're ready for some serious mistakes, digging the foundation. Whatever goes down has to come up. Digging the hole too deep (which is relatively cheap—it's only dirt), can get real expensive bringing the foundation wall back up. The block or concrete that makes up your foundation goes all the way around the house. It is real expensive to miscalculate how tall the wall should be. Estimating how tall this wall is supposed to be is your first real test of math skills. Get it wrong and it comes out of your pocket. Flunking math has real value in construction. In fact, the first cost overrun on a job usually starts with the foundation. The best laid plans go out the window due to poor supervision of the dig or simple mathematical mistakes.

This is also an area where you're all alone. The guy supplying the concrete or block doesn't care how much you put into the job. They get paid for what is used. It is easy to count or measure once it's in place. Beforehand, it is difficult to measure and even the most experienced of builders miss this estimate on a routine basis.

Getting the foundation wall wrong is about as wrong as it gets. Everything else depends on it. The problems are threefold. First, there is a possibility that the wall is improperly built and hence unsafe. Fortunately, this is rare, most probably because it is such a large mistake that people are very careful to avoid it. The second problem is much more common and that is where the wall is out of level, out of plumb or out of square. Out of square is the most common of these problems. We'll discuss these later but believe me, foundations built out of square continue to haunt you throughout the entire construction process, right down to the very last nail.

The third problem has to do with how you enter the house as well as a tendency for the house or yard to flood. If you bring the house too far out of the ground, you'll have to deal with too many steps into each door. You'll be climbing extra stairs for the rest of your life. However, if the house doesn't come out of the ground high enough, you'll be dealing with wet basements, flooding yards and a foundation that will have to be replaced in half it's normal life span.

Later mistakes have to do mostly with counting and math errors. Ordering too much or little of a material. Miscutting or misapplying materials. Many of these mistakes are latent, having been there since the beginning and only showing up when the parts are installed, i.e. siding and trim.

Another common problem is damage to materials. Your house is going to be built in the rain. Baby, it's cold out there and sometimes it's hot and sometimes the wind blows hard. Rain, wind, cold, and heat will play havoc with a house. You'll never be able to avoid this problem without a lot of luck and good fortune. Damage gets real serious when it's not the weather, but some oaf who drops a window or scratches the tub or countertop. Especially worrisome is if vandals get into your house and replay *A Clockwork Orange* in your living room.

Theft is also a concern. Theft is so common in construction that most builders don't even insure for it. They make allowance for it (it's very common and occurs on almost every job) and you wind up paying for "average" theft in the cost of your home. Most often it's simple things like 2x4s ($2.75 each) or a box of nails ($4.25). What's a couple of these for someone's tree house? Well, it adds up to big bucks, usually several hundred dollars if the thieves stay to the small stuff. Theft gets real expensive when the pros go to work. Usually it's windows and appliances. Heat pumps are also so popular that they are sometimes stolen *while running*.

So while everything can go wrong, it seldom all goes wrong. Be aware and be forewarned, but also be assured that this too will pass.

What Usually Does Go Wrong?

Usually small things, very consistent things. Things that are the nature of the beast. There is a saying in construction that might upset those of you who are perfectionists. That is, "There is no such thing as a perfect house." Houses are just too complicated, with too many players *building in the rain* to be perfect. Your house will most probably be over budget, behind schedule and almost never on autopilot. If that realization is too much for you, maybe you should start working for world peace rather than building a perfect house.

But what usually does go wrong? Often it's very simple. What you were expecting and what the supplier, banker, building inspector, machine operator, carpenter, mason, etc. really heard was probably not the same thing. You want a cheap house but you don't want cheap materials or labor. In the specifications phase of planning, you are shown so many options that you get confused. When these parts finally are installed (months later) they are not what you thought you wanted or agreed to. You can use the wrong words and not get at all what you wanted.[1]

The second most common thing to go wrong is for the subcontractors to be late to the job. This single problem keeps the liquor business booming and is the number one complaint of builders. It's not just a matter of someone not following the rules, their obligations and commitments or making the job take longer. It's a problem because everything else that needs to be done *next* hinges on what the late or missing sub has to do *first*. Among the reasons that the sub is late to your job is that he's behind on someone else's job. Or it could be that Johnny had a rough night last night and couldn't quite get in this morning. He was probably out drinking with your builder, who was commiserating about how late the subs always are.

Mathematical errors, minor theft and damage are going to happen. You can

War Story

#1: I recently was ordering parts to repair a porch. Without thinking, I asked for porch brackets to be delivered to a job and got nothing. I should have asked for porch braces. The frustrating thing was that the supplier knew that the job required porch braces (and that they never supplied brackets). However, they chose to do nothing because I didn't use the right word.

I think those guys used to work for the government because I got the same treatment in the Army when I didn't use the exact word (we called it nomenclature).

reduce them or even get lucky and have very few of them. Chances are, however, that some of these maladies will occur. You should just be aware of them and don't get too upset. Realize too that you cannot buy your way out of these problems. I've seen just as many mistakes in mansions as I've seen in starter homes and cabins. The main difference has always been in how the homeowner approaches the project. Good attitude—good house. Bad attitude—bad house.

The worst projects I've seen were the ones where the homeowner had been too critical and overbearing about the project. This bad attitude and approach permeates over to all those who come into contact with the house. Most subs and suppliers truly want to do a good job for you. If you're being critical or being a pest, they're going to get you, either through spite in ways you'll probably never see *or* they will just leave. There's plenty of work to do—why do you think they're always late? They're also in the business because they like their freedom and they are not going to put up with a hard time from anyone. Realize too that no one in the business likes to come in to replace a sub. They just don't like it and most probably are not going to like you (or charge you fairly) if you've run off a sub through bickering and a bad attitude.

What Can You Do To Prevent It From Happening?

There are lots of things you can do to prevent things going wrong with your house. Building a house is a cooperative event. You and about 200 other people are going to build your house. The vast majority want to do the very best they can for you. Most of the tradesmen involved in the project are self-employed and not only highly skilled but also highly sought after. They expect to be treated fairly. To them it is not a hobby or a burning passion. It is a job they like doing but they are not going to take a lot of abuse. If you approach the project aggressive as a bear, with determination that this will be the best built, lowest cost house ever and no one is going to get in your way, you're headed for disaster.

The profession is wrapped in laws that are typically a nuisance. I have spoken to people who were building their homes and they bragged of ironclad contracts and lawsuits. Their house was going to be built perfectly because their attorney wrote this wonderful contract. They could push their subs around because the law was on their side. They were sadly mistaken about how those contracts and the law works in home building. The honest, reputable tradesmen isn't going to be affected by any laws or threats of lawsuits. The dishonest, unqualified tradesman won't be either. They'll just leave the state in a business that is controlled by state laws, not federal laws. Since each piece of your house comes in small bundles, seldom more than $5,000, it's difficult to pursue a bad deal. Planning on the law to help you out of your mess is a really bad plan.

One of the best things you can do is to take your time in planning. Rushing to get a house built is a blueprint for disaster. This (lack of adequate and timely planning) usually occurs because building a house is such an emotional event. You're hot to get started, you've waited long enough (a lifetime?) and the time is *now!* Everyone should jump when you say "boo." Well, get in line. You should have been here yesterday. It will take time and there are few shortcuts. We'll talk

HOW TO PREVENT PROBLEMS

▲ Good attitude

▲ Careful planning

▲ Get it in writing

▲ Stick with your plan/don't change your mind

▲ Study and specify well

about timelines later, but following a timeline will save you thousands of dollars and tons of heartache.

The next thing you can do is not change your mind. In building your house, you've started a finely tuned machine into motion. That machine does not want to be stopped or slowed down. In fact, it does not slow down. Any changes causes a train wreck the likes of which you've never seen. Changes cost you three times what careful planning cost. The first cost is the original plan and work. The second cost is to tear it out or replan. The third cost is to put it back in. There probably is a fourth cost added in for the aggravation you've caused the builder. Plan well and stick to the plan.

The third thing you can do is to be very specific about what you want done. There are literally millions of choices in a house, from materials selection to how things are to be done. If they are not clear as a bell, at about a third-grade level (some of your subs live very well in that world), there is going to be a problem. A set of plans drawn by an architect, with details, sections, tables, and schedules (we'll talk about what these mean later) will help considerably. Even if they are ignored or misread, they'll at least help your case in working your way out of a mess. Everything has to be written down and not left to (mis)interpretation.

Beyond allowing adequate time for the process, you have to do a lot of study and just hard work. You have to ask lots of questions. Everything you fail to do, fail to question or leave for later will most likely be a problem in the future. It is going to take days and weeks of reviewing, selecting, comparing, and making decisions. It is not something you can leave up to someone else because they will make *their* choices, not yours. This custom house is your baby and you have to work to get it right. ■

One of the best things you can do is to take your time in planning. Rushing to get a house built is a blueprint for disaster.

4

The History of Building

Why Are Homes Built the Way They Are?

Building a home today is not very different from the way homes were built in Biblical times. Many of the same principles of building still apply. You build on rock, not sand (Matthew 7:24–26). You use a plumb line to determine the straightness of a wall (Amos 7:7). You build with wood and brick and span distances with beams and arches, nothing new under the sun.

There are five basic elements to why American homes are built the way they are today. All have roots in our history. These five elements are: the materials used (wood), the connecting devices (nails), delivering these pieces to the job site (transportation systems), cutting the wood (saws and saw mills), and the system of building (stick framing).

First is the building material itself. In America, homes are mostly built of wood. There are other systems of building (like steel), but wood is predominate. The reason is simple, there are a lot of trees around and they are easy and inexpensive to get. If they weren't so readily available, such as in arid climates like South America and the Middle East, they wouldn't be used. Those parts of the world use rock, brick, clay, or other non-wood products to build their homes because they are readily available and cost less.

The price of wood went up sharply in the early 1990s and the result has been the growth of a new building material—steel. A number of metal building companies sprang up overnight and took a stab at the future of American building. The wood manufacturers (from tree growers to lumber wholesalers) took notice and the price of wood went down (somewhat.) Steel is now less novel and people are not as interested in building steel houses. However, that industry got its foot in the door and it will be interesting to see where it goes in the future.

The original settlers built their homes out of whatever was growing on their land. It worked out well because they had to clear the trees anyway to get farm land. (Most settlers were farmers or at least grew some of what they ate.) The trees came down, they built their homes and barns with it and they were left with

> **In This Chapter . . .**
>
> ▲ The five elements of modern construction
>
> ▲ How past is prologue
>
> ▲ How Thomas Jefferson helped build houses

pasture land for the animals and farm land for the crops. It all made sense and worked very well for the 100 or so years of the settlement of America. While not yet a renewable resource (the pioneers were by no means conservationists), there were still plenty of forests and trees in the settled areas of our new country. As we all know, the easy-to-get to land was taken by the earlier settlers, forcing those who came later to move further west.

Nails were so rare and expensive in pioneer times that abandoned homes were burned down to salvage the nails.

The next thing that affected how houses were built was how the pieces were connected. Everyone knows that nails are a cheap, efficient way of connecting wood. You go to any home under construction and you see hundreds of nails littering the job site. Who cares, they're cheap and easy to get. It didn't used to be that way. Nails were so rare and expensive in pioneer times that abandoned homes were burned down to salvage the nails. Nails were hand made and expensive. In fact, the earliest homes were built using wooden pegs or trunnels just because nails were so rare, costly and imported.

If you ever have the chance to visit a truly remarkable site, you ought to go to Monticello, Thomas Jefferson's home in Virginia. Besides being one of the founders of our country and the writer of our constitution, Jefferson was a farmer with a vision. Jefferson did not want to depend on anyone, the least of all mother England. His home was the epitome of self-sufficiency, with shops or *dependencies* that made as many of his needs as possible. He had a furniture shop, a blacksmith and a medicine shop. This was doubly important to him because most of what couldn't be made in America was imported from England. There was no love lost between Thomas Jefferson and mother England. This really hit home after the War of 1812. If you recall, the British were still upset about losing their colony and came to Washington to burn it down. Bad blood. Well, at that time, almost all the nails used in America came from England. Nails were made from iron ore called nailrod. England and America were at war and no nailrod was coming in. Jefferson decided to get into the nailmaking business and did so, as did the rest of the country. Not only did this make us self-reliant as a country, innovation in nail making that came from this reduced the price of nails sixfold. A positive result of the War of 1812 was the availability of inexpensive nails made in America.

Another element that makes houses the way they are has to do with the sawing of trees. Imagine that you are a settler. You've just cut down an oak tree that is three feet around and you want to make a house with it. How are you going to lift it? How are you going to connect other pieces of wood to it? All you have is the ax and handsaw you brought from England. Some settlers were able use the rivers to power reciprocating saws that went up and down, cutting the trees into smaller pieces of wood. It took a long time and breakdowns were common. It worked, but barely.

Those that couldn't get to sawmills just cut the wood themselves and used the home building technique prevalent in Europe at the time. This system was called timberframing or post and beam, where larger timbers were joined to span a certain distance. These pieces were carved so that they joined into each other and were held together with pegs. Since this was a technique also used in shipbuilding, a number of former shipwrights became home builders. The joinery

method is called mortise and tenon. It worked, but was tedious and took a fair amount of skill.

As time went on and America became more industrial, better saws were made and eventually a round or circular saw was developed. Rather than going up and down (and breaking frequently), this saw went in a circle and cut the wood not only faster but in a more uniform manner. The end result is what is called dimensional lumber or lumber that is roughly the same size each time. The modern day equivalent is called a "2x4." As simple as this seems, it revolutionized home building.

The next element that made a significant difference was the development of a reliable transportation system. Two major elements were at play. First was the building of canals in upstate New York, the most famous of which was the Erie Canal, which was completed in 1825. This not only made it easier for people to get about, but also made it easier to move raw materials, especially trees.

The second major development was the railroad and the expansion of lines out to the West. The target was the upper Midwest, Ohio, Illinois, Indiana, and eventually into Chicago, the boom town of the middle 1800s. Reliable transportation networks like the canals and railroads made it possible for people to settle the Western (now Midwest) regions of the country. Trees were less plentiful in the West, but land was cheap and there was room to grow and expand. New transportation systems helped bring these trees to the West and thus house the new settlers.

Other forces that played into this change were the vast increase in immigration into this country. America was teeming with new settlers. These people were mostly unskilled and broke. The farms and lush lands of the East were not available to them. They had to go West and therefore headed towards Chicago. Along with them was the future of housing. All the elements necessary to radically change how houses were built came with them.

First was the need for housing. Quick housing. Simple and easy to put up. Inexpensive. Not only were there fewer and fewer craftsmen going West, their work couldn't be afforded anyway. Home sites were smaller near the big cities and trees were less available. Because of this, they had to be shipped in. Fortunately, there were still vast forests in upstate New York that could be logged and brought out West. The railroads and the canal brought the raw goods and the new sawmills, with their new circular saws, cut them into dimensional lumber.

A revolution was going on. Nails were plentiful and cheap. Dimensional lumber was easy to work with and few skills were needed to build these houses. There were plenty of unskilled immigrants to build and live in these houses. And it all centered around the city of Chicago. Guess what they called this type of construction? "Chicago style." You know it as "stick." Technically, it's known as "balloon" framing. That term can best be seen if you can visualize a house being built like a balloon. The term *stick* most probably came because dimensional 2x4 building materials look more like sticks when compared to the larger, heavier timbers used in timberframing, the original building method used in America.

The current style of home-building is called platform framing. It is a slight evolution of the balloon method. In balloon framing, the vertical support pieces were usually two stories tall, using a single vertical piece of dimensional lumber and putting in braces to support the second floor. While there were some economies of effort and material in this system, it had one major drawback that became most evident in the Great Chicago Fire of 1871. The single member two story framing methods served as a flue for fire and made these houses easier to burn. It was quickly replaced with platform framing. This method of framing is, as its name implies, building with platforms. First, the first floor is built and then the second (or more) floors are built on top of them. Not only is it an easier system, it is more fireproof than balloon framing.

How is Home Building Different Than It Was in the 19th Century?

The short answer is not much. I'm quite sure that if you could dig up a 19th century carpenter and put him on a framing crew, he would fit right in. The advances over the past 100 years have more to do with machines doing the very same operations as before than with anything really revolutionary. Concrete is pretty neat, but essentially serves the same function as mortar and sand. Drywall and plywood is new, but not much more than the lath, plaster and strip paneling

Home sites were smaller near the big cities and trees were less available. Because of this, they had to be shipped in. Fortunately, there were still vast forests in upstate New York that could be logged and brought out West.

of 50 years ago. Probably the biggest improvement has been in the area of insulation and energy efficiency. Older homes had no insulation and glass was glass. Houses leaked like sieves and people put up with the cold—they wore more clothes and had more blankets. Air conditioning certainly helped build new cities (like Houston), but people have always lived in hot climates. They had broad overhangs and raised foundations to keep their houses cool. Mint juleps, while not as good as central air, at least kept their thoughts off how hot it was.

The innovations of new construction have more to do with faster and cheaper than better or stronger. As the price (of everything) goes up, inventors are looking for ways to do a better job cheaper. In reality, it has to be much better and a whole lot cheaper. Housing is not an industry that embraces technical innovation. There are too many train wrecks and lawsuits along that path, like aluminum wire and fireproof plywood. Aluminum wire, used in the 1970s, was a cheaper alternative to copper wire. It conducted electricity just fine and certainly cost less. However, because it expanded at a different rate than copper, it had a tendency to arc and start a fire. Fires in houses are like Kyptonite to Superman—a real bad plan. It wasn't a problem in a specially made sockets where things were permanently plugged in, like ranges and electric dryers. It was a real problem everywhere else—retrofits and lawsuits.

Fireproof plywood was mostly used in apartment roofs. It probably was somewhat fireproof, but it also caused the roof to rot a whole lot faster. Here the problem wasn't only public safety, but also the cost of removing the plywood (and the shingles) and all the other associated expenses. The jaundiced eye towards new products is well deserved. New almost always means cheap and people don't want houses built with cheap components (they only want cheap houses).

Are They Still Making Them Like They Used To?

No. But you can get close and if you do, you've got a much better house. It's difficult to make a horrible house. No one can stay in business (much less go into business) without adhering to suitcases full of regulations and red tape. While the cost versus benefit of government regulation is sometimes debatable, good products do work themselves through the system. For example, you are not going to find a bad toilet fixture. They might range in price, but any one will function, at least at first and probably for a long time. Every piece of lumber that goes into your house is graded, stamped and certified; every window, socket, length of wire; every window and door and the shingles on the roof. You will have a government inspected, grade A certified house. It's almost impossible to do otherwise, because no one is producing parts that don't meet some minimum specification by some government agency.

The quality of the part is another matter. Are top quality components, as good as were used in Grandma's house, still available? You bet. They just cost a lot more and are not the norm. The "standard" quality level of a house has gone down overall. It's just too expensive to match the specifications of days gone by. Some items have been replaced with truly superior products. Some just do an adequate job. Some products are really quite flimsy, but you get what you pay

No one can stay in business (much less go into business) without adhering to suitcases full of regulations and red tape.

Newer can be better and certainly is the aim of the industry. A lot of people are trying to give you the very best house that you can afford.

for. I'm always amazed when I hear people talk about how cheap their house is. This is because the buyer sets their own quality levels. If they think the doors are cheap (hollow core plastic), they can request solid wood doors. They cost four times as much, but they are available. And it's not the builder's fault. The customer sets the standards and quality levels. The very best things are available. They just cost more.

There are a lot of things that make your house so much better than houses have ever been. Things last longer, look better, fit better and are easier to maintain. Roofing products have made tremendous progress, from durability to appearance. Windows are light years ahead, with R-values that now exceed the R-value of *walls* not too many years ago. Paints last longer, are easier to apply and clean up. Your house is environmentally safer, more fireproof and healthier. Your home is built much faster and with much less impact on the surrounding community and environment. It is more comfortable, easier to heat and cool, and stays cleaner. It is safer from outside crime as well as from inside hazards. Newer can be better and certainly is the aim of the industry. A lot of people are trying to give you the very best house that you can afford. ■

5

A Brief Discussion of Architecture

What Period of Architecture Are We In?

Who cares? Well, not everyone, but you should. Styles of architecture are like fashion. There are fads and things go in and out of style. While architecture doesn't change anywhere near as quickly as hem lines, it changes enough in the life of a house to drastically affect its value. A "hot" new style this year might devalue your house 10 years in the future. The neat thing about architecture is that there are a few safe bets that you can make. The safest bet is probably a Colonial. Since this is America and the Colonial style (sometimes called Williamsburg) is the first style seen in America, it remains just as popular today. Most of New England was built in the Colonial style as was the rest of the original 13 colonies. It is simple, easy to build and easy on the eyes. It generally costs less to build as well.

The current period we are in today is called "Post Modern." *Post* means "after" and thus we are in the period that is after the *Modern* era. The Modern era covers the architecture of the 1930s, '40s, '50s, and '60s. Styles of the Modern era include *Art Deco, Art Moderne* and *International.* While these styles have their own specific details, they shared a rather boxy, plain look with limited ornamentation (except Art Deco, which had the misfortune to be popular at the onset of the Depression). Huge, skyscraping buildings of almost all glass facades, like I.M. Pei's "Hancock Tower," are typical of the Modern era. Like all new trends, Post Modern was a reaction against the previous period.

Post Modern houses reach into the past and bring back styles of earlier eras. These are typically simplified and made at an exaggerated scale. A common example is the revival of turned gables from the "Greek Revival" era. The use of stucco for siding material and colored metal for roofing is often seen. Half-round shapes are also seen in windows and gables. Even so, Post Modern is seen more often in strip shopping centers, malls and small public buildings. Some details, like the turned gable and the Palladian window, cross over into the styles seen more often in modern residential designs.

In This Chapter . . .

▲ The most popular styles of today

▲ How you can design your own home

▲ What an architect can do for you

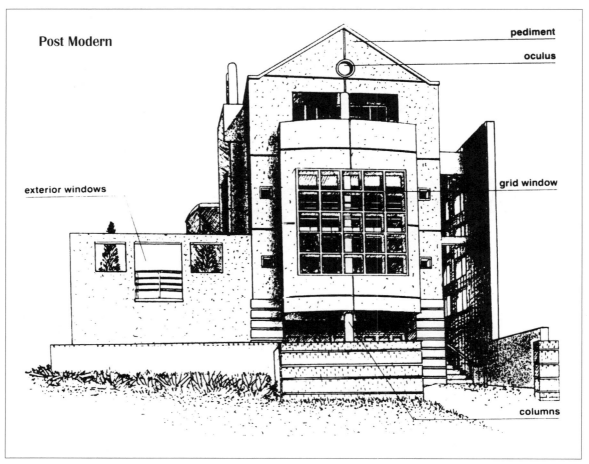

Post Modern

pediment

oculus

grid window

exterior windows

columns

While Post Modern is the current style, it is not followed in its purest sense in residential architecture. While beauty is in the eye of the beholder, the Post Modern style will probably become "dated" in the years to come. The huge Palladian windows might possibly go the route of the huge "picture" window of the homes of the 1950s. While Post Modern is seen in residential design, the more common style is what is called "Neo-Eclectic." *Neo* means "new" and *Eclectic* means "choosing from diverse sources or styles." Essentially it is a style of architecture where older styles (many older styles) are made new or modernized. Styles most copied are *Colonial, Tudor, French, Victorian, Classical Revival,* and *Mediterranean.* The "copying" of these styles is in a general sense and details thought to be unimportant or too expensive to replicate are simply left out. In keeping with the Post Modern style, Palladian windows are often incorporated into the houses somewhere as are turned gables.

People like to duplicate the styles of the past and close replicas are still being built. *Colonials,* and it's variations like *Georgian* and *Adams*, are still very popular, especially in the New South. The *Craftsman* era style homes have made a slight resurgence in the past few years. Regardless of style, Americans still incorporate what they want in their homes and have no problem with violating some of the purest rules of architecture to get the home that they want.

Architecture, Smarchitecture, What About Houses for the Average American?

You're right. Not everyone cares about the style of their home. Nor can they afford to pay much attention (or dollars) for it. Most people are living in very simple ranches and two-story homes with minimal decoration or detail. Where are they in the world of architecture? Well, as you learn more about architecture, you'll see that architectural historians can't resist giving every style and nuance of architecture a name. There is a name for these typical style of homes. It's called "Minimal Traditional." Creative, huh? It's a real term for the typical American home. This style of home usually has one roof line, a low pitch roof and very little else. Simple trim. Narrow overhangs.

It is inexpensive to build and inexpensive to own and it houses most of America. It's also not a bad start for those trying to get into their first house. There are economies that this style provides and they are easy to design; simple houses for bread and butter, meat and potatoes Americans.

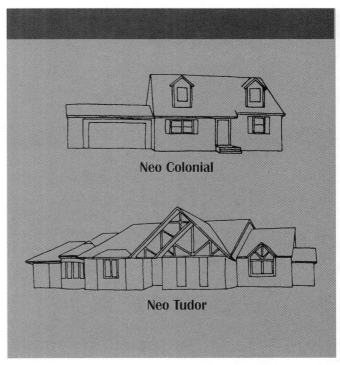

Neo Colonial

Neo Tudor

FROM "A FIELD GUIDE TO AMERICAN HOUSES"

Who Can Help Me Design My Home?

We discussed earlier that almost everyone wants to design their own home. This book can help with that goal. It certainly will give you a head start regardless of how you get your house designed. What I'd like to show you are the options available to you and let you decide. There are advantages and disadvantages to every route you take. Some of the choices can be combined.

The first choice you have is to do it yourself. You can generally do two things. Either take an existing plan and adapt it to your needs or start from scratch. The biggest advantage is that you know what you want. The biggest disadvantage is that you don't know what you're doing.

Let's start with doing it from scratch. The napkin approach, or it could be the sand approach, because I know of at least one $500,000 house that began at the beach, drawn in the sand. While this method is probably the hardest one to bring to fruition, this book provides an excellent starting point for this journey. Realize too that you are not alone. Lots of people design their own home and are sure to tell you that they've done that. Usually it's very obvious. It can be a great joy as well as a great struggle. Designing your own home is fully covered in Chapter 6, which will give you enough information and direction to design your own home with a reasonable chance for success.

The next way to design your own home is to adapt someone else's plans. You're in luck because you have thousands of plans to choose from. The plan book industry is booming. There are probably 30–40 plan books published every month, each with an average of 200 plans. Let's see, 40 times 200 times 12 equals 96,000 plans produced every year. Since most people dream about their homes at least five years before they do anything, they have a chance to look at

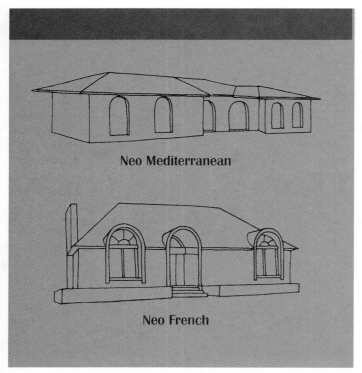

Neo Mediterranean

Neo French

FROM "A FIELD GUIDE TO AMERICAN HOUSES"

480,000 plans. Let's say half a million plans to review. We already know that the chances of finding one perfect plan from these half-million choices is about zero. You will want (and probably need) to alter these plans to meet your needs. One room will need to be made larger or smaller or made into something else. Your lot conditions might require the plans to be reversed or windows moved, enlarged or made smaller. Finding the perfect stock plan is virtually impossible. Even if one is found, you'd feel an overwhelming urge to change something to make it yours, if not during the planning stage, certainly while the house is being built. You'll want to change something.

Not all is lost. It's actually a pretty good start. It's certainly easier than starting from scratch because you'll find at least some part of the plan that makes sense for you. Often it is almost all of the plan. A tweak here, a twist there and you're in business. It is a worthy pursuit and one that I recommend you do regardless of how you get your home designed. What you should do is start a scrapbook and every time you see a plan you like, clip it out and put it in the book. You should not limit yourself to house plans, but also parts of a house, from windows to flooring; interior shots of rooms, especially kitchens and baths. Look for interesting finishing details: wall paper and paint combinations, built-ins and decks. Save these for later. It might be interesting to also date the plans and pictures to see how your tastes might change in the process. Tastes that remain after five years should be an indication of what should remain in the design. Fads you liked five years ago but don't like now are like a gift from heaven. Thank goodness you didn't put *that* into your house.

Let's say you're comfortable with coming up with the design of your home but lack the technical skills or time to make it into a blueprint. It's still your baby, but you want to hire a mechanic to draw the plans *on blueprint paper*. Your design, their paper. Oh, yes, you don't want to spend a lot of money. What are your choices? Well, there is probably at least one option in every town in America and that is at your local high school. Provided someone there teaches drafting. There are two ways to go here. Either the drafting teacher themselves or one of their star pupils. You probably will not be the first person to ask the local teacher to draw a house, but this teacher might not be interested.

If so, ask for their best student. Realize though, if you go for the student, you'll be dealing with a teenager. Not to be prejudiced about teenagers (I have two of them at home), but you're not dealing with a professional here. You can expect every evil in the American labor force to be teeming in their blood. Work ethic, attention to detail, eagerness to work or to do an *excellent* job. You can get lucky. Ask them to show you their work. It might look wonderful but you need to ask the next important question, "How long did it take you to do this, son?" The answer might be "All semester," which is not what you want to hear if you ever expect to get your plans back. If things look good and the student appears to be a decent bet, you must next negotiate a price and payment schedule. Your best bet might be to ask the teacher what is fair. It needs to be a fixed price and not by the hour or you'll become part of that kid's car payment. A fair price for a simple set of plans should be well under $100 but you'll have to determine the going rate. At the end of this project, you should at least get a set of plans on blueprint paper at it's cheapest possible rate.

The next choice is to see if anyone else in your community does drafting by moonlight. Drafting is a fairly common occupation and many companies employ draftsmen. It is also a common skill needed by local government and utilities. A little research should uncover a few draftsmen in your community. While drafting pays a decent wage, these guys are not getting rich on the boards. Also, don't forget your local community college, which is quite a step up from the high school program.

The biggest drawback to hiring a moonlighting draftsman is that it is, as they say in the computer world, garbage in, garbage out. You're not going to get much help here. Chances are real good that your moonlighting draftsman knows nothing about construction, much less architecture. They're not going to be critical of your plan or very suggestive. They'll figure you know what you want and they'll draw what you've given them. You get what you pay for.

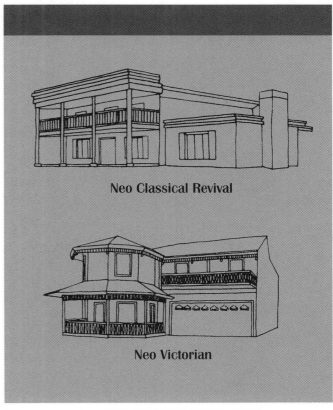

Neo Classical Revival

Neo Victorian

Your last choice in the do-it-yourself mode is to try to convince a moonlighting design professional to do it for you. There are two basic choices. First is the professional residential building designer. Second is someone from an architect's office. You need to go for one of their newest junior members and contact them outside of their office. Their boss will not be happy about this venture and therefore you should be discrete about the project.

There are two basic reasons for this. First is that you're taking business away from the firm. Drawing plans is their business and they don't appreciate what you're doing (getting professional work at less than professional prices) and certainly don't want to be part of it. Second is that if a member of their firm draws your plan, the firm might be liable for the plans to work. Your sworn and written waivers that you won't sue them if something goes wrong are of no value. It happens all the time. Let no good deed go unpunished. Most of the lawsuits in the building business come from people who try to cut corners and build on the cheap. This is well known and those in the business stay out of that mine field. If you can get someone from a design firm to help you, more power to you. You'll get the best job you almost paid for. You might even get some advice on the design, but don't plan on it. It will be mercenary work and held at arm's length.

Oh yes, there is one more avenue open to you and that is a CAD program you

Minimal Traditional

FROM "A FIELD GUIDE TO AMERICAN HOUSES"

can buy for your own computer. There are lots of choices and it is worth exploring. It might be cheaper in the long run to just sub it out unless you really like designing houses and want to put a lot of money and time into the program. Like all computer programs, it will take a while to master it and it might slow you down. Nevertheless, it's worth a look.

Boy, That Guy Was an Idiot! Who Else Can Help?

Someone once said that a man who defends himself in court has a fool for a client. This can apply in the design of your home. The greatest fear is always that it is going to cost too much to use professional services. What is the most it could cost? The standard line is as much as 10 percent of the total budget for the project. If this were always true, that really is scary. Fortunately, it rarely is. The reality is that the cost of design is negotiable. It could be as simple as a dollar figure per square foot. It could be broken down into phases, any one of which you could drop out. It could be a flat fee.

One interesting way to look at it is as a total budget fee. Let's say you want to spend $200,000 for a house. You could tell the architect that you want him to design a house that could be built within your budget and specifications *including his fee.* If he can meet your design and space needs as well as your total budget requirements, who cares what his fees are? While there are no guarantees in life, architects can and do live under these conditions.

Before we start talking about architects, let's first explore the new guy on the block, the residential designer. These guys are like architects but only design houses. Some are actually better at house design than typical architects. They cost less than architects and have their own professional organization and certification process. It's called "AIBD" or the American Institute of Building Design. Member of AIBD (and nonmembers, not everyone is a joiner) are almost always full-time residential designers. While there are no specific college program requirements for these guys, they've been at it long enough and have enough experience and reputation to make a living at designing houses. They often work for a series of upper end custom builders, designing homes that sell well in a local area and are within the capability of the custom builders who use them. They also are available to people who want their custom home plans drawn. While not inexpensive, they cost less than architects and generally do a pretty good job.

Architects generally don't like residential designers. They definitely take business away from them. Architects are critical of their work and their creativity. The architects are usually right, but the problems are so subtle that they are almost never noticed or observed by the untrained eye. Their plans usually copy other plans and seldom go beyond a few standard, popular styles of architecture. Architects sometimes argue that the home might not be structurally sound or buildable, but that is debatable. Some architect plans are also virtually unbuildable. To lend credibility to that argument, just ask a builder of custom architect plans. In defense of residential designers, they are not going to go far in pushing the engineering of a plan. It will generally stay well within the bounds of routine construction. Architects can go beyond this through their own knowledge and skills as well as through the use of engineers. Residential designers are not going to bite the hand that feeds them. Builders hate engineers and hate to use them. They would prefer plans that don't require engineers and the residential designers know this.

Residential designers are a pretty good bet. They fill a void in the business and do a fairly good job at it. Their designs are attractive, well within the norms, usually appropriate for the area and relatively easy to build. Since many architects do not like or specialize in residential design, the field is left wide open for them. They definitely cost less, can take your needs and wants and help you develop a workable set of drawings. They would welcome your input and the drawings you might have already come up with. They will offer suggestions to problems and point out things that won't work or would look better done another way. They can meet most people's needs and provide a valuable service at a fair price.

Why Would Anyone Use an Architect?

Johnny and Jeffrey graduate from high school together. Both are smart young lads and know what they want to do with their lives. Johnny wants to be a medical doctor and Jeffrey a registered architect. Who will reach their goal first? Neither. It takes just as long to become a doctor as it does a registered architect. Doctors have four years of college and four years of medical school. Architects have five years of college and three years of apprenticeship in an architectural firm before they can be certified as an architect. Doctors put M.D. after their name after the eight-year period. Architects put AIA, which stands for the American Institute of Architects, after their name after the same eight-year period.

It takes just as long to become a doctor as it does a registered architect.

Architecture is an interesting field and an unusual combination of talents. While best thought of as a field of great creativity and artistic nature, it is also a solid, hard science. Engineering and physics. Usually people are one or the other, seldom both. Scientist or artist. Cowboy or Indian. This combination makes for an interesting person and architects are definitely interesting people.

The world of architecture also demands a degree of salesmanship, diplomacy and tact. Architects who specialize in residential design seldom have more than a few projects going on at any one time and thus are constantly looking for new projects. Projects usually last from six months to a year. Every project is a big deal to the architect and losing a project can make for lean times. The other side of this is that their clients are usually very demanding and, while usually rich, want more than they can afford. Spoiled and undisciplined is probably a good description for a typical architect's client. Not used to following the rules or the advice of experts. It's a tough world and it's no wonder that fewer and fewer architects go into the residential side of architecture. It certainly accounts for the growth of the AIBD residential designer.

A residential architect is an independent businessman and an entrepreneur. They probably love designing houses and are constantly looking for a client with the budget to do a house proud. Occasionally they find one and have a grand old time. Architecture is a matter of subtlety. It is small things that make the difference. Like the thickness of the piece of wood (mullion) that divides the panes of glass in a window. The height of the fascia board, the reveal of the siding, the pitch of the roof. These small things mean a lot to an architect and to the way your home looks. There is a science to proportion, to mass, to texture and reveal. An architect can get it right even when you can't see it unless it's pointed out to you. They can determine how high and how intricate to make the baseboards in your house. They can make the traffic patterns work and the kitchen efficient. To save you money, they can select materials that will not only give you the look you want but add an elegance that belies it's low cost. They can design and spec a house that will more than pay for their fees. And, in the end, you've got a house you can treasure and enjoy for the rest of your life. Pretty neat deal.

The best way to deal with an architect is to have your homework done.

So why doesn't everyone use an architect? It has a lot to do with money. It is not free and it cost money at the beginning of the project when you're worried most about being able to afford the house. You fear they're going to design something you cannot pay for. You are intimidated by them, that they would ridicule that cute little detail you want in your house. You're afraid you're going to lose control of your house and it's going to be a monument to them and not you. There is a little truth to this. Many architects have a signature to their design. I know of one architect who likes round walls and puts one into every house he designs. While not a bad detail, it might not be what you want and it would be difficult to upset your architect's ego.

An architect would probably not ridicule your ideas. They need the business and are going to satisfy you as best they can. What they're going to have a hard time doing is to violate what they know is improper. If you are suggesting something that is just plain inappropriate, they are going to tell you. I suggest you listen. It's like debating closure techniques with your heart surgeon. You might have read a lot of books and articles and have a second cousin who is a scrub nurse but that surgeon has had their hands on a lot of hearts (and yours soon) and they know what they are doing. This is not to say that you shouldn't tell them what you want. Hopefully, they will ask you this wonderful question, "What are you trying to achieve?" Chances are that they will have a much better way to give you what you want than you originally thought of. In fact, architects love to solve problems through design. One of the most popular design contests that architects participate in is the "Small House Design" or "Low Cost House Design" contests. Here they experiment with low cost materials and dual purpose space to solve design and budget problems. It's a great contest, often sponsored by home magazines and material suppliers. The results of these contests ought to go into your scrapbook for future use, especially if you're facing a budget problem.

The biggest way to demystify the world of the architect is to go shopping for them. What most people don't realize is that the first meeting usually doesn't cost anything. You just call up a local office or get a referral from someone who knows or has used an architect. Tell them what you have in mind and ask if they'll see you. Of course they will. At that meeting you will outline what you're looking for and they will show you what they have done in the past and outline their fees. It would probably be well worth your while to see several architects.

This will allow you to not only see how their fees are different but also to see what kind of work they do. It will be quite different. You'll determine a number of things.

First, you will see if you like them and their work. It's going to get a bit intimate with this person trying to reach deep into your emotions to give you what you want. If you don't like or trust them, try someone else. While you might see a certain theme to the homes they've done (e.g., ranches with lots of stonework), it doesn't necessarily mean that they are locked into a particular style and can't do what you want (a two-story brick Georgian). Believe me, they can do anything. If the chemistry is right, the plans will work themselves out.

Next are the fees. If you have shopped around, you have probably seen a variety of fee structures. If the structure you like doesn't match up with the architect you like, ask them if they will do it the way you like. Chances are good that they will to get the business. A typical initial fee is to come up with conceptual drawings. These can be very exciting. While relatively rough, these are often done in color (sometimes a water color—an original work of art), are done in perspective and often show how the house will actually sit on the lot, complete with landscaping and existing trees. They also will show a rough floor plan. The cost for these conceptual drawings (if this cost is separated out) usually range around $1,000.

It's a small investment to see if you're on the right track and is usually all that is needed to cement a relationship with the architect and to confirm that you are headed in the right direction. If you are dissatisfied and it doesn't work out, it's a good point to bail out of the deal. It could also be all that you need. You might want to work out the details yourself and take over the project from there. While I would not necessarily recommend this, it is an option open to you and it might give you just what you needed from the architect. I would, suggest, however, that if this might be where you're headed, tell the architect about this ahead of time so that there are no hard feelings or misunderstandings.

Fees beyond this will differ from architect to architect and is usually very negotiable. There will most likely be an established hourly rate. This could be for office visits and site trips (plus mileage). Site visits might have their own fee or could be included in another fee, i.e., draw the plans plus two site visits for "X" dollars. Fees are often broken down in phases, with so much money for initial floor plans and elevations, another payment for foundation and working drawing and then another at final approval plans. Again, it will vary so you'll have to get a fee schedule to see exactly what it will cost and when you have to pay.

The best way to deal with an architect is to have your homework done. Bring your scrap book and whatever notes you have taken over time. If you've made progress on a plan, bring it with you. In this case, the architect will point out what works and what they would suggest be changed. They need as much input from you as they can get. The architect really wants to please you and do a professional job for you with your needs, desires and budget in mind. If they can't do that, they'll tell you.

TYPICAL ARCHITECT'S CONTRACT BREAKDOWN

Schematic design	10%
Design Development	15%
Construction documents	60%
Bidding/negotiations	5%
Construction administration	10%
	100%

There are a number of reasons for an architect to tell you they can't help you. While money is high on the list, it often is because you seem to lack the flexibility to explore the possibilities first. You have to be honest with your budget. Everyone wants it as cheap as possible. That is of no help whatsoever. There is an absolute amount of money you can afford to build the project. It's OK to say you want to spend less, but the architect needs to know the most you can afford. At least then they know the upper end of the budget and can work back towards the desired budget. ■

6

Design By Lists

Make a List and Check It Twice

Designing a house is a lot like making a Christmas wish list. You're excited, want everything under the sun and don't want to leave anything off the list. A list puts everything in front of you and helps you arrange your thoughts. It's an excellent organizational tool and can be quite helpful in designing your new home. A couple should make a list together, though you can start separate lists first and then combine them. What we've developed here is a thing called "Design By Lists," a proven method of determining what you want and need in a house as well as a starting point for putting your design together. Whether you're going to design the home yourself or eventually bring it to an architect, you need to fill out the list. You'll be surprised how helpful it will be.

In This Chapter . . .

▲ An easy way to design your home

▲ Making a list makes it easy

▲ Using a list as a starting point

Gotta Have It

You have to know what you can afford and what you have to have in a house to make it worth building. If you cannot have certain things, there is no reason to start the project. The first list is the "Gotta Have It" list. This list should include code or covenant requirements as well as things that have to be there to get permit or subdivision approval. You should include the minimum number of bedrooms and baths. The minimum (or maximum) square footage should be listed here. Required or prohibited materials should be listed. Setbacks, maximum height of building, tree removal guidelines, etc., ought to be on this list. It is an absolute list. Maximum budget (from the bank, not what you'd like to spend) ought to be on this list. This list will establish the parameters of your

GOTTA HAVE IT

1. ....
2. ....
3. ....
4. ....
5. ....
6. ....
7. ....
8. ....
9. ....
10. ....

Continue on another sheet if necessary.

DREAM ON!

1. ....
2. ....
3. ....
4. ....
5. ....
6. ....
7. ....
8. ....
9. ....
10. ....

Continue on another sheet if necessary.

house and will require some compromises and tough choices. Fill out the *Gotta Have It* list on the left.

Dream On!

Whew! That was tough. Now on to something fun—a real wish list. Go for the gold, reach for the stars. With the absolutes out of the way, you can now list the things you'd really like to have, budget provided. Here you are challenging yourself and your designer. If you're using a design professional, this list gives them a chance to shine, to win your undying gratitude. This is because some of your dreams, once known, can be incorporated into the design. Let's say, for example, you've got a lot of good looking books and you want to show them off in a home library. It's not necessary to your house and could very well be a budget buster. But boy, would it be nice. If you don't mention it in this list, you'll never get a shot at it. Remember what I said about building designers being able to solve problems from a different perspective ("What are you trying to accomplish?")? Do you want a separate, single function room or just a nice place to show off your books? There is a trend nowadays for people to expand their formal dining room slightly (one foot for each wall of book shelves) and letting it serve double duty. The formal dining room is little used, usually has beautiful furniture and would be greatly complemented by a wall or two of built-in book shelves. A problem solved at very little cost only because you asked. Go ahead, fill out your *Dream On!* wish list in the space provided. Put your wishes in priority so that your designer will know what to attempt to solve first.

The Way We Were

This list is especially useful because you've already got a track record of likes and dislikes in a house. Certainly you've lived in a number of different homes, apartments, college dorms or tents. (I lived in a G.P. Medium tent for a month on the DMZ in Korea; mice were a problem; I always check for mice in the homes that I live in.)

You probably have at least one opinion about each of your former residences. This list asks you to list everywhere you've lived before and state at least one thing you liked about living there and one that you didn't. It could be anything from where the sun set on a particular room, e.g., the kitchen, making it hot when you cooked supper to where a light switch was located.

THE WAY WE WERE		
HOME	**LIKED**	**DISLIKED**
1.		
2.		
3.		
4.		
5.		
6.		
7.		
8.		
9.		
10.		

Continue on another sheet if necessary.

How You Doing Now?

This list will be crucial when you develop a house plan (see the space provided on the following page). Simply, measure the rooms in the house you're currently living in and comment on how that size works for you. If the size is OK, say so. If it's too small, try to estimate how much larger it needs to be for it to work. Do the same thing if you can afford to downsize a particular room (common in older houses).

Putting It All Together

A sample list is provided on the following page that we will develop into a house plan in a later chapter. ■

HOW YOU DOING NOW?

ROOM	SIZE	COMMENTS
Living Room		
Dining Room		
Master Bedroom		
Kitchen		
Family Room		
Master Bath		
Hall Bath		
Powder Room		
Foyer		
Dinette		
Bedroom #2		
Bedroom #3		
Bedroom#4		
Laundry Room		
Hallway		
Stairway		
Garage		
Patio		
Front Porch/Stoop		
Deck		

PUTTING IT ALL TOGETHER

GOTTA HAVE IT

1. 1,500 square feet (covenant requirement)
2. Three bedrooms
3. 2 1/2 baths
4. House no wider than 80 feet (covenant requirement)
5. Separate living and dining room
6. Family room open to kitchen
7. Two-story
8. Two-car attached garage
9. $150,000 maximum budget including lot

DREAM ON!

1. Wide halls
2. Colonial style
3. Nine-foot ceilings
4. Walk-in closets
5. 4th bedroom/study
6. Four piece master bath

THE WAY WE WERE

	Home	Liked	Disliked
1.	Charlotte	Breakfast bar	Slab foundation (cold)
2.	Atlanta	Colonial style	Small lot
3.	Savannah	Large dining room	Small foyer
4.	Atlanta	Shady deck	Sun in MBR
5.	Birmingham	Large foyer	Tiny windows
6.	Brunswick	Wide front porch	Small MBR
7.	Pensacola	Large family room	Flat roof
8.	Charlotte	Large master bath	D/W blocked door

ROOM	SIZE	COMMENTS
Living Room	12'6" x 13'8"	Too small
Dining Room	11'4" x 12'7"	Too small
Master Bedroom	13'3" x 12'6"	Need 1 foot each way
Kitchen	9'9" x 14'6"	Too narrow
Family Room	14'4" x 13'5"	OK
Master Bath	5'1" x 10'2"	Too small
Hall Bath	5'1" x 9'2"	OK
Powder Room	3'5" x 8'2"	OK
Foyer	4'2" x 5'3"	Too small
Dinette	9'9" x 11'3"	Too small
Bedroom #2	10'9" x 12'4"	OK
Bedroom #3	10'8" x 11'7"	OK
Bedroom#4	n/a	
Laundry Room	n/a	
Hallway	3'	OK
Stairway	3'2"	OK
Garage	19'2" x 21'11"	OK
Patio	n/a	
Front Porch/Stoop	3' x 4'6"	Too small
Deck	10' x 16'	Too narrow

7

Design Guidelines

The Science of Design

Many people think that home design is an art done by creative, sometimes flighty people. They're half right. Home design is also a very unforgiving, hard science with rules that don't like to be broken. Break the rule, stay after school. Not really, break the rules and your house is a mess, sometimes forever. Some of the rules are just common sense. Others are required by codes. The remainder make the house safer and easier to live in. Some of the rules are suggestions that don't have to be followed. Really, it's your house and if you don't mind that your house will never be resold (it's a design disaster), that's your right.

I've been told by more than one person that they're going to do what they want because they're going to die in that house. I happen to live in a area where there are a lot of retired people. Believe me, they do not die in their homes. When they get feeble and unable to care for themselves, they move into assisted living apartments or condos: very expensive apartments or condos. Ones that the quick sale of their homes would really help get them into. Good design will sell your house. Self indulgence and violation of the rules of design will not.

This chapter will give you room-by-room guidelines that provide rules of thumb and suggestions on how to design your home. Not all are absolute and usually there is more than one solution to a design problem. Realize too that these are by no means all the rules of design but merely some of the more important ones that will keep you out of trouble.

In This Chapter . . .

▲ Simple do's and don'ts

▲ How codes help you design

▲ How to use standard sizes in design

KITCHENS

▲ Place near the dining room; you should not have to go through another room to get to the dining room from the kitchen.

▲ Place near a service door to the garage/driveway/basement for ease of bringing in groceries.

▲ Use a durable, all-weather floor that continues all the way to the outside.

▲ Use a crank-out (casement) or sliding window over the sink for ease of opening.

▲ Arrange the "big three" (sink/range/refrigerator) so that they range between 12'-22' apart in a "work triangle." This will make the kitchen more efficient. There should be at least 4', but no more than 9' in each leg of the triangle.

▲ Keep refrigerator and dishwasher doors away from entries to the kitchen.

▲ Dishwashers should always be placed next to the sink.

▲ Typical sizes of appliances:

· Standard, single door refrigerator — 32"-34" wide, allow 36" of space

· Double door refrigerators take more space, check the actual size

· Dishwashers — 24" wide

· Range/Oven — 30" wide

· Standard double bowl sink — 32" wide

▲ Typical sizes of cabinets and countertops:

· Base cabinets (including top) — 36" tall, 25" deep

· Upper cabinets — 12" deep, placed 15"-18" above base cabinets

· There should be at least 24" of countertop on one side of the sink and 18" on the other. This is not absolute, but highly recommended.

· There should be at least 15" of countertop on the latch side of the refrigerator. Again, this is a strong recommendation.

· There should be at least 9" of countertop on one side of the cook top and 15" on the other. Also, a strong recommended minimum.

▲ Shapes of kitchens:

· "U" shaped is the most efficient

· "L" works well for an eat-in kitchen

· Galley or corridor works well in a small house or apartment

▲ General space: You need at least 36" of space between cabinet/appliances and other cabinet/appliances or islands; 42"-48" separation is strongly recommended though. This becomes crucial when trying to incorporate an island cabinet. It takes a lot of room and shouldn't be squeezed in.

BATHS

▲ Smallest three-fixture bath is 5'x8'.

▲ Smallest two-fixture bath is either 3'x7' or 5'x6'.

▲ Minimum suggested door size is 32", though doors as small as 24" are seen.

▲ Standard sized tubs are 60"x32" wide; 6' tall with shower surround.

▲ Standard showers are 36"x36" or 48"x36", 6' tall; minimum size shower is 32"x32" (but you'd better be a small person at this size).

▲ Standard toilets are typically 28" deep by 20" wide and need 24" of clearance in front and 12" on each side.

▲ Bathroom cabinets (vanities) are typically 31" tall by 18"–22" deep (including countertop). A double bowl vanity should be at least 5' wide, single bowl vanity sinks should be at least 18" wide, though 2' is a suggested minimum. Sinks need at least 30" of clearance in front.

▲ Bathroom plumbing is most cost efficient when placed back-to-back and stacked floor-to-floor to other bathrooms.

▲ Never place a window above a shower; if you can't resist, be ready for leaks, rot and mildew.

DINING ROOMS

▲ There are two ways to properly size a dining room:

1. Allow 42" from the edge of the table to the wall or furniture (e.g., a 3'x5' table needs 10'x12' of space).

2. Allow 30 square feet per person (e.g., 6 people x 30' = 180 square feet or a room 12'x15').

FAMILY ROOMS

▲ Near the kitchen, often open to the kitchen.

▲ Usually in the rear of the house, private and not seen from the front door.

▲ Primary choice for fireplace, entertainment centers, bookcases.

▲ A small family room is typically 12'x16', average size is 14'x18'.

LIVING ROOMS

▲ Usually in the front of the house, often opposite the dining room.

▲ Should have at least one long wall for sofa and for hanging formal pictures/paintings.

▲ Minimum recommended size is 12'x16'; average size is 12'–14' wide by 16'–18' long.

FOYERS/ ENTRY HALLS

▲ 6'x6' is a minimum size, 6'x8' (or larger) is better.

▲ Try to incorporate a 4' (or larger) coat closet.

▲ Separate from rest of house by using either wing walls or a different flooring, usually all-weather rather than carpet.

BEDROOMS

▲ Plan for at least one long wall for the head of a bed. Placing the head of the bed on an inside wall is better (for warmth).

▲ Try to place closets towards other rooms (to reduce noise) or on an outside wall (to help with insulation) if possible. (These are suggestions and not always possible.)

▲ Minimum and suggested sizes of bedrooms:

Size	Double Bed	One Twin Bed	Two Twin beds
Minimum	10'x12'	8'x12'	12'x12'
Suggested	11'x12'	9'x12'	14'x14'

DINETTE

▲ Remember the rules for dining room sizing; often dinettes are smaller because dining rooms are planned for guests while dinettes are only for those living in the house.

▲ Dinettes are often pushed into a corner or a nook or bay. This gives more space and is an attractive part of most houses, both inside and out.

CLOSETS

▲ Closets are typically a minimum of 25" deep.

▲ A separate broom closet can be as little as 2' wide, a linen closet 3' wide.

▲ Bedroom closets should range from a minimum of 4'–8' wide.

▲ A foyer closet should be at least 4' wide.

▲ Walk-in closets provide more free wall space than wall closets. They are usually "U" or "L" shaped.

▲ Closet systems (usually ventilated plastic or rubber coated wire shelving) will usually provide a much better use of closet space and thus reduce the size needed for closets.

GARAGES

▲ Garages are typically 22' deep.

▲ A minimum one-car garage is 12'x22'.

▲ A minimum two-car garage is 22'x22'

▲ Other standard widths of garages are 14', 20' and 24'.

▲ Garage doors are typically 7' tall by 8' or 9' wide; a single door for a two-car garage is 16' wide.

▲ Optimum sized garage doors are 7'x9'; two separate doors for a two-car garage is recommended over one single 16' door. An automatic door opener is a true luxury well worth having.

▲ If you plan to use your garage for storage, plan for it in the design. These suggested sizes don't allow for a lot of storage.

HALLWAYS

▲ Hallways are always at least 3' wide; 4' is nicer but 3' is adequate.

▲ Plan for a durable, scuff resistant paint or wallpaper in hallways. Also consider a more durable flooring because of the excess wear in a hallway. Plan for good lighting there as well.

The Art of Design

The art of design is much more subtle. While these are not necessarily absolutes, they are generally accepted and applied rules of good design. There is a lot of common sense in the art of design and these suggestions have their roots in what is normally done. As was mentioned in the chapter on the history of housing, a lot of outside influences affect how your house will be built. While you can have just about anything you want (for a price), you are still limited by what is available locally.

Brick is an excellent example. While brick is a more expensive siding material, it is also more available in some areas than others. You will see brick houses in rural South Carolina that cost less than $80,000, while brick might not appear on houses in Michigan under $200,000. The reason is that brick is readily available in South Carolina (there's a lot of sand and clay there) than in Michigan. There is also a cultural bias (hillbilly heaven is a brick house) towards a brick home in South Carolina and thus there are a lot of very small, inexpensive brick homes there.

There is a saying in housing that, "Houses are built with whatever can be shipped down the road." Things still have to be shipped down the road and there are some very real limitations on how large a building component or system can be made readily available in a certain area. Examples of this include pre-assembled trusses and modular housing. The general rule is nothing more than 14' high, 14' wide or 60' long can be shipped down a U.S. Highway. While you probably have never noticed how high bridges and overpasses are, the trucking industry certainly does and the magic number hovers around 14'.

Sometimes the components of a house are limited by the availability of craftsmen or the necessity of the component. Clay tile roofs are common in the Southwest and California. The sun is brutal on roofs there and, even though more expensive, houses are typically built with tile in those regions. While tile is available almost anywhere, you'll usually only see it where the climate demands it. The availability of craftsmen also varies around the country.

There is a continuing debate of the benefits of poured concrete foundations versus block foundations. The costs are similar as are the durability. However, it is rare where both foundation systems are done in equal amounts. In fact, in many areas, only one type is available. It's usually just a matter of where there are block masons readily available, you'll see a lot of block foundations. Where there are companies that specialize in poured concrete foundations, you'll see more poured walls. (Go figure!)

The point of all this is that when you start designing your house, you're going to start the process of thinking about components of the house. While we'll be going into much greater detail in this area later on, realize that the components of your home will affect it's design.

Beyond the practical side of design and designing with readily available materials, you need to design with how the materials typically come.

Beyond the practical side of design and designing with readily available materials (with regional differences in availability and cost), you need to design with how the materials typically come. As we mentioned in the review of history, houses are built with dimensional lumber, often called "2-bys" or "2xs." This means that the wood will range in size from 2'x4' to 2'x12', in various lengths. Sheathing (plywood) and drywall typically comes in 4'x8' sheets (though drywall also comes in 4'x12' sheets). What you have here is a building block to design with. These blocks are typically divisible by two and four. Lumber comes in 2' increments, starting with 8' and ending with 16' (though longer pieces are available, usually up to 20' without special ordering). With this mind, houses should be designed in 2' and 4' grids to take best advantage of the size of normal building materials.

The following are some typical rules of thumb in roughing out the size and design of your house:

GENERAL SIZE OF THE HOUSE

▲ Always work in even numbers, round up and down in numbers divisible by two.

▲ Make the house wider rather than deeper. A rule of thumb is to try to keep the houses no more than 32' deep. This is crucial if you're planning to use trusses (most houses nowadays do) because trusses longer than 32' often require special engineering. This means extra cost, extra time and a more complicated house.

▲ Typical house depths range from 24'-28' deep. The 28' might be a bit shallow if you're planning to put a room front and back and want each to be 14' wide (it won't work). Go up to 30' or 32' if that is the intention.

▲ If you need the house to be deeper and can not design your way out of it (have you considered intersecting wings or a two story?), go ahead and make it deeper. Just plan for the extra time and cost in your estimates. It's not the end of the world.

ROOFS AND ROOF LINES

▲ The steeper the roof, the better the house looks. A shallow roof pitch (steepness of the roof) is the mark of a cheap house. It is cheap because a shallow roof is cheaper to build; however, more than anything else, it makes your house look cheap. A minimum 6/12 roof pitch is very desirable, followed by a 9/12 or a 12/12. The small extra cost is worth it in many cases. Also, a 12/12 roof pitch allows for extra room on the second floor and is an inexpensive way to add square footage to your home. By the way, most Cape Cod style homes have a 12/12 pitch, which not only gives them more room but makes them look more attractive. In many areas around the country, the Cape Cod style home is always a best seller.

▲ Most 12/12 roofs are made with rafters rather than trusses. However, trusses are available that allow second floor room for additional rooms or storage. There is a limitation in depth for these "attic" trusses, but they usually provide at least 10' of living space within them, which is a workable amount of room, especially when used in conjunction with dormers.

▲ When designing a building with multiple roof lines, they all should have the same pitch. Do not mix roof pitches in a house.

▲ When choosing roofing materials, realize that the best looking stuff (shakes, tile, metal) also costs the most. Labor costs are more as well as the extra cost of the materials.

SOLAR ORIENTATION

▲ Almost all you need to know is that the sun rises in the East and sets in the West. East is warm and bright, West is hot and dark. Rooms that would appreciate the morning sun, like the kitchen and your bedroom (if you're an early riser) should face East. Rooms that you don't want to get too hot (the kitchen) shouldn't be facing West.

▲ You also need to know that the north side of the house is always going to be colder than the other sides. It might be a good idea to reduce the size of windows on this side as well and possibly increase the insulation there, also.

WINDOWS

▲ Traditional homes typically use double hung windows, contemporary homes use casement or sliding windows.

▲ Don't mix the types of windows if at all possible. You can probably get away with the use of true divided lites in the front of a colonial house and snap in grills on the unseen sides and rear. A casement over the sink is forgivable.

▲ Line windows up outside the house. It should not have a hodgepodge look. Doing this might cause you to rework the floor plan, since the floor plan is usually done first and often doesn't match how the windows should look on the outside.

▲ Try to avoid a "bug-eyed" look to the house that is created by putting larger windows above smaller windows in a two-story. There is an art to getting the windows right, but balance and symmetry are the guidelines to follow.

▲ Consider using smaller, better insulated windows on the north side of your house to help with the energy efficiency, if possible.

STAIRS

▲ Stairs are always at least 3' wide; 4' wide (or wider) is nice but 3' is normal and adequate, albeit a bit boring.

▲ Changes in ceiling heights greatly affect stair design. Increasing the ceiling height might cause a total redesign of the house. Each foot of extra ceiling height requires two extra treads (steps). It is especially crucial in shallow house designs because of the extra room longer stairs take up in the depth of a house.

▲ Circular and winder stairs are especially tricky. They are not a good choice in smaller houses (unless you're copying "Tara") and should be avoided. They often violate local codes. Find another solution.

The Code of Design

Codes have a dramatic affect on your house design. Violate the code and you have to take your house apart (at least the offending part) and rebuild it. While we'll go over codes in more detail in another chapter, we'll explore some basic areas of a typical building code that affect the design of your house.

Codes are usually common sense things. They are made by the government "and all they want to do is (to protect and) help you." (You've heard that before?) Why do so many people resist this help from the government? It costs money to meet codes and many people feel they don't need the government's help, thank you very much. While some of the codes border on the ridiculous, they are based in fact and usually in reaction to actual events. The state of North Carolina recently beefed up its code on how well decks are attached to houses. It appears that a deck fell off a house in Raleigh (with some high up *muckity mucks* from the state capitol on it). Some people got hurt and a grand investigation was conducted. Discovered first was that the deck was built to meet current code. Discovered second was that current code was not adequate for a deck party of the magnitude of that unfortunate event. The result was a much tougher deck code.

Codes are there to protect your well being and to make sure your home is built better. It's not necessarily a matter of quality (specifications do a better job there), but a matter of better technique and function. And again, they are based on common sense. Along with common sense is how human beings function in real life. As an example, how much room does an average human being need to turn around, walk down a hallway, to balance themselves on a stoop or to keep from falling over a deck rail or down the stairs? The answer is 3 feet.

There are two major areas where the code people take notice. One is in the area of fire prevention. Bad houses burn down and kill people. It is quite avoidable in most circumstances. The second thing code people know is that people fall down a lot in homes. They slip in the shower, they fall down the stairs, they go over or through a railing.

From the study of ergonomics (or klutz study), scientist (geniuses) know how much room an average human being needs to walk in. (Three feet, remember?) So, guess what? A lot of codes have a "three-foot rule." Hallways are 3' wide. Stairways are 3' wide. Stoops and landings are 3' square. Main doorways are 3' wide. These scientist also know how big the typical fireman is (with all his gear on) and prescribe the size of things firemen have to get through to stop fires and rescue people. Like windows in bedroom and access holes to attics. These are prescribed by code and rigidly enforced. Remember the great Chicago fire that caused the framing methods to change from balloon framing to platform framing? Balloon framing increased the risk of fire so it was eliminated. The code guys don't mess around with public safety and it is reflected in how you design your house.

A specific area where codes play a major role in house design is the design of the stairs, which have a prescribed height (rise) and depth (run) to each tread. While there are some regional differences in stair design, the codes are pretty much the same. Ergonomics tells you that the average human being can only climb a certain steepness of stair. The normal rise ranges from 7"–9". The average run averages from 9"–12". Your code will be very specific on this, down to the last quarter inch. Ergonomics also tells how to trip someone. The steps have to be uniform the entire way. If the top or bottom step is off as little as an inch, the chances are that you are going to trip. Or your 90-year-old grandmother with the weak hip. If she lives in California, where the state sport is lawsuits, she's going to sue someone.

The ergonomic people have also measured the heads of little kids because they are prone to poke them through railings and get stuck or worse. Therefore, they've prescribed how far apart each picket of a rail should be (6"). They know how far you can fall before you're probably going to get hurt (32"). Therefore, stoops higher than this have to have a protective railing. They know how high most people can climb and therefore prescribe how high a window can be off the floor (44") to let a fireman in or you out. While they'll tell you how high a doorway has to be, it's hard to goof that one up because no one makes a door that violates code. (Why would they?) Even so, the clever do-it-yourselfer could build his own doors and violate the heck out of codes if they didn't know the prescription (6'8").

The code people even tell you how much natural light and ventilation a room should have, thus helping you select your windows. They'll tell you how well to insulate your house and where to use caulk to seal it up. They'll make sure your plumbing works and that the wiring probably won't burn your house down.

Codes vary from state to state and from county to county. This book cannot tell you everything. Besides, codes change every year. Nevertheless, this chapter and the one on codes will give you enough information to keep you mostly out of trouble. Don't fight the codes (for a lot of good reason) and remember, the government is there to help you. Really. ■

8

Bubble Diagrams

Tiny Bubbles . . .

Circles actually. Or maybe balloons. A great way to start designing your house is by assigning a relationship between rooms. Write down what the room is and draw a circle around it. Write the other rooms as they relate to the first and circle them as well. What you're creating is a bubble diagram. Pretty simple. The best way to show this is with an actual house plan. We'll use the notes from the *Design by List* house seen in Chapter 6.

The First Bubbles

Let's start with the *Gotta Have It* list and lay out the first floor. Item #5 lists separate living and dining rooms, so we put these words side-by-side like such:

In This Chapter . . .
▲ How to lay out a basic house
▲ How to determine the size of a house
▲ How to use Design by Lists

Now a number of things come into play. From our *Design Guidelines* (Chapter 7), we know that the kitchen should be near the dining room. We also know that the living and dining room (formal rooms) should be in the front of the house and that the kitchen and family room (private rooms) should be in the back. Therefore the house should lay out like this:

FR	Kit.
LR	DR

(Front of house, facing west)

Notice that we placed the living room on the left and the dining room on the right. This forced the kitchen to be in the right rear of the house. This might not necessarily be the best place for it. Two things can affect the placement of the kitchen. First is solar orientation. What you want to avoid is having the kitchen facing west. This is because the sun will be setting in that direction and it will get hot in there while you're trying to cook supper. Wouldn't it be nicer for the kitchen to be bright and warm in the morning? Face the east and you've got it!

The second thing to affect the placement of the kitchen is which side of the house the garage or driveway is going to be on. It needs to be next to the kitchen for ease of unloading groceries. This requirement should outweigh any other factor, including solar orientation. Sometimes lot condition dictates the design of your house and you just have to do the best you can. Of course, buying the lot and designing the house to it makes good sense. We'll talk about that later. Let's assume that the solar orientation and the garage placement works out here.

Another consideration was that the *List* (item 7) called for a two-story house. It also requested a Colonial style (*Dream On!* #2). While you might not know at lot about Colonial style plans, if you look at enough of them you will know that the living and dining rooms are split by the foyer/hallway and the stairs going up. Therefore, it makes sense that this house has the same arrangement. With four primary rooms downstairs and a fairly modest-sized house, you're probably OK with the first floor as it is.

Before we move onto the second floor, we should first work on the basic size of this house. Look at the *How You Doing Now?* list. Are there any sized rooms that you've determined to be OK? How about the family room at 13'x14'? We know that the living room is too small at 12'x13'. We also know from the *Design Guidelines* that an average size of 14'x16' is adequate. How about assigning it a size (for now) of 16' wide by 14' deep? This meets the size criteria and is also divisible by two, the typical size of lumber. It would look like this:

—16'—

14'	FR	Kit.
14'	LR	DR

—16'—

We've assigned these number based on several factors. We know that 12'x13' is too small for the living room (from *List*). We know that 13'x14' for the Family room is OK so that 14'x16' would not be a problem. We also know from the *Design Guidelines* for living and family rooms that 14'x16' is within reason. We are also staying with the typical sizes of lumber. By the way, we probably have, by default, determined the depth of the house at 28'. While this might not work, it is a typical size of a house's depth.

Let's next look at the center hallway. We know that a set of stairs takes up 3' of room. We also know that a hallway is at least 3' wide (we know these things from

Design Guidelines). So, we're at a minimum of 6'. However, 10' would work a lot better because we know that houses seem to lose inches and feet as we design them. We also know that Colonial houses have generous foyers and center hallways. So let's make the center hallway 10' wide as thus:

—16'—/—10'—/

14'   FR Dinette Kit.

14'   LR Foyer   DR

—16'—/—10'—/

Next is the kitchen/dining room. Obviously they will most likely be 14' deep to match the other side of the house. If not, at least that side will be a total of 28' deep. Let's work with the dining room next. Our *List* tells us that the 11'4"x12'7" dining room is too small. We could match the living room in size at 14'x16' but that might be a bit too large; 12'x14' might work if the furniture placement is known and there is no furniture placement problems. It would work if furniture wasn't going to be placed on the north or south walls of the dining room. Chances are pretty slim of that happening because most dining room sets have hutches and the east wall is the entrance to the kitchen and the west wall will have windows in it.

The debate is whether to go with a 14' or 16' wide dining room. At 16', the total width of the house is 42'; 42' times 28' (depth) is 1,176'. Since this is a two-story house, we're looking at 2,352 square feet. At 14', the total width of the house would be 40' or a 2,240 square foot house, 224' smaller. Using a very rough cost estimate of $70 a foot, we are looking at $15,680 for these extra 2'. Let's go with 14'x14' and see if it works. It would look like this:

—16'—/—10'—/—14'—/

14'   FR Dinette Kit.

14'   LR Foyer   DR

—16'—/—10'—/—14'—/

Does it work? We're certainly over the covenant minimum. How about the maximum width of house requirement? Remember that we also want an attached two-car garage. We know that these range from 20' to 24', so we'll be at least 60' wide with this house. Have we forgotten anything? What about a downstairs bathroom or laundry? Where can they go?

You've got two basic choices. They can be worked into the hall or between the kitchen and dining room or they can go into their own separate room between the house and the garage. Either will work. However, a separate room between the house and garage is often used in this house plan. Sometimes called a connector, it is efficient and looks pretty good from the outside. I'll show you how this works here:

$$-16'-/-10'-/-14'-/$$

| 14' | FR | Dinette | Kit. | Bath |
| 14' | LR | Foyer | DR | Laundry |

$$-16'-/-10'-/-14'-/$$

First, what is the typical size of a powder room? Either 3'x7' or 5'x6'. What is usually done in this case is a 3'x7' rather than a 5'x6'. We will use a 3'x7'. We know that we have to get by this bath to get from the kitchen to the garage. Therefore, we need another 3' of space. Next we need room for the laundry. A washer/dryer side-by-side needs a space of at least 5' wide and 3' deep. We might also want to add a broom closet or pantry plus room for a freezer. Why not? Using even numbers, let's expand the width of the connector to 12'.

Now let's look at the depth of this small connector. We need at least 9' of room. Three feet for the powder room, 3' for the passage way and 3' for the washer dryer/freezer/closet. If we had at least three more feet, we could put the washer/ dryer in a room rather than a closet. Twelve feet in depth seems to work. The total connector would be 12'x12', thus adding 144' square feet to the house, making it 2,384 square feet. That little connector is going to cost you, in theory, about $10,000. But, you've now got a nice powder room (that's not crammed in the house), a nice laundry room, a pantry/broom closet and room for a freezer.

Not a bad deal. It would look like this:

$$-16'-/-10'-/-14'-/-12'-/$$

| 14' | FR | Dinette | Kit. | Bath/Hall | 3' |
| 14' | LR | Foyer | DR | Laundry | 6' |

$$-16'-/-10'-/-14'-/-12'-/$$

Next is the garage. Our covenants say we have to have 20' setbacks on the side yard. The lot is 120' wide. Minus 40' (both setbacks), we have room for a house that is 80' wide. The main house is 40' plus the connector, which is 12', giving us 52' total and allowing 28 more feet for a garage. A 24' garage would leave 4' to play with. We'll probably need that 4' to take best advantage of the slope of the land. Therefore, a 24' garage would work. We also know from our *Design Guidelines* that the typical depth of a garage is 22', so we'll make it 22' deep.

The bubble diagram for the first floor of this house would look like this:

```
        −16'−/−10'−/−14'−/−12'−/−24'−/
14'  FR  Dinette  Kit.   Bath/Hall 3'  Garage
14'  LR  Foyer    DR     Laundry  6'     22
        −16'−/−10'−/−14'−/−12'−/−24'−/
```

The Second Set of Bubbles

Let's now look at the second floor. We know we have a space of 28'x40' to work with. The stairs and foyer will take the majority of the center of the house. Our *List* tells us we want at least three bedrooms and two baths upstairs. We'd like to have a four-fixture master bath and 9' ceilings. While we are now looking at the second floor, we did want 9' ceilings on the first floor. We are looking at it now because it will affect the layout of the second floor as well as the first. An extra foot of floor height will use up about 21" of floor space. The house is 28' deep. Normal stairs take up about 3'x12' of space. To be safe, let's say the stairs will take up 14' with 9' ceilings. Subtracting 14' from 28' gives you 14'. What do you need to do with these 14'? First, you have to have a foyer. We know that it is 10' wide. Our *Design Guidelines* recommend a foyer to be 6'x8'. We also know from our *The Way We Were* list that we like large foyers. So, we're down to 8' (14' minus 6'). Behind the stairs in the back is where the dinette goes (between the kitchen and the family room). That's a little tight. A solution? How about a bay that pushes part of the dinette out towards the back of the house? Great idea. We need to remember that when we get into more detail later.

Now let's look upstairs. At the top of the stairs, we've got about 8' from the top of the stairs to the rear wall. We need 3' for a hallway; leaving 5'. Is that enough for a hall bath? Maybe? Some solutions. How about a deeper house? Thirty feet works. What will it cost? Rough calculations tell me over $18,000. How about we dump the 9' ceilings downstairs? That will help. How about we grit our teeth and see what happens? Might work also. With a compromise of a few inches here and there (a 5'x10' foyer?) or some other magic, it might work. The real answer will come when the plans are drawn to $\frac{1}{4}$" scale, by a professional who, hopefully, doesn't make mistakes. The choice is yours. For this example, we're going to forget about the deeper house right now. We'll rely on the draftsman to tell us if we can have 9' ceilings and what will have to be adjusted to make it work.

OK, we're upstairs, got the stairs in and the hall bath is going to work *somehow.* The hall bath is 5'x10', which, as we know, is a decent size for a hall bath. The 5' came from the room left over when we put the stairs and hall in (plus the 6' or so foyer downstairs). The 10' came from the width of that center section downstairs. Next are the bedrooms. We've got three to put up there and we know whose is going to take the most space—yours. Which side do you put in on?

Remember when we talked about plumbing on the *Design Guidelines*. Where below are a lot of plumbing fixtures? The kitchen, right? Put the master bedroom on the kitchen side. Now you've got two bedrooms left. Put them on the other side. It looks like this:

−16'−/−10'−/−14'−/

14'	**BR**	Bath	Master Bath
14'	**BR**	Stairs	**MBR**

−16'−/−10'−/−14'−/

We need to determine how large the master bath and bedroom should be. We know we've got 14' of width to work with. We also have the same 5' from where we enter the master bedroom from the hall to the rear wall. Five feet works well for tubs and it would be economical to back the master bath up to the hall bath. So with 5' dictating the width of the master bath and having a total of 14' to the outside wall, we can develop a pretty decent master bath. We do have to put some closets into this room and would like large walk-in closets (from our *Dream On!* list).

There is a problem with the hallway being so far back in the house. To get to the front bedroom from the top of the stairs, you will have to have a turn in the hall to get to that bedroom. This detail will be worked out later. You also have some more space available to you. That's the space at the front of the house over the foyer. There are two typical uses for this space. First is to leave it open to the ceiling of the second floor. This adds drama and space to the foyer and can serve as a source of light if you put a window or skylight there. The second use is as a pretty good sized closet for the front bedroom. Since the hallway to the front bedroom is going to take a good bit of room, you should strongly consider a closet as a possibility.

Are you done? No, there's lots to do, like figuring out closets, placing windows and doors, etc. However, you've come a long way. You've satisfied all of your *Gotta Have It* list, knocked out a few of the *Dream On!* list and incorporated a lot of your experience with other homes into this one. It's a great start. We'll be drawing this house up in Chapter 12. ∎

9

Design To Fit Your Land

Buy the Right Land for What You Want

Most people start their home design projects years before they purchase their land. They've been tearing out plans and drawing on napkins forever. This isn't a bad idea and this book has been set up to help those that do. However, the proper way to design a house is to design it to fit your land. Fortunately, you will (or should) discover that you will have to design your house to fit your lot once it has been purchased. If you've put a lot of time and effort in designing your house and don't want to change it, then you should purchase land that fits your plan. While not especially easy, it can be done.

The first thing to look for in selecting land is whether it is suitable for a basement. Obviously coastal property is not suitable for a basement. You also might not want a basement. If so, do not buy a basement lot! If you do want a basement, you should be looking for land that slopes away from the street, not towards it. The basement or downhill side of a house is generally not attractive and best not seen from the street. Most homes built with basements also have decks. Decks that are high off the ground are also not especially attractive. Most people try to hide the underside of decks with lattice. While better looking than nothing, lattice is not a good architectural detail.

In searching for a basement lot, you should look for a lot that would be gently sloping to the rear. A perfect basement lot would be 8' out of level. This would accomplish two things. First is minimum excavation. You want to dig as little as possible because it costs money to dig. The second is that you're looking for minimum foundation work. If the lot is more than 8' out of level, you've got to make up that difference in foundation, which also is expensive. A steep mountain lot can require more than twice the foundation than a gently sloping lot.

The second thing you should look for in selecting a lot is solar orientation. If you want the morning sun to come into your kitchen or bedroom, you need to find a lot that matches your house plan. I live in the mountains and once worked at a development where most of the views faced towards the north. Obviously people wanted to capture these views with lots of glass. Glass is one of the worst insulators and therefore, people building on these lots were setting themselves up for very high energy bills. While it was not the end of the world and certainly lots of homes have views that face north, it was a problem. In the case of this development, it went under and the north facing views contributed to its failure. Another development several miles down the road (with south and east facing lots) sold like hotcakes.

The third thing to look for in a lot is where to place the driveway. If you plan to enter the house on the same level as the main living area rather than through the basement, you need to place the driveway and garage on the high side of the lot. The reason for this is that you want to have the least amount of stairs into the house from the driveway or garage. If you're on the low side, you could have a flight of stairs to climb. In addition, these stairs could interfere with the space needed to park your car.

The fourth thing to look for is how the slope of your land will affect where the entry doors are. Obviously, the goal is to reduce the number of steps at each entrance. Optimally, you want no more than three steps out of any door. This is especially true with the main entrance door. With a sloping basement lot, this won't be possible on the downhill side but should still be achievable for the main entrance door if you selected the right land.

The way production builders and production plan companies sometimes deal with this problem is to flip or reverse their plan to meet lot conditions. You might have seen plans that have been stamped, "Build in Reverse." What this means is that the plans, as drawn, do not fit the lot, but will if the plans are inverted or "reversed." I've built lots of houses with this condition and it is pretty doable. I cheat by flipping the plans over and looking at them through the light to get a full sense of how the house would work. It's always a concern that the house would be put in wrong or numbers mixed up. While I rarely had a problem with "Build in Reverse" plans, it would be better for the plans to be drawn to exactly fit the lot.

How Does It Lie?

Probably the most important thing a builder does is what is called *set* the house. It takes a fair amount of skill, should involve some math and, in doing it wrong, can have disastrous results. *Setting* the house has to do with where you place the finished floor. It's how deep you dig and how high you come up with the foundation. Obviously there is an optimum amount and everything beyond that "perfect" setting will cost you money or could put your house at risk. Sometimes the *set* of a house is predetermined. If you are on a public sewer, the plumbing has to have positive drainage or *fall* to the sewer. In other occasions, your finished floor is predetermined by flood conditions. In well-planned master communities (or areas with lots of building inspector types), the finished floor is preset for every house.

Where there is a sewer involved, you always go for a positive slope towards the sewer. Gravity never fails. Mechanical devices, like lift stations and sump pumps, are costly and don't work when the power is off. While these devices do exist and are required sometimes, they are best avoided. What you have to do when a sewer is involved is to raise the foundation high enough to get positive drainage to the sewer. The rule of thumb is ¼" of rise for each foot of distance. As an example, if your house is 100' away from the sewer, you will need 25" of fall in your sewer connection pipe, starting at the front of the house and going towards the sewer lateral (where you hook up your sewer to the main line). Obviously, you need to know how deep the sewer is before you can make that judgment. You also have to allow for the bend of the pipe inside your house as well as the distance the pipe goes while it travels underneath your house. Let's say, for instance, that the sewer lines started 24' back into your house. You would therefore have to add an additional 6" of slope or a total of 31". You might also want to add another 6" for the bend of the pipe, so now you're dealing with 37" of slope to get the sewer to work.

The next trick is to determine how deep the sewer lateral is in the ground. Here is where it can get very difficult or impossible without other information. I used to build in subdivisions that had what we called sewer stakes. These were 10' long 4x4s that were placed by the developer right on top of the lateral. Since we knew (we just knew) that they were 10' tall, we could determine how deep the laterals were and take measurements from there. While not hard to do, you needed a transit and confidence in your math skills. The worst thing you could do as a construction superintendent was to screw that up. It literally meant your job and was understood by all. I never got it wrong. However, there were enough "war" stories floating around of those that did. A few narrow escapes occurred when someone, in need of a small piece of treated 4x4 post, cut off the top of a sewer post. Or the case where the developer ran out of 10' posts and used eight footers, fully intending to tell someone but never did. Whew! While I could show you how to do the math on this, I would suggest you get some help. It's too important to goof this up.

If your site doesn't have a sewer, you'll be dealing with a septic tank and the drainage issue might not be as big a deal, especially if your have a decent slope on the lot. However, if you're digging a basement and plan to put plumbing in the basement, you have to do the same calculations as for a sewer to ensure you get positive drainage to that septic tank. In some areas, the health department (or whoever is responsible for approving septic tank and drain field permits) will require that the septic system be *in place* prior to building the house. While this might seem like a nuisance, it is not a bad idea and certainly would prevent heartache if you built your house too low for the septic system to work. Remember, gravity never fails—don't rely on a lift station or pump unless absolutely necessary.

The typical "off-site" (non subdivision lot) condition usually does not involve a critical sewer or septic system issue. You will have some leeway in how deep to set the house and therefore have a chance to do it right or wrong. The rule of thumb for setting a house is for the house to come out of the ground 8" at the high corner. Eight inches is because the foundation has to be 8" above grade (the

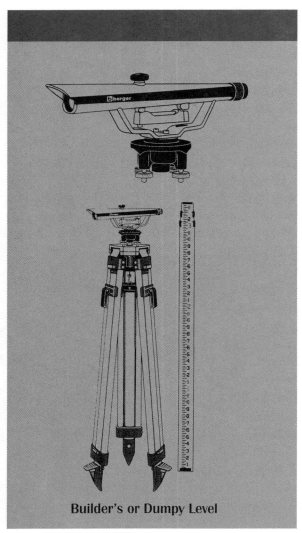

Builder's or Dumpy Level

dirt) by code. Among the things you need to know is how tall the foundation wall is, how thick the footing has to be and where the frost line is. We'll go over these terms and issues later in the book, but they do have an impact on setting the house. Foundation walls typically range in height from a few feet to 8' depending on a lot of factors we'll go over later.

As we mentioned, the goal is to use as little foundation material as possible. Everything beyond the minimum is called "wasted" or "buried." You also have to be concerned with the number of steps going out of each door. The goal is to have no more than three steps out of each door, if possible. The way you determine this is using a transit or builder's level and "shooting" all corners of the house. Transits are essentially levels with a scope. The scope has some magnification so that you can see for a considerable distance (hundreds of feet) and still read a ruler down to $\frac{1}{32}$ of an inch. The scope had cross hairs (like a rifle scope) and is very accurate. It rests on a tripod and is made level for 360 degrees. It pivots so that you can "shoot grade" in any direction and has a range of focus from a few feet to infinity.

Actually the word transit is a misnomer. A transit will do the job but is usually used by land surveyors and can do a lot of other amazing things. What most builders use are devices that are called "builder's levels" or "dumpy levels." These are very simple (and far less expensive) transits that shoot a level grade and that's about it. They can cost as little as $200 or so and are usually available for rent from equipment rental stores. Another device that will do a similar job is called a "lock level." This is an inexpensive, hand-held level that can do the trick, even though I've never been that pleased with a lock level. I prefer a *dumpy level.*

There are a number of advanced tricks you can do with setting a house. While most people just come out of the ground 8" at the high corner, you can, by studying the lot, come out less, and then *shave* off the high corner when you're back filling, thus saving a course (row) of block or 8" of concrete. Studying the lay of the land around your foundation can also save you in finish foundation material. This is especially important if you're using a brick veneer. The reason for this is what is called "brick to grade." Brick to grade means that brick will be showing from where the framing begins down to grade (the dirt). What you want to do is only have brick where it will show and not covered up by the dirt. Your mason would love to start the brick right off the footing because he makes more money doing that. However, if you study the lay of the land around your foundation, you can see where the brick will be exposed and where it will be buried. While many masons determine this for you (fudging in their favor), I always told my mason where I wanted the brick to start and where he was to use cheaper concrete block. While this will save you some money, you have to be careful that none of the block (or waterproofing) shows above grade. While it might be too difficult or risky (exposed block or waterproofing looks terrible), you should at least talk to the mason about it and let them know that you're concerned about "burying" too much expensive veneer brick.

Another aspect to setting a house is getting the water to drain away from the house and out of the yard. This is usually no problem on a lot with some slope to it. It's a real challenge when the lot is relatively flat, like in the Midwest and along the coast. The best way to look at setting a house on a flat lot is to think of it as an island. The top of the wall should be the highest point on the lot or at least the highest point at least 10' away from the foundation.[2]

Like the positive drainage for the sewer and septic, the ground should slope away from the house at least a $\frac{1}{4}$" a foot for about 10'. This will ensure that the house does not flood in a normal rainy season. Beyond the 10' you still have to get the water away from the house and off the lot. This is usually done by the grading contractor who establishes rough *swales*, which are finished graded by the landscaping contractor. "Swales" are broad, shallow trenches that direct surface water away from the house and off the home site. What you don't want is to have standing water on your lot, a common problem with new homes.

Many subdivisions have a master plan done by an engineer that shows where every lot in that development should drain to. Sometimes it drains toward the

War Story

#2: I had taken over a sub-division of townhouses once and noticed that one seven unit building was set too high. The spec was for the building to have poured concrete steps to the front door. These steps were as many as five steps up and some were starting to fall off due to the extra weight of the concrete. Like all townhome developments, the lot conditions were tight and there was a fair amount of slope to the site. Each unit, though 20- to 24-feet wide, was individually set. The first buildings in the development were built on slabs and then followed up with buildings that were built on full basements. The units that had the steps falling off were on basements and one reason the steps were falling off was because the fill dirt was settling. This is a common condition with any basement house, but I attributed the steps falling off to the fact that they were just too many of them. When I set a house, I always think about the number of steps involved because I know that people will be walking up those extra steps for the next 50 years. That's a lot of steps that could be eliminated if someone took the time and effort to optimally set a house. Anyway, I found that a site plan for the entire development had been made and that the finished floor of each unit had been predetermined by a surveyor. So why were these houses set too high? I called up the surveyor and explained the problem. He said that he determined the finished floor level based on the first building built and used the same calculations. Essentially, he used the existing curb height and, allowing for some slope away from the house for drainage, set the finished floor an average of eight inches above the curb. This worked great on the slab units. Unfortunately, the surveyor also used this calculation for the basement units. Aha! The top of the foundation wall of a slab house is the same as the finished floor. The concrete floor is poured level with the top of the wall. However, in a basement unit, the top of the wall is not the finished floor. You have to build a wooden floor system, above the top of the foundation wall which places the finished floor 12 inches higher! No wonder there were two extra steps on every one of those basement units. Not the end of the world but think about all those steps people have to take into their houses every day for the next 50 years. Needless to say, I threw away the site plan and individually set the rest of the units in that sub-division by myself.

street and is carried away in the curb's gutter. Sometimes the water will drain across a neighbor's (or your) yard to a drainage ditch. Regardless of where it goes, the drainage plan has already determined where the water should go and if you're having a problem with drainage, you should ask to see the master plan for the development and see if it is going to the right place.

Setting the house is an art and a science and I believe one of the most important things a builder does for you. It is a skill that is tough to master and is admired inside the business by those who can do it well. It is especially critical in the mountains and cannot only save you money and heartache, it can made your house look and function better. If you're unsure of your ability to set your house, by all means find an experienced builder or even a land surveyor to do it for you. It is an important part of your house and it lasts forever.

Setting the house is an art and a science and I believe one of the most important things a builder does for you. It is a skill that is tough to master and is admired inside the business by those who can do it well.

The Stars, The Moon and The Sun

The next thing you must do to your house is site it on the lot. While not as treacherous as setting the house, it too is important. Siting a house means placing it on a lot. There usually is a lot of freedom in siting a house, but there are also some limitations and restrictions. We'll talk about the legal aspects of sitting a house later in this book, but you should realize that codes and covenants restrict where you can locate your house on the lot. This usually has to do with how close you can come to a property line. While it will vary considerably with the size of your lot and whether it's in a subdivision or not, you generally can place your house on at least 50 percent of the available land on the lot. The covenant restrictions will take away the outside fringes of the lot (on all four sides) and, if you're on a septic system, this will eat up a fair amount of the land. Driveways and parking will also consume some land. Still, you'll have some flexibility depending on the size of the lot.

You should first identify how much land is available to "site" with. Mark off the lot itself with flagging material or string. This can also be done initially on your plot plan if done in scale. This will give you an envelope to work in. Next you need to determine what you want out of that lot and how to maximize the use of that lot. If you're building a basement, you'll want to position the house so that you would waste as little foundation as possible. Move the house up or back, left or right, or at an angle to get the most efficient use of the lot relative to the digging of a foundation. If there is a view to be captured, position the house to take best advantage of the view. You should realize that there are probably going to be some compromises to be made. The best view location might also be the most expensive to build. Tough choices.

Consider solar orientation. You might gain that morning sun by cocking the house in one direction. You might want to be cautious doing this as it might affect the way your house looks from the street. Most houses look best head on from the street or driveway approach. Not the end of the world, but a consideration. The contour of the land could be a factor. Let's say you really don't want a lot of steps up to the front door. Moving the house could help improve that situation. Privacy might be a consideration. Hiding the house in the trees or behind a rock outcropping might help. You might want to consider camping on your lot to get the best feeling about the lot. This will certainly help with the solar orientation and might give you clues to the noise level of the lot. Doing it at different times of the year will be instructive because the sun sets in different places as the year wears on.

If you don't want to go to the trouble of renting a level, you can site the house using stakes, mason's string and a string level, which should cost less than $10. Level up the strings on all four sides and see what you get. If it looks like a problem, move the house some place else and try again. Even if you don't use a string level, staking out the house will give you a much better idea about how it will look on the lot. Some people even bring out ladders or build small decks to see how the view would look from approximate floor level. However you do it, you should look at all the options when siting your home.

The Real Cost of Land

Most people looking for land focus on the sales price of the land and not the real cost of land. A $20,000 lot might cost more in the long run than a $30,000 lot. While location is the most important part of land value, a number of other factors play a major role.[3,4]

Land usually comes two ways: developed and undeveloped. Developed land usually has something more to it than raw or undeveloped land. It could have utilities already installed. Power, water, sewer, phones and cable. It could also have paved streets and a gate guard; swimming pools, club houses, golf courses and tennis courts. Some of these you might not want, but some things you're

War Stories

#3: I know of a person who wanted very badly to get into an exclusive neighborhood. They chose the cheapest lot there, one that was very steep. In clearing the lot, they discovered that they would have to site the house much further down the hill than they originally thought. The end result was that they built in a hole that was deeper than the roof of their two-story house. The house was also $25,000 over budget, mostly in retaining walls, driveway and foundation. The house plan was gorgeous—beautifully executed and well laid out. Out the back of the house was a lovely view. Out the front of the house, 15 feet away, was a raw cliff two stories high. The driveway had to be made of concrete because it was so steep. The people are very unhappy with their dream house. The problem could have been solved by purchasing a more expensive, but more buildable/livable lot. The customers are so upset that they are trying to sell their house. It has been on the market for more than two years. A real tragedy.

#4: Another story is about a friend of mine who bought some nice raw land out in the country. It was cheap and he was building as he could afford it. When he started, he didn't bother with temporary power (too expensive) and built the house with a gas powered generator. When it came time for him to apply for power, he met the utility company engineer to discuss getting power to his site. It so happened that he was one half mile from the nearest power line. The cost was $8,000 to run a line. Wow? That extra cost was no where in his budget. Well, my friend was also a strong environmentalist and wanted to be self sufficient (plus he didn't have $8,000). He got real interested in solar energy, root cellars and windmills. I still don't think he has power and has moved back into the stone age.

going to have to pay for anyway, like power, phone and water. The $30,000 lot could be a bargain if it already has many of the items mentioned and a much better deal than the $20,000 undeveloped lot in the middle of nowhere.

Another aspect of the cost of land is the degree of slope. A gently sloping lot for $30,000 could be cheaper than a steep lot being sold for $20,000. The extra cost of excavation, retaining walls and extra foundation materials could easily eat up the $10,000 cost differential.

The requirement to bring in fill dirt or accomplish certain site improvement and engineering such as pilings on a beach lot could greatly affect the true cost of land as well. Covenant restrictions could also make an impact. One subdivision might require an all brick veneer while another would allow other less costly materials. The speed of construction could be a factor. Some developments require you to be finished in a certain amount of time, within one year as an example. This would not work well for the do-it-yourselfer who wants to pay as they go.

So, when you're shopping for land keep these factors in mind. And don't go for the cheapest lot available until you know the true cost of building your home. ■

Don't go for the cheapest lot available until you know the true cost of building your home.

10

Blue Prints

Why Are You Blue?

I'm blue because I've always been blue. I'm printed through an emulsion process that uses blue ink. In fact, I'm a lot like a photograph because a strong light is used to cause a chemical reaction to make me print. I smell like ammonia, because the chemicals of ammonia are used in printing me. Where I'm printed has to be strongly vented though the smell can never be totally removed from the print room. If you don't like the smell of ammonia, stay out of the print room! I'm really only a copycat because the original drawings of a house are done in pencil or by my new cousin CAD. These original drawings are often copied for permanency on special paper called "Mylar." Often certain drawings for a house, called "standard details," are copied over and over again and use mylars. Mylars make sure these drawings don't get torn or damaged, which is what eventually happens to original drawings. You have to be real careful with original drawings and keep them unfolded in a large, wide drawer.

In This Chapter . . .

- ▲ The parts of a blueprint
- ▲ The many ways to look at a house plan
- ▲ How to read plans like a pro

What's the Plan, Stan?

Everyone calls blueprints "plans." While not incorrect, the word *plan* actually has a specific meaning. If someone asked you to bring a copy of your house plan only, you would probably bring more than your plan, probably the elevations, some details and a few sections. What a plan is best described as is a "birds-eye view" of your house. It's as if you're standing above (way above) your house and looking down at it.

Each level of the house has a plan. It starts with the foundation/footing plan (usually on the same sheet) and continues with a plan for each floor level and ends with a roof plan. If the roof is fairly simple and straightforward, the roof plan is often not done or necessary. While the word "plan" does have a specific meaning, it is also used to represent all the drawings of a house. It is certainly all right to call any part of a blueprint a plan. We'll do so through this book (even though we *know* now the technical definition of a *plan*).

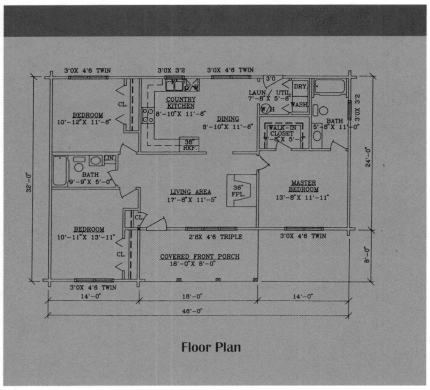

Floor Plan

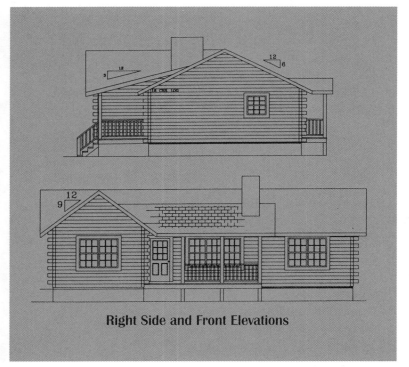

Right Side and Front Elevations

How High is the Elevation?

If you use the word "elevation," most people think of the height above sea level. *Elevation* has a totally different meaning in house plans. What it means is the outside appearance of a house.

Elevations will show each side of the house and will be listed as either a compass direction (north, south, etc.), if this is already known, or as front, rear, left, and right side if a standard plan. A small house usually has two elevations per page, a larger house one side per page.

In some cases, an interior elevation is also drawn, usually highlighting a particular room in a house to show how this would look once completed. Most elevations are drawn head on in two dimensions. Three dimensional or perspective drawings are used occasionally, but usually for the most unusual or attractive exterior side(s) of the house or interior.

Planning with a Chain Saw

Another way of looking at a house is through the use of a "section" drawing. A *section* is best explained by imagining that you cut your house in two vertically using a chainsaw and then drew the results. It will show the house from the footings all the way to the peak of the roof. A section drawing will show how thick the footings and foundation are. Then it shows the components of the exterior wall, including the parts of the wall, how thick the framing and insulation are, the sheathing and siding, and how the roof is built and covered.

Sections are sometimes a little hard to read because there are so many components in the wall or "skin" of a house and the layers are very thin. A lot of lines are drawn to these layers telling what they represent and you have to have a sharp eye to read the section plans. Many times the sections of a house plan are the only place that tells you some very vital information. For example, whether the walls are built of 2x4s or 2x6s or how tall the ceilings are on the first floor. Many a poor subcontractor lost their shirt by not carefully reading a section and placing a bid on work based on misinformation. It could be something as simple as the thickness or type of plywood, which could translate to hundreds, possibly thousands of dollars of misestimates. Sections are also used to show the components of a window and door.

The Devil is in the Details

Words can mean so many different things. We already know that *plans* and *elevations* mean different things in a house plan. Now there is another word that means something else and that word is "detail" as it relates to a house plan.

The word *detail* can be a noun or a verb. The noun detail means a drawing of a small, but complicated part of a house. It often is drawn as a section, but shows only a small part or series of parts of a house. Often it is of intricate parts of a house, like moldings and trim. Sometimes it is something that is repeated through the house or a series of houses. In this case, it is called a "Standard Detail." Since these are often repeated from house to house, many firms put these all on one page and issue them with each house plan. This is especially true with a building system or partially manufactured or pre-cut house. It often shows various ways to build foundations. Since there are two general types of foundation materials (block or poured concrete), several different finishes of foundation walls (stucco, brick, stone, etc.), and three different types of foundations (crawl, slab and basement), all of this information is pre-drawn and included on a standard detail sheet. The builder uses whichever applies to their particular house.

Unlike a section, a detail would show only part of a wall. In the case of the foundation detail, it could show the house from the footing to where the first piece of lumber is attached to the house and not continue up through the roof. Like sections, details often show very complicated parts of a house and are often hard to read. You must be careful in reading details.[5]

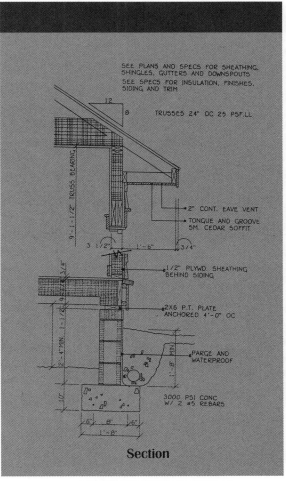

Section

COURTESY OF WILLIAM HUNTER O'CAIN, AIA

War Story

#5: I once was involved in the remodeling of a house that an architect had drawn the plans for. We were converting a minimal traditional house into a Craftsman style house. One of the distinctive details of a Craftsman style house are the porch posts, which are usually thick at the base and taper up to the porch ceiling. The architect drew the elevations showing these, but not any details on how to build these or what size to make them. He said the builder should be able to "scale" them off the blueprints and get them right.

While it is not uncommon to leave off some details (they cost money to draw and can be scaled off the plans), in this case they lead to a compromised house. The carpenter not only didn't "scale" the plans, he used the smallest pieces of wood he could find, barely enough to cover a 4x4 post. The column should have been at least a foot wide at the base but wound up about six inches and destroyed the look of the house. The details are important.

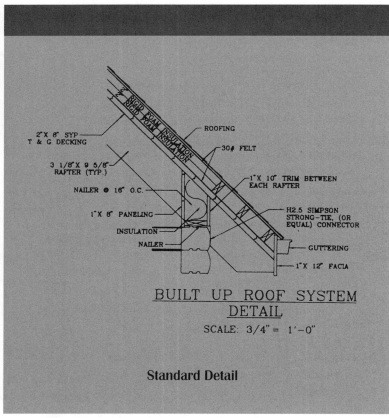

2" X 8" SYP
T & G DECKING

3 1/8" X 9 5/8"
RAFTER (TYP.)

NAILER @ 16" O.C.

1" X 6" PANELING

INSULATION

NAILER

RIGID FOAM INSULATION

ROOFING

30# FELT

1" X 10" TRIM BETWEEN
EACH RAFTER

H2.5 SIMPSON
STRONG-TIE, (OR
EQUAL) CONNECTOR

GUTTERING

1" X 12" FACIA

BUILT UP ROOF SYSTEM
DETAIL
SCALE: 3/4" = 1'-0"

Standard Detail

COURTESY OF ANTHONY LOG HOMES;
© ANTHONY FOREST PRODUCTS COMPANY

Detail is also a verb and means to draw a small section or group of components of a house. Fledgling architects in their three-year apprenticeship often are assigned the work of detailing plans. It is hard and exacting work and involves little creativity or excitement. It is, though, very necessary to the success of a house and not only shows the subcontractors what needs to be bid on and built, but also can make a vast difference in how the house will look. The details are what gives the house its charm and small details like the specific sizes and types of molding used in crown molding, chair rail, door trim, and baseboard can make all the difference in a home. It is something that should not be ignored or treated lightly.

What's the Schedule?

Yet another word with a different meaning. A "schedule" is a list that lays out the components of a house, usually in chart form. The two most common items in a schedule are windows and doors (millwork) and nails or fastening devices. Often the plans will use a code that refers back to a schedule. For example, rather than drawing all the specific information about a window or door, the plan and/or elevations might use a number or series of numbers and letters to refer back to the window and door schedule or chart. The chart shows the name of the window, the rough opening, the style and color, the manufacturer, the screen size, the mullion type, and other vital information.[6]

As you can see, this is too much information to place on a floor plan or elevation. This also is true on a nailing schedule. Could you imagine a plan that showed where every nail and bolt went?

The nailing schedule is important to not only tell the carpenter which size nails to use (they'll use whatever is in their apron if you don't tell them), but to

Millwork Schedule

		Type	Quantity	Size	Material	Finish	Swing	Location
	Windows							
		D.H. twin	4	3/0 4/6	Pine	Paint/stain	n/a	BRs, DR
		D.H. single	2	3/0 3/2	Pine	Paint/stain	n/a	Bath, Kit.
		D.H. triple	1	2/8 4/6	Pine	Paint/stain	n/a	LR
	Ext. Doors	9 lite x buck	1	3/0 6/8	Pine	Paint/stain	L/H	Rear
		6 panel	1	3/0 6/8	Pine	Paint/stain	L/H	Front
	Int. Doors	6 panel	3	2/8 6/8	Masonite	Paint	L/H	BRs, Bath
		6 panel	3	2/8 6/8	Masonite	Paint	R/H	BRs, Bath
		6 panel	1	2/4 6/9	Masonite	Paint	R/H	Foyer
		6 panel bi-fold	2	6/0 6/8	Masonite	Paint	n/a	BRs
		6 panel bi-fold	1	5/0 6/8	Masonite	Paint	n/a	Laundry

satisfy engineering requirements. This is especially important in an area that has earthquake or hurricane codes. Many code books will have standard nailing schedules that tell you what size and type of nails to use to connect standard sizes of wood used in specific locations. Plans often don't have nailing or fastening schedules in areas where there are no engineering concerns or strict enforcement of codes. In areas where there are strong codes, you're going to see not only schedules but also connection details.

Head for the Border

The information that is on the border of a set of plans is very important to the plans and provides a wealth of valuable information.

The first thing typically seen on the border of a set of plans is the scale of the drawing. Most plans are drawn at ¼" scale. This typically includes the floor plans and elevations. If the house is huge and won't fit on standard blueprint paper, it could be drawn at another scale. When looking at plans, you should always check to see the scale. Realize too that the scale can change from page to page or within a page. This is often done to get a detail or section to fit on a page. It is a common mistake to misread the scale of a plan or page, so be careful.

The second vital piece of information in the border is the date of the drawing. The date of the original drawing will show prominently and this date will never be removed. If the plans are changed or revised, that information will be placed in a block usually directly below the date of the original drawing. The difficulty lies with ensuring that you and your builder or subcontractor are using plans with the latest revision. This again is a common mistake in construction. Many builders will number each copy of their plans and keep a record of who they gave these plan to. When revisions are made, they sometimes ask for the earlier

The nailing schedule is important to not only tell the carpenter which size nails to use (they'll use whatever is in their apron if you don't tell them), but to satisfy engineering requirements.

War Story

#6: This has to do with Hurricane Andrew in Florida in 1993. As you know, a lot of houses blew down during this storm and charges of builder and building inspector misconduct and incompetence flew as furiously as the hurricane itself. One of the concerns focused on the use of OSB, a type of plywood, and nailing and fastening schedules. While there were instances where inadequate nailing occurred (there is no such thing as a perfect house), OSB took a beating. At the root of many failures was nail guns being used in conjunction with OSB. When you nail with a hammer, you know when you missed the framing member below. You also cannot nail the nail too deeply because the hammer head is wider than the nail. However, with a nail gun, you wouldn't know for sure if the nail went into the framing member below (though some people can hear if it "hits"). Also, a nail gun has settings for different types of nails and these settings are rarely changed.

What happened in Florida was that many carpenters were using nail guns and either missed the sub framing or drove the nails so deeply that they wouldn't hold in the OSB. Most people blamed the OSB and sales of that material plummeted. The code people were also thinking of banning OSB in Florida, but cooler heads prevailed. What they did do was add to the connection schedule of all homes in Florida and are now requiring what is called "hurricane straps" and other metal connectors that are stronger than was used previously. Inspectors are also checking the setting on nail guns and educating builders on how to use and set them properly.

plans back and issue new, revised plans. Still, mistakes are made and it is always best to not issue any plans out to the field until after final revisions are made. If changes are made, you have to ensure that your house is being bid and built off of the latest set of plans.

The third thing you'll see in the border is the initials of who actually drew the plans. This means less to you than it does to the firm drawing the plans. While it gives the architect or draftsman "ownership" of the plans, it also tells you who made mistakes on the plan. It will also let you know if the architect drew the plan himself or gave it to someone on his staff.

Additionally, it also lets you know if your plans are being passed around the office with each revision. It is best for the same person to make each revision. This is also common practice in the industry. It is not uncommon, however, for an architect to have someone on staff detail or draw your plans. The only cause for concern would be if you were told or expected the architect to personally draw all of your plans.

The *fourth* thing you'll see on a set of plans will mean a lot to you, but not especially be vital to the building of your house except making sure it's your house being built. This is your name and probably the address (city/state) of where the house is being built. Instead of plan B1254 or "The Oakwood," these plans (if you use an architect or building designer) are the *Jones* plans or the *Smith* plans. It is a bit of an ego trip. Make sure they spell your name right.[7] ■

If changes are made,

you have to ensure that

your house is being bid

and built off of the

latest set of plans.

War Story

#7: You can bet that sometime in the history of building that someone built the wrong house on the wrong lot. You need to pay attention. When I was building production houses, the company I worked for got mad at their masonry contractor and fired them. These guys were great and did more than their share of the work. In fact, they did their job so well that I really didn't know much about masonry. When they were fired, we hired a bunch of smaller masonry crews whom we had not established a track record with.

We had a popular style of bi-level house that had what is called a garrison overhang. The upper story hung over the lower story 18 inches. We left the foundation plans on site in a weather tight tube for the contractors to use and then leave for the next person. The footing man put his footings in and now it was the mason's turn. Everything was going smoothly and the job was completed.

A superintendent's job is to check the foundation to make sure it was square, level and plumb. Since the foundation was a rectangle, this was easy to do and I pulled diagonals and sure enough it was square. It looked like I had a good crew here. I then measured the foundation and found the foundation to be 18 inches too deep. Whoa! I looked at the footings and saw that while the block was resting on the footings, they were shoved almost off the footings front and back. I called the mason up and asked to meet him at the site. I asked him to show me what plans he used. He reached into the weather tight tube and pulled out the upper story floor plan. He then said that these were the only plans he had and he used them to build the house. It was 18 inches too big. I later found that the footing contractor had taken the foundation plans with him. I told the mason contractor, "Good guess, but no cigar, make it right," which he did. He knocked down the front and rear wall and relayed them. This just shows you how important plans are. If it had been a two-story house with both floors the same depth, he would had been right on. I kept this sub because I was impressed he could build a perfect foundation based on a floor plan rather than a foundation plan. I also met every mason from then on to ensure that they were using the right plan.

11

The Tools of the Trade

Become an Architect for Under $10

Like many people, you probably want to take a stab at drawing your own plans, at least initially. This is not a bad idea and can be a lot of fun. If the plan is fairly simple and does not involve a flight of stairs or more than one ridge, you could probably build your house safely from the plans you drew. If your house has a second floor, reduced head room on the second floor or you're building where there is an active building department, you might want to have a draftsman, building designer or architect draw your final set of plans. Still, whatever work you do ahead of time might be very helpful to the draftsman or architect in getting a clearer picture of what you're trying to accomplish in your home.

You don't need any special tools or equipment to draw your own house plans but a few supplies could be helpful and probably cost less than $10. The first thing is an architect's rule. These are usually triangular in shape and have different scales on each side. There is one trick with this and that is that an architect's rule also looks like an engineer's rule. Their shape is the same and there are different scales on each side of the rule. The difference is that the engineer scale is in tenths and centimeters, while the architect's scale is in fractions of an inch and includes ⅛", ¼", and ½" scales. The two scales are incompatible. They usually say what they are on the scale or in their packaging. Just check to see that the scale you buy has an ⅛" and ¼" scale on it. Realize too that in the field, builders often use their tape measures to scale plans. While crude, it works because a tape measure has hash marks for ⅛" and ¼" measurements. Also, while you can use a tape measure or ruler to scale with, an architect's rule is also used to draw with, serving as a stable straight edge.

The next thing that is useful to use is a mechanical pencil with a fairly fine point. A sharp regular pencil will do, but you will have to constantly re-sharpen it because drawing requires very sharp lines. You also need a good eraser. I recommend an eraser that is not part of the pencil, but is refillable and in an adjustable holder. While usually not available in department stores, these can be found

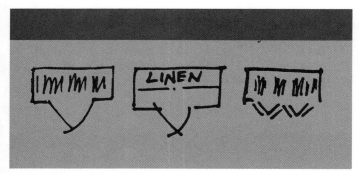

Clothes in closets are represented by squiggly lines. In a linen closet, you should label the closet "Linen."

Bi-fold doors are represented by twin hash marks.

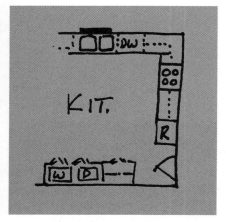

Appliances are usually drawn with templates and labeled with one letter. "R" is for refrigerator, "W" for washer, "D" for dryer, "Fr" for freezer, "Lt" for laundry tub or tray. Sinks, toilets, and stove tops are usually drawn with a unique shape that doesn't require labeling. Dishwashers are labeled "DW" and also use a dotted line to show where they actually are. Upper cabinets in a kitchen are also represented with a dotted line, which is drawn on the countertop.

good office supply or a blueprint supply store. If you re-want to get fancy, you can buy an electric eraser for around $50. These are more like neat toys and are not at all necessary. Some people want to have the tools of a pro, however.

Next is a plumbing template. Your plan will show plumbing fixtures and these templates can be used to draw these fixtures neatly. These templates can be purchased from a good office or blueprint supply store. Make sure they show the fixtures as they would appear from a *plan* view and have fixtures in ⅛" and ¼" scale. Since these templates might be the most expensive thing you buy (though usually less than $5), you can also obtain a template for free from a plumbing fixture supply house. The bigger brands of fixtures, like Kohler, usually have these available as promotional pieces. You can visit one of their offices, look at their products and see if you can talk them out of a template.

The next step is to get some paper. I recommend that you start drawing at ⅛" scale rather than ¼", which is the standard scale used in house plans. There are two basic reasons for this. First is that most house plans will fit on a standard-sized 8½"x11" sheet of paper if drawn at ⅛" scale. Going to ¼" will require larger, more expensive paper. Since there will be numerous revisions (there will be), it's less costly and easier to draw your home initially at ⅛" scale.

The second reason is that the width of a pencil lead is approximately the same width of a 4" wall at ⅛" scale. At ¼", to be in scale, you would need to draw a double line to accurately depict a 4" wall. Essentially, you would be drawing the house twice to get the same result. Again, because you will be doing a lot of revisions, you can get the job done quicker at ⅛" scale. The down side is that it is not as accurate and if you're trying to squeeze things into a house, like stairs or headroom, a plan drawn at ⅛" scale might not work when drawn at ¼" scale. In this case, don't get emotionally attached to the dimensions of the house and be prepared for additional compromises when you go to full-scale drawings.

You should draw on graph paper initially rather than unlined paper. The lines will help you draw and count the space. You can use paper pre-drawn with ⅛" squares (8 squares to an inch is what the cover sheet of the paper will say) or at 4 squares-per-inch. If you go with ¼" squares, you can still draw at ⅛" scale by remembering that each square represents two feet and not one. This graph paper is readily available at discount stores and will be least costly there. You can get more expensive paper from office supply and blueprint supply stores, but expect to pay a premium for it.

There are a few neat tricks some of the more expensive paper can do for you. First, you can get paper that shows the lines when copied. Most graph paper is printed in blue ink that does not copy. If the lines don't copy, you have to show every dimension or rely on a scale to determine the relative size of rooms.

The second neat kind of paper is paper you can see through. This is especially useful if you're designing a two-story house, because it is helpful in lining things up like stairs and bathrooms. It is much easier to start drawing the second floor

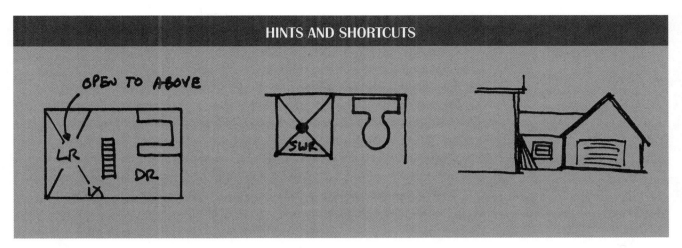

Open space is represented by a lightly drawn "X" that fully covers the space, with the words "open to above" or "open to below" depending on which level you're on.

Showers use a similar X but a small dot is placed in the center of the X to show that it is a shower rather than an open space. You can also write the initials "SWR" in this space.

Shadow lines could be added where there is a change in depth in a building, for example, where the connector recedes in our drawing.

Doors are drawn with a straight line showing the door and an arched line showing the swing. These representations should be shown exactly where they are in the house. If the door has a threshold, it should be represented with a straight line that closes it up.

You can draw corner boards and fascia. Windows can be drawn in more detail with moldings, muttons and trim. Glass can be represented by a squiggly line as well. You can also draw in some of the siding, roofing and brick using a line with a squiggle in it to show only part of it.

You can also draw in the foundation as it would look on the actual lot showing how the grade slopes. You can add steps and decks and even smoke from the fireplace.

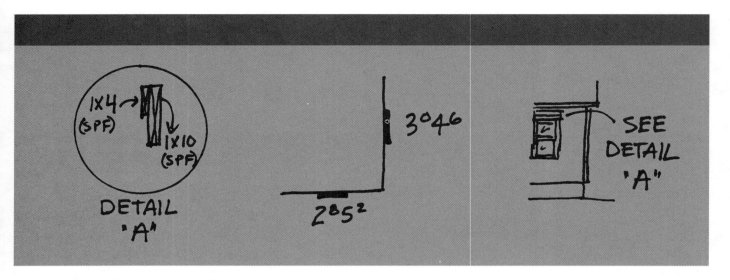

L–R: Detail drawings should show exactly what parts are needed to construct the house. Details should list the size and type of materials used; details are sometimes placed inside a circle.

Windows and doors are normally labeled on the plans only and not the elevations. Often they are labeled with a number or letter that refers to a millwork schedule. However, in rough draft, they can be labeled by their size (i.e., 3/0 4/6 on the plans).

You can label unusual items provided it too does not clutter up the drawings. If it is important to you to do so, draw a detail and/or section to show what you mean. Refer to it in the plans, such as "see Detail A" and then draw the detail somewhere else.

by laying a transparent sheet over the first floor and tracing in the stairs and outline of the house.

You can also get some tracing or tissue paper to help you make temporary "what if" drawings without having to draw the entire floor plan. While there are no lines on tracing paper, it is useful to make trial revisions to see how it fits. You can get this paper at discount stores in 8½"x11" sheets or on a roll of various sizes at a blueprint store. While not terribly expensive, it is not necessary to go this route unless you're planning to do a lot of drawing or you just want to show off.

Tricks of the Trade

There are a number of tricks and short cuts to make your drawings look even better. Up to now, your drawings should have been pretty precise. You've counted squares and put things where they belonged. Now you can add some flair to the drawings and maybe even save some time. While ⅛" scale drawings lack the detail of ¼" drawings, a few touches can improve their looks dramatically.

The sketches above and on the previous two pages show these neat, easy-to-do tricks. ■

12

On Your Mark, Get Set, Go!

Why Not Start at the Beginning?

Now you're ready to start drawing the house plans. We are going to convert the bubble diagrams in Chapter 8 to an ⅛" scale house plan. You always draw a floor plan in its entirety before beginning the elevations. The first thing you must do is determine the overall size of the plans and then center them on the paper.

In this example, the bubble diagram house is 76' wide and 28' deep. An 8½"x11" sheet of paper has 88 squares on it at ⅛" scale. Our house will use 76 of the squares, leaving 12 squares for borders. If the house were to have a side porch or deck, it might not fit on one sheet of paper. Even so, you should not go to larger paper just because a deck or patio doesn't fit. In the case here, you would center the drawing on the page, leaving 6 squares of margin on the left and right sides.

The 8½" side of the paper has 68 squares on it at ⅛" scale. Since our house is 28' deep, there will be 20' of margin on the top and bottom of the drawing. You should start the drawing at the left bottom corner, coming over 6 squares from the left and 20 squares from the bottom. Make a dot at this point. From here count up 28 squares, make a dot and then draw in the left side of the house plan. Next, measure over 40', make a dot and then draw in the line for the top and bottom of the house plan. Since you do not know at this time where the connector will attach to the house on the right side, leave this line off for now.

Now go back to your bubble diagram and start laying out the main rooms of the first floor. You can start with the 14'x16' living room. Draw a horizontal line in the center of the house dividing the living room from the family room. Come over to the right 10' (beyond the foyer/hallway) and lightly draw the line separating the kitchen from the dining room. You should do this lightly because you will later need to erase some of this line to show the entrance from the kitchen to the dining room. Next you can draw the vertical lines from the front wall that separates the living and dining rooms from the foyer/hallway. These lines should also be drawn lightly as part of them will be erased to show the entrance from the foyer/hallway into these rooms.

Now you have to make a decision—where do you put the stairs? On the left side or the right side of the foyer? We need to look at a number of factors. An absolute is that there has to be room to get by them to get into the living and dining rooms from the foyer/hallway. We also do not want them to interfere with the dinette or reduce the size of the upstairs hallway or bath. We have 28' to work with. We know the foyer needs at least 4' of room in depth (we'd like 6') and the upstairs hallway needs 3' and the upstairs bath a minimum of 5'.

Stairs for an 8' ceiling need about 12' of run. Add to this 3' for the upstairs hall, 5' for the bath and 4' for the foyer, and we have 24'. This gives us 4' to spare. Since this is a fairly shallow house, we will leave some of this extra room at the rear of the house for the two upstairs baths. The stairs can start 6' from the front of the house (giving us a 6'x10' foyer). We will place them on the left side of the foyer (although the right side would work as well). Counting from the front wall, come backwards 6' and start the stairs. They should be 3' wide and continue for 12'. This leaves 3' for the upstairs hall and 7' for the bath.

You should realize that different locales have different codes for how steep stairs can be.

You should realize that different locales have different codes for how steep stairs can be. Their exact measurement will be determined once these plans are done at ¼" scale. Realize too that the width of each intersecting wall takes up 4"–6" of space that is not accounted for in ⅛" scale drawings. This will cause some compromises as well once the plans are drawn at ¼" scale. What typically happens is that the plans are shifted to make them work or a design problem is created that has to be solved. The 12' used here for the stair run is a liberal allowance. Even so, most of the plans that I have drawn at ⅛" scale always seem to wind up with compromises at the stairs. Just don't get too emotionally attached to your plans until they are drawn at ¼" scale.

It looks like the stairs have defined the entrance to the living room. There is an approximate opening of 6', 3' of which is needed to get into this room. Probably the only two choices here is to leave the opening alone at 6' or build a 1'–3' wing wall starting at the front wall. This wing wall would better define the foyer space visually as well as physically separate the two rooms. However, either solution is fine and becomes a matter of personal choice. If a wing wall was not used, a different type of flooring in the foyer should be used to visually separate the foyer from the living room.

Let's now look at the wall between the kitchen and dining room. While we know we need 3' of space to enter the room, we'll allow 4'. This might be reduced when we go to ¼" drawings. We'll center the opening in the room with 5' walls on either side. Doing this will also help define the wall space available in the kitchen as well as giving wall space for furniture (extra chairs or a small buffet?) in the dining room.

The next space to define is the wall between the foyer hall and the dining room. While there are many suitable solutions (based on personal taste), let's bring a wing wall from the front of the house and end it opposite the stairs. Then, create a 4' opening and complete the wall. The wing wall defines a 6' (approximately) by 10' foyer. A problem we have though, is where to put the foyer closet. Since we usually want a 3'–4' foyer coat closet, we need to see where it could go. In a layout like this, there are several choices which again go back to personal taste.

One typical choice is only available if there is no basement. If that were the case, placing the closet under the stairs is a viable solution. If you were to do this, you would place it towards the rear of the stairs near the kitchen to get adequate ceiling height. The next choice would be to put it in the foyer at the front wall next to the dining room. While this would work, it would take 2' out of the foyer, which we wanted to remain spaciousness. Again, a matter of personal taste. A third choice is to put in no foyer closet and plan on a coat tree in the corner of the front wall and the dining room. This would work and is not a bad idea. A fourth choice is to work it into the kitchen. In this example house, we'll leave that choice for later. However, you can at least see the problem and the range of choices.

Let us now look at how to define the space between the family room and the dinette. The stairs help define it on the bottom of the room, but it is wide open from then on. While our *Design by Lists* tells us we want it to be open into the kitchen, it could be closed in somewhat and still achieve that goal. In this case, we need to think about furniture placement. A single chair needs about 3' of space, while a chair and small table needs about 5'. We still want to retain a large opening into the family room, but it might be helpful to have a small wing wall or half wall to define space. These walls will give something for furniture to back up to and also define the dinette space. On the rear wall, we'll use a 5' "half" wall that will accommodate room for a chair and small table. The half wall will still leave the room open to the kitchen, yet define the space and make the chair/table space more private and separate from the dinette. This will also physically define the dinette space. Doing this also leaves an opening into the family room about 5' wide.

Of all the rooms downstairs, the kitchen is the most challenging and also has the most choices. The kitchen design industry is well organized and has its own certifying organization "CKD," which stands for Certified Kitchen Designer. Many of the larger home centers like Home Depot and Lowes now also have kitchen design services that use CAD design systems. These are excellent resources and I highly recommend using them before you go to ¼" drawings. Since most people are using stock cabinets today, you need to be reasonably precise in determining the layout of the cabinets. While filler strips, usually no more than 3" wide, are commonly used, it is best to get this space down to 1"–2", if not to fractions of inches.

I usually rough out a kitchen, making sure the general space is how I want it and then go to a home center or kitchen designer to finalize the plans. The service is there, they are usually very good, and I trust them. In the case of this kitchen, the first thing I like to do is locate the kitchen window. A reasonable choice is to place it in the rear wall, centered in the room. Typical kitchen windows are 3' wide and a little over 3' tall. The industry standard is a double hung 3/0 3/2. If you recall, we suggested that the kitchen window not be a double hung because it is hard to open reaching over a sink. When you open a window, you usually get closer to it for leverage. The base cabinet interferes with this. In this

Of all the rooms downstairs, the kitchen is the most challenging and also has the most choices.

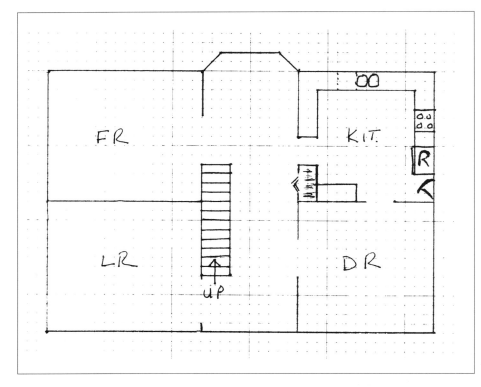

First Floor Plan

case, I'm going to allow space for a window up to 4' wide. We will size this window later. There is a current design trend for kitchen windows to be larger than the standard 3/0 3/2, making kitchens brighter than in the past.

Since we know that base cabinets are 2' deep, we can draw these in along the entire rear wall. However, before we do that, we need to decide if these base cabinets will return into the room or end right there. In making this determination, we need to decide if we want to have a bar that separates the dinette from the kitchen. This is common and makes sense—we'll do it! How long we make it is a matter of personal taste, but it ought to be 3'–5' long. In this case, we'll make it 5' long.

On the other side, we need to get a refrigerator and a range in, still leaving room for countertops between these appliances. We have 14' of space to work with here. We know we need a door to the outside that will take up 3'. The refrigerator will also take up 3' and the range 30".

Let's look at the range first. It can be placed 12" after we turn the corner. Twelve inches allows for a one-foot wide base cabinet, which is a standard size. The range will take up 30". Next, 18" of counter space and then the refrigerator. This 18" gives us both the 15" the range needs and the 15" the refrigerator needs (from *Design Guidelines*). This space is shared, but that is allowable. Eighteen inches is also a standard-sized cabinet.

Next is the kitchen sink. Most sinks are placed on an outside wall under a window. It is not required nor always placed there. Since there is a trend towards kitchens being open to the family room (and the family), some designers place the sink on a bar that faces the family room. It is not a bad choice and more a matter of personal taste.

There are two other considerations in our case here, however. These are the placement of the dishwasher (there's not enough room in the bar for both a sink and a standard dishwasher) and that the sink takes away from countertop space. A bar between the dinette and kitchen is typically used as a serving bar. A sink would interfere with this use. In this case, we'll place the sink under the window.

Let's see if our "work triangle" works. *Design Guidelines* tells us that it should be no more than 22'. A quick measurement between the "big three" shows it to be about 18', so it fits within the 12-to-22-foot rule.

Other considerations in the kitchen are where to place the dishwasher and how doors open. The dishwasher should be next to the sink, typically to the left of the sink for ease of rinsing and loading the dishwasher. We'll do that in this case. If it were placed to the right of the sink, it would interfere with the opening of the oven door. The next door to look at is the refrigerator door. Since the countertop is on the left side of the refrigerator, the latch side should be on that side. The hinge is on the other and therefore, the refrigerator would open towards the door to the connector/garage. As you recall, we don't want the block entrances to the kitchen and we don't want doors to open into each other. Since the refrigerator, when open, could possibly interfere with someone coming into the kitchen, we will hinge that door in the corner so that it opens towards the dining room wall.

We've got the kitchen just about finished. By locating the kitchen door to the outside, we've fixed the position of the 12' wide connector, which we'll get to shortly. However, we've got a little more space left in the kitchen. This often happens in design. We've been following some pretty strict rules about space and now we have a space about 4'x5' (at the wall that backs up to the dining room.)

If you look at the space carefully, you can see a number of possibilities. First is that it could really be a space of 5'x6' if we shortened the bar and shifted the dining room opening down a foot. Why this 5'x6' space is interesting is that it is the size of a powder room. If you recall, we had that concern when we were doing the bubble diagram. We chose to move it into a connector. While there are other useful things in the connector (like a laundry room, room for a freezer and pantry, etc.) these items could go in the basement if the home had one. This space could also serve as a coat closet. We struggled with the location of the foyer closet earlier. It could also be a small pantry.

The point is that, as you design your house, you might find solutions to problems you couldn't solve earlier. Sometimes these solutions don't come to you until the house is framed and you see the space. The coat closet idea is not bad. Nor is the pantry. However, you'll have room for a small pantry in the connector. The bath idea isn't far off the mark though it would be a bit snug. If your budget goes haywire, the idea of dropping the connector might need to be revisited. Again, there are a lot of personal taste and choice decisions.

In this case, I am suggesting that this space be used for both a small coat closet and a small desk. The coat closet can be 4' wide by 2' deep. It will close the entrance into the kitchen from the dinette to about 3'. If this is too snug, the bar could be shortened or the closet made smaller. The desk area can be made by using a 12" wide base cabinet and a desk top 3' wide. Do remember, though, that a desk top is lower than a kitchen countertop. Leave the 12" top on the base cabinet at normal height (you really don't have a choice here because it comes at standard height). Drop the top 6" to make the desk top 30" high. You might want to consider using upper cabinets in a shorter height so that you're not staring into a cabinet. Many people put a bulletin board below the shorter upper cabinet.

This desk in the kitchen idea is not new or original. It too is a trend and your cabinet salesperson will help you design it and make sure the tops and upper cabinets are the correct height. You should also remember to put extra receptacles in this space for a computer (very common) and don't forget the phone jack, as this is the logical place for a phone.

Let's next look at the dinette. Is it large enough to sit down at? How many people can eat there? Is it in the flow of traffic? Most are. What size and shape of table is going there?

Good questions. If the table used is 3'x5' (a standard size), it might be just fine. That gives the people sitting with their backs to the kitchen and family rooms 3½' of room. Our *Design Guidelines* tell us that they need 3½', so we're in luck with a 3' wide table. In the other direction, we've got a total of 7' of room if we want to stay out of the traffic from the kitchen to the family room. *Design Guidelines* suggests 12'. Tough problem.

Solution? Compromise! *Design Guidelines* are there to guide. You can get away with as little as 30" from the edge of the table. The 42" in the *Guidelines* provides room to get *around* you. Thirty inches will get you seated, but no one will be able to get around you comfortably. We've only got 7' of clear space and 5' of it is taken up with the table. We need at least another 3' (through compromise). Where is it coming from?

One solution is to bump out the rear wall with a bay. It can easily go out 2' and is an attractive detail in a house. Bays can be squared up or have angles. In this case, we'll have angles. While this solution is still shy one foot, it will probably work. Check it again once the plans are converted to ¼" scale.

Let's Go Upstairs!

Rather than go out into the connector, let's go upstairs and tackle it. If you have tracing paper, it will be a lot easier to draw since all you need to do is trace the outline of the outside walls and the stairs. If not, you just need to carefully duplicate the same outline and stairs as you have downstairs. At this point, the only dimensions that you're sure of is the hallway and bath (determined while placing the stairs on the first floor plan.)

Start with the hall itself. It would be nice to be at least 4' wide at the top of the stairs. This will leave 6' for the bath, 5' of which will be taken up by the tub. The extra foot would be an excellent place for a cold air return chase (part of the heating/cooling system—what you will see there is a vent cover.) Let's place the tub on the left side with the drain towards the rear wall. Next draw in the commode along the rear wall and then the vanity. You have about 6' to work with, so a double bowl sink is certainly called for here. You might want to bring the rear sink out a bit away from the toilet so that it can be reached easily. The last thing to do is figure out the swing of the door. A rule of thumb is to swing a door towards a wall rather than a cabinet. In this case, swing it towards the tub where the chase is.

Now we have to figure out how to get to the front bedroom from the hallway. We know we need at least 3' of room for a hallway. We're going to have to go into the rear bedroom's space and take 3' for a hallway. This will make the rear bedroom nominally 13' wide instead of 16'. The space created by the hallway also creates a nook in the rear bedroom that is perfect for a closet. This 3'x7' closet will also help muffle the noise from the hall bath. The hall should make a left turn and then go down to the center of the house and stop. This will make both bedrooms nominally 14' deep. The door to the front bedroom should swing towards the wall that backs up to the stairs.

Placement of the door to the rear bedroom takes some thought. If you enter the rear bedroom, head on from the hall, there is nowhere for the door to swing against. If you move down towards the front bedroom, it can swing against the wall that divides the two rooms. At this point, there is no clear location for the door. Either way will work. In this case, we're going to place it head on into the room and swing it away from the closet

Next is the master bedroom and bath. Since we know it is good to "stack and back" plumbing, we'll

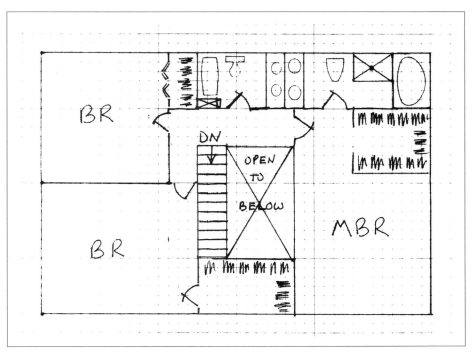

Second Floor Plan

put the master bath in the rear of that room. It will be backed to the hall bath and stacked over the kitchen. There are so many choices with this space. It would be well worth it to discuss the master bath with a kitchen and bath designer to get ideas. It is also worth it to review magazine house plans and see how they do it. The bath depicted here is only one of hundreds of possibilities.

You can start by backing the master bath vanity to the vanity of the hall bath. Pipes can be shared this way. Then work down the room to the toilet. Since you have the room, keep it away from the vanity so that the sink can be slid back further, thus allowing you a knee space between the sinks for a makeup area. Remember that the countertop will need to be dropped between the sinks for this makeup area.

There has been a trend lately where the toilet is in its own room complete with a door for privacy. Again, this is a personal choice. In this case, this plan will have no separation for the toilet. Going down the wall, we'll use a 3'x4' shower. While 3'x3' is standard and adequate, 4' feels luxurious and costs very little extra. It also allows for a seat in the shower, which can be especially pleasant. Beyond the shower and in the corner is a luxury bath. It can be a garden tub or a whirlpool. I suggest that it be oversized and comfortable. A garden tub is just an oversized tub without the whirlpool jets. Obviously it costs less. If you're interested in a whirlpool tub, you ought to talk to people who own them and see how they like them. I think you'll find that many people use them rarely after the first few times. Again, it is a personal choice, yet it could save hundreds of dollars by forgoing the jets.

The tub was placed in the corner. If it would be difficult to get in the tub, it can be pushed out a bit. This "dead" corner can have built-in shelves for towels/toiletries and even a spot for a TV or books and magazines. If it is your intention to sit in this tub facing these shelves, make sure the tub is ordered so that the most comfortable side of the tub faces the corner. Many luxury tubs have faucets that are on the side rather than one end so this might not be a problem. Nevertheless, make sure you can sit in that end of the tub without interference with plumbing or the contour of the tub.

If you do choose a whirlpool tub, realize that there has to be an access panel to the motor of the tub. It cannot be in the corner, because it cannot be reached there. In this case, the closet backs up to the tub and, if it were a whirlpool, the access panel would be in the closet.

The walk-in closet forms the wall between the bath and the bedroom. This positioning dampens the noise from the bath. Placing the door into the walk-in closet near the entry to the bath allows for the long closet wall to not be interrupted by an opening. This helps in furniture placement in the bedroom. The use of closet systems can make the space allowed for the closet seem cavernous.

Master bedrooms are the second most important room (kitchens are first) in most houses today. The design of this master suite is by no means the only way to arrange this room. The choices are endless and there are multiple sources of information on how to design this space. Feel free to go wild with this room provided you keep the basics in mind. You still need 3' to get around and bath fixtures come in standard sizes. Get those right and you can have a little fun in the bedroom (design).

How Do We Connect?

Let's now look at the connector. Our bubble diagram showed this connector to be 12'x12'. After connecting the building at the 3' wide hallway, we leave room for a 3' wide powder room at the top of the connector plan. Since we have 12' and we need only 7' for a powder room, we have approximately 5' left over. This space can be used as a pantry/broom closet. We are going to place this closer to the house for easy access to the kitchen.

Now the laundry room. We have a 6'x12' space here for this. Six feet makes it possible to walk into this room. A washer/dryer takes up 5' of room. We mentioned space for a freezer, which will take up another 3', leaving about 4'. This leaves room for a laundry tray, another closet or an ironing board. The choice is yours. In this case, we chose a laundry tray. This completes the design of a connector that will make this house very pleasant.

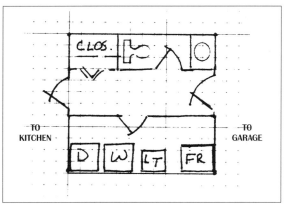

Connector Plan

The Garage

The garage can be flush or even with the front of the house. This is only one of many choices. It could be pushed forward or back, or built at an angle. It could also be what is called front or side "loaded," which means where the doors are. Some areas have covenants that require the garage doors to not be visible from the street, thus requiring side-loaded garages. This is done for aesthetic reasons and homes do look better with the garage side-loaded. In this case, the lot doesn't allow for this and it's not the end of the world or even unusual for a garage to be front-loaded. In fact, most are.

Making this 22' deep garage flush with the front of the main house places the door to the connector 5' from the back of the garage. If there were a number of stairs from the garage into the connector, they could interfere with the parking of cars. This often is the result of not putting the garage on the high side of the lot. If this condition occurred (it could also not be your fault but the result of a very steep lot), you might want to push the garage forward and place the door in the last 3' of the garage. This would take up less space in the garage.

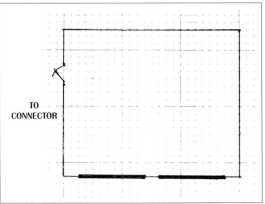

Garage Plan

Let's now look at the garage doors. My favorite is 9' wide doors (versus 8') and thus we'll design with them. We have 24' of space, 18' of which will be doors, leaving 6'. We'll need returns on either side of each door plus space between the two doors. Two feet of the space can be used in each of these three locations and give a balanced look. You should also consider using another door out of the garage. It can be placed on the far side or rear of the garage. Placing it on the rear might interfere with storage space you might have planned. It will give you the best access to the backyard, however. Placing it on the side, where storage probably would not be, would work but will cause extra steps to the backyard. It's a personal call.

Never Enough Closet Space

We now have the entire house, connector and garage roughed out. Let's go back inside and figure out the closets. The rear bedroom has a perfect space for a 3' deep wall closet that is almost 7' long. At this length (and shallow depth), it ought to have bi-fold doors rather than swinging doors.

Typically bi-fold doors have a one-foot wing wall on either side and sometimes a one-foot wall between sets of bi-folds. They can also be flush to the side wall with no wing wall as well as having no center wall between them. A single door bi-fold can be as narrow as 12" with one single door. The most common size bi-folds are 3', 4', 5' and 6'. In the case of the rear bedroom, the 7' closet will use a 5' bi-fold door, with one-foot wing walls on either side, closing the rest of the opening.

We will assume that the front bedroom uses the space over the foyer as closet space. Since it is a deeper closet, it should have a swinging door rather than a bi-fold door. At 10' deep, it is a good-sized closet. You could steal from this closet to give yourself an additional wall closet in the master bedroom if you want. I would reserve this decision until you're at quarter inch drawings to see how the space is working out.

The master bedroom closet is good sized and can be helped even more with a closet system. It is definitely a walk-in closet. A door is not necessary and could be a nuisance. Using a door is a matter of personal choice and lifestyle. Look at the door of your current closet and see if it's ever closed. If not, why waste the money on a door?

Let's Look at the Outside

The Roof Pitch

We've got the inside going, now let's look at the outside. One of the primary things that makes a house look good is the roof line. One of the identifying details of a Colonial house is the steepness of the roof, ranging anywhere from a 9/12 to a 12/12 roof pitch. Over the years, roof pitches on less expensive Colonial style homes have been as low as 4/12 and often 6/12. These *Minimal Traditional* houses are not especially attractive. I would suggest at least a 9/12 pitch on this home. If you wanted to use the attic for finished space, a 12/12 would be more suitable as it would give the most room and would be in keeping with original Colonial style homes which used the attic as living space. Additional room and light could be brought into the third level with dormers. This would also add greatly to the look of this house, but is a personal and budgetary decision.

The connector should be the same pitch as the main house, while the garage could be shallower or steeper depending on how the upper level of the garage is going to be used. Since the garage roof is going the other way than the main house and connector roof (a common design for this type of house), it does not have to be as steep as these other two roofs. If, however, you wanted the garage to have upstairs storage or finished off into an apartment or extra bedroom, it needs to be at a 12/12 pitch.

Remember, however, that you will need stairs to get up there and that stairs will take up some room. You should also take a close look at the available headroom upstairs. A general rule of thumb for usable space is one that has at least 4' of headroom, but preferably 5'. At a 12/12 pitch, you will gain one foot in height for every foot in depth. With the garage being 24' wide, you'll lose 10' (5' on each side) of headroom while gaining 14' of usable space in the middle of the building.

If you choose to not have access to the space over the garage, I would recommend that the garage have at least a 9/12 roof pitch (for aesthetic reasons.) In our example house, we'll go with a 9/12 pitch all the way around and forgo the extra space that would be available in the main house and garage if they had a 12/12 roof.

Let's Draw the Elevations

Since the front of this house is so large and fills almost the entire page, we will have to place the front and rear elevation on their own separate page. The left and right side elevations can fit on one page, however. You should start drawing at the bottom of the page, about 10 lines up and 6 lines over. Draw the bottom horizontal line first representing all 76' of the house width.

Using a scale will be easier than counting individual squares. Then go up the left side of the paper and draw a vertical line 17' high. This 17' represents 8' for the first floor, 8' for the second floor and one foot for the thickness of the second floor system. Bring this line to the right horizontally for 40'. Then draw the vertical line that represents the right side of the main house.

Next draw the horizontal connector eave line and right side vertical line. You can also draw the right side vertical line of the garage. What cannot be drawn at this time is the roofs of these buildings. You need to draw the side elevations first to determine how high the roofs are. This will be done next.

The Side Elevations

The next consideration is which way the roof goes. The main house's roof will have the ridge or peak going left to right as will the connector. The garage roof can do the same, but turning the roof so the gable shows from the street would be much more attractive. This is also a common way this is done. There is a little more cost because of the way the connector roof attaches to the garage roof, but it is well worth it. Draw a horizontal line 28' wide, starting at the bottom left side of your paper. Leave 10' of margin to the left and bottom edge of the page. Then draw a vertical line 17' high on both sides.

If we had chosen a 6/12 or 12/12 pitch, it would be easier to draw the roof. A 12/12 roof is drawn by rising one square for each one drawn horizontally. A 6/12 roof is drawn by rising one square for every two squares drawn horizontally. A 9/12 roof is exactly halfway between these two. Rather than draw the lines for both a 6 and 12/12 roof, just place dots for each of these on one side. You will find that the 12/12 roof is 7' higher than the 6/12 roof. Half of seven is 3½. Go down 3½' from the highest 12/12 mark and make another mark. Draw a line from this mark back down towards both sides of the house. This will represent a 9/12 roof pitch for a 28' deep house.

By counting from the eave line to the peak of the roof, you can determine the height of the roof. In this case, it is 10½'. You will use this information when you draw the front and rear elevations of the main building. Since we've first drawn the left side of the main house, we must next draw the right side to see how the roofs of the connector and garage look. From the left elevation, you would not be able to see these buildings because they are shorter than the main house.

We will draw the connector gable first. Realize that the connector will not be visible from either the left or right side elevation. The main house blocks it on the left, the garage on the right. You can still represent it with dotted lines, though. First draw the right side elevation of the main house. It is drawn exactly the same as the left side. Then, using dotted lines, starting from the rear of the main house and go to the left 8' and draw a vertical line 8' high. Go forward another 12' and

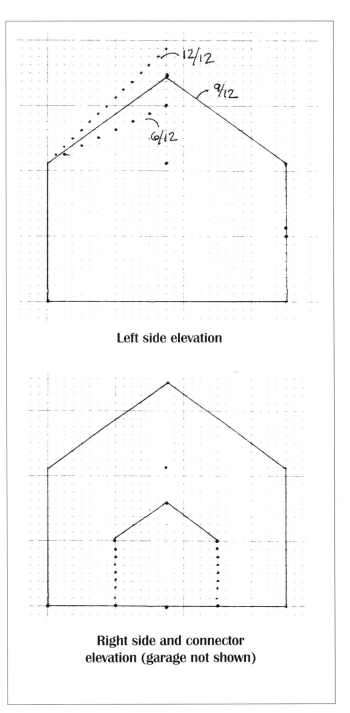

Left side elevation

Right side and connector elevation (garage not shown)

then draw another vertical line 8' as well. Using only dots, draw in the 6/12 and 12/12 roofs and then determine the 9/12 height. In this case, there is 3' of difference between 6/12 and 12/12. This makes the roof of the connector 4½' above the eave line. You now know how high the roofs are for both the main house and the connector.

You need to next determine how high the garage roof is. Since it is going the other way (sometimes called a reversed gable), you need to know how tall it is before you can draw the roof of the connector at the front elevation. Go back to the front elevation drawing. Drawing both the 6/12 and 12/12 roofs using dots, determine the height of the garage roof. You will find that the 9/12 roof height is 3' lower than the 12/12. You should also see why the garage roof had to be drawn in before the connector roof. If you drew the connector roof first, you would not know where it tied into the garage roof.

Go ahead and draw the main house and connector roofs on the front elevation. On the main house, you should draw it one foot wider on each side to represent the overhang at the gables. Draw in the connector roof and you're done with the front elevation.

The rear elevation is the same as the front except that it will be reversed from the front elevation. The garage will be on the left side of the page. The rear elevation will also show the small bay at the dinette. We will show the front, rear, left and the right side elevations (with the garage) when we take these plans a step further and draw in the windows. ∎

13

Designing with Windows and Doors

Codes Again

Building codes are very strict on windows and doors. We'll talk in more detail about this in Chapter 18, but you do need to know a little about windows and doors to select and locate these items in your drawings.

First, you need to know that each bedroom has to have what is called an "egress" window. This window has to be a certain size and a certain distance from the floor. This is to meet building code and essentially is to let either a fireman into your home or you out during a fire. While there are a number of choices, the most common egress window used is a double hung 3/0 4/6 window. It is 3' wide and 4½' tall. It also has to be no higher than 44" off the floor (where the sill starts).

With our house well on its way in design, the next step is to select the millwork (another word for windows and doors) for the house. We will select standard-sized windows for now and can alter them in the future if we need to. The biggest advantage of using standard-sized windows is that they are readily available and most window companies have the same sizes. This makes it easier to compare price and quality of similar windows.

We get a little help by the fact that this is a Colonial style house. We know that we should be using double hung windows. The toughest part of selecting windows is making sure they are placed where you want them on the inside, but still look right on the outside. With a two-story house, you have to make sure they line up floor to floor (at least on the front elevation). Placing windows is quite an art and you might not get it right the first few times and need to go to an expert for assistance. Like the kitchen cabinet business, window suppliers and home centers can be of considerable help in selecting and placing windows. They will be the experts on selecting windows, but might not have the design skills you will find with the kitchen and bath suppliers.

You should start in the front of the house with the first floor. Windows should be placed at least 2' from the corner of the house in order to not interfere with the

strength the house gets from corner bracing. A window close to a corner is hard to trim, does not have enough room to place a decorative shutter, and could be expensive because of the possibility of alternate bracing or extra engineering to re-engineer a corner.[8]

I would suggest 3/0 5/2 windows for the living room. The distance windows are apart might be dictated by a piece of furniture. For example, a typical sofa is 5'–6' long. Placing windows this distance apart might make sense provided it looks right on the outside. In the case of this house, we'll start the living room window 2' off the floor and 2' from the corner. Since this room is so long, we'll add another same sized window further down that wall. We also need to keep this second window away from the foyer/living room wing wall so that it does not interfere with the trim and moldings that might be used there. Two feet away from the foyer wing wall would work, so we'll do that.

Another consideration in placing windows in a wall is that they are placed at the same level at the top of the wall. The most common placement is starting 6'8" from the floor, which lines the top of the window up with the height of the front door. This placement also gives plenty of room for a structural header in the wall.

The front door is tricky and a number of concerns need to be considered here. First is that doors typically swing towards a wall. The dining room wall is long enough for it to swing towards it, but we might not want the door there, especially if we plan to place a coat tree or closet there. (While this plan decided against this idea, your plan might not. Placing the door wrong could take that option away.)

Another concern with the front door is that it not interfere with the flow of traffic. If we put the door towards the living room, people coming down the stairs would be trapped when the door opens. So would people in the living room. While we probably don't have this problem here, many homes with very

The front door is tricky and a number of concerns need to be considered here.

War Story

#8: I worked for a company that had a house featured in *Country Living* magazine. A customer built a copy of that house with a few modifications. We made the plans and the customer submitted them to their local inspections office for approval. They came back disapproved. They were told that one of the bedrooms did not have an adequate egress window. Since we had built numerous copies of this house before without a problem, we were perplexed. What was different about this plan? We had not changed the window size. We compared this plan to the original plan. The only thing different was that a permanently built step below a skylight had been taken off this plan in the offending bedroom. I called the design department and asked for an explanation. They said that the bedroom window was never meant for egress. The egress requirement was met by going through a skylight that was hinged, and thus opened. It was placed higher than 44 inches above the floor and therefore, a permanently installed step had to be placed below it to satisfy this requirement. The customer omitted the step from their plan as they didn't see the need for it. We thought the window gave us egress and never even thought about the step or the skylight as a means of egress. Since the customer still did not want the step, we changed the plans using a bigger window and got code approval.

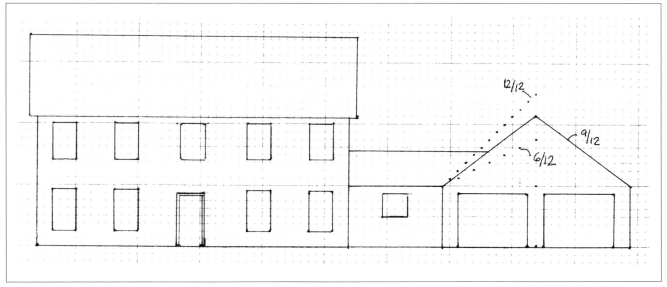

Front elevation with windows

small foyers get a big surprise when the stairs are trimmed out in the foyer. Which has happened at least once (if not hundreds of times) is that the front door hits the banister or bottom tread of the stairs. The typical solution is to take the door back out, re-frame the rough opening for the door and then re-hang it. Since this is a Colonial house, we should consider centering the front door between the windows of the living and dining rooms.

Next is the dining room windows. While this is a smaller room than the living room, it will be dark because most dining rooms are heavily furnished and need extra brightness. In keeping with the "look" of a Colonial, two windows should be used here as well. They should be the same-sized windows as was used in the living room. They should also be balanced with the rest of the front of the house. They should start 2' from the side of the house and then come over another 5' for the second window, duplicating the living room side of the house.

To draw these windows on your plan, you have to constantly be looking at both the floor plan and elevation. Use the grids to locate the windows. They should be located exactly where they are on the plan so that you can see not only how the home will look in the elevations but also how they will work with the floor plan. To represent them on the floor plan, you should darken the outside wall line where the windows actually fall.

In the case of a door, show the swing of the door like on an interior door. Be careful to place it in scale and at the correct location. Always favor how they look on the outside to how they function on the inside, especially on the front and most visible elevations. An example of this is that the living room windows are balanced inside the room while the dining room windows are not. It is more important that the outside of a Colonial be balanced than the inside. If this is a problem for you, widen the house to make the dining room 16' wide like the living room.

With the first floor windows drawn, it will be easier to locate and draw the upstairs windows. What you want to do is locate them directly above the win-

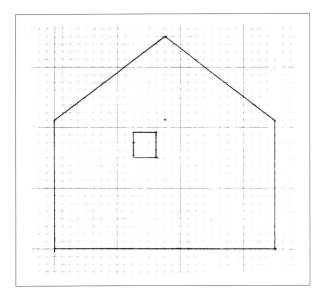

**Left side elevation
with windows**

dows below. To locate these accurately, you need to note on the elevations where the second floor is. We've designed this house to have 8' ceilings on both floors. Realizing that the second floor framing takes up about one foot of space, we've drawn our house to be 17' high from the first floor to the ceiling (eave) of the second floor. Mark the front elevation to show where the second floor begins (9' above the first floor).

The upper windows should be slightly shorter than the lower windows so that the house doesn't get a *bug-eyed* look. These windows do not have to be the egress windows, but typically are. Egress windows can be on the side of the house for the master and front bedrooms if you choose to do so.

Knowledge of how the furniture will be placed could help you decide if you even want windows on the side of the house or not. If you choose not to place the egress windows on the sides, the front windows must be egress windows. In this example, the front bedroom windows will be egress windows. We'll use standard 3/0 4/6 windows here with no side windows. To help balance the house and give natural light to the front bedroom closet, we will add a 3/0 4/6 window over the front door. All upstairs windows will be installed at the same header height and line up with the windows below.

Let's now go to the left or north side of the house and work our way around from there. As you recall, the north side will always be the coldest side of the house. If you can reduce or eliminate the windows on that side of the house, your house will be easier to heat.

On the first floor in the living room, we already have two fairly large windows. Therefore, we do not need more windows on the left side, thus allowing more room for furniture placement and wall space to hang pictures. In the family room, the end wall is usually reserved for a fireplace and book shelves. Windows here would interfere with these items and therefore will not be placed here.

On the second floor, we decided we wouldn't place windows on the left wall of the front bedroom since we've met our egress requirement with the front windows. The rear bedroom is another story. This room is 3' smaller than the front bedroom and could use two windows, one in each outside wall. One or both of these can be the egress window. Since we're concerned with the cold on the north side, we'll place a smaller, non-egress window on the North wall. We will use a 3/0 3/2 window here. While it can go anywhere on that wall (except within 2' of the corner), we need to consider a number of factors.

Furniture placement should play a role here as well as personal taste. The balance and look of this wall is of secondary importance since this side of the house would most likely not be seen. We do, however, have to be careful that the window not get in the way of the fireplace below. A typical fireplace is about 5' wide. Since it will most likely be centered in the family room, we have to be careful to keep this north wall bedroom window at least 6' from the center of the room. This 6' allows for window trim and irregularities in the fireplace design.

It's Ugly Out Back

The rear of the house is where you can usually get away with mismatched windows. You can use several difference kinds (double and casement). Windows do not have to line up or even look right. While this is typical, many architects do attempt to get the back of the house to look as good as the front. Many residential designers, do-it-your-selfers, etc., can't and don't. It is usually not a problem and, unless your rear is exposed, not worth worrying about.

In drawing the rear elevation of the house, you have to remember that it is the opposite of the front of the house. In our example, the garage is on the left side of the drawing, the house on the right. Everything else should be the same. Since we left at the corner of the family room, we will start again there.

The family room typically is not as bright and cheery as many of the other rooms of the house. It usually has a fireplace, bookshelves and a lot of furniture for sitting. Wall space is at a premium and is often covered with bookshelves, knick knacks and pictures. Windows in family rooms are usually not as tall as those in the front of the house. You really do not want to interfere with the furniture in this room. In this case, a window no more than 4' tall would work. Since we're trying to bring in adequate light but not take up too much wall space, the windows ought to be banked (joined together). We'll use two 3/0 4/2 windows mulled (another word for joined) together into one unit. We will place them higher in the wall than the windows in the front, keeping them tight to the top plate and header. Depending how the furniture and shelves fit in the room, these windows will also be placed three to 6' from the corner of the room. This would allow you to turn the corner inside the room with furniture or shelves while getting far enough from the TV for comfortable watching. Chances are that the TV is going to be in the outside corner of the room because it will be closest to the cable connection and that the fireplace will take up the center of the room. The room ought to work OK with just these windows.

Next is the bay in the dinette. The window glass here could be achieved through

Rear elevation with windows

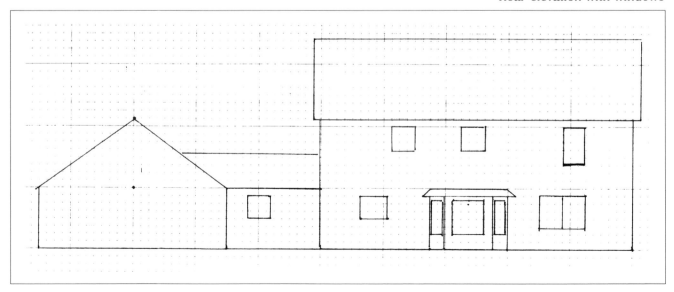

individual windows or through fixed glass or a combination of both. Realize that there is very little room here and that the 45-degree corners will be taken up with a lot of moldings. Plan for windows/glass less than 18" wide in the two corners. Some people like for the dinette bay to be bright and cheerful with lots of light. This is not a bad solution but you have to be careful that the glass does not get too close to the floor or someone's foot is going to go through it. Placing the window/glass 2' from the floor would work. It should be about 5' tall to bring in plenty of light. The center piece could again be fixed glass or another window. In this case, we'll use a fixed glass, making sure that all three windows are placed in the bay at the same height.

Kitchen windows typically are about 45" above the floor. Countertops are 3' above the floor and there usually is about 9" left for the back splash and window trim. The width of the window depends on the amount of upper cabinets desired and personal taste. There is a trend for larger kitchen windows than in the past when the typical over sink kitchen window was a 3/0 3/2. The loss of upper cabinet space is generally made up with a pantry or more efficient cabinets and shelving systems.

As we mentioned earlier, the window over the sink ought to be a casement or sliding window for ease of opening. In this case, we'll use a 3/4 4/0 casement window. Realize that many upper cabinets do not go up to the ceiling and are attached to soffits that might interfere with the window height. Since the soffits are usually built after the windows are installed, it should be obvious to the carpenter that the soffits, if continued across, would interfere with the kitchen window. Leaving the soffits out across the top of the window would make perfect sense to everyone except a gorilla.

Let's go upstairs and finish out those windows. Starting at the right side where the rear bedroom is, we remember from earlier review that we need an egress window here. While it could be placed anywhere in this room, keep in mind furniture placement. In this case, we'll place a 3/0 4/6 directly above the family room window below, flush to the outside corner. Again, it could go anywhere in this room.

The hall bath can get along with a smaller, standard window placed high over the toilet. A 3/0 3/2 would work just fine here. Over the toilet is the normal location and about the only room left. The shower wall precludes it from being placed there and the vanity wall usually has a shelf or mirror placed there. Place it about 3½' off the floor, leaving space above the toilet for a small shelf for toiletries.

The master bath often has larger and/or more windows than the hall bath. Often the larger window is over the tub and the smaller one behind the toilet like in a hall bath. If a professional is designing your bath, they should also determine the windows. In this example, we will place a 3/0 3/2 over the toilet like the hall bath and allow for a more interesting window over the garden tub. Windows in master baths are often stained or frosted glass or glass block. These windows bring in plenty of light while ensuring privacy.

The Hidden Side

Often in drawing plans, a side of the house is hidden from view. It is true in this case because some of the right (south) side elevation of the house is hidden from view by the garage. In this case, there is one window and one door hidden from view. These are the window in the master bath over the tub and the door between the house and the connector and the connector and the garage. The floor plan will show these doors and windows while the elevation can only show and label the windows (with dotted lines) and the door (again with dotted lines but probably no labeling).

An important reason for drawing the windows on the south elevation is to ensure that the roof of the connector not interfere with their proper placement. This is a real and consistent concern when two unequal buildings are attached to each other. There is a section in the center of the south wall of the master bedroom where the peak of the connector roof would interfere with the placement of a window. The window has to be on one side or the other of this area. Furniture placement, view, personal preference, etc., ought to be considered. In this example, we will place a fixed 4/0 3/0 piece of stained glass over the garden tub, starting 2' from the rear corner.

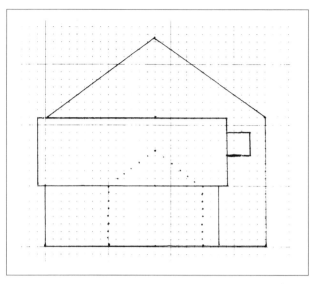

Right side elevation (partially hidden by the garage)

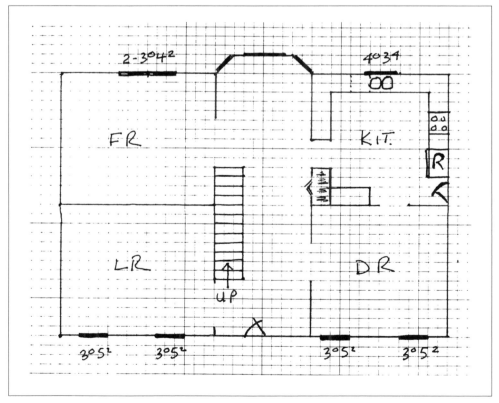

First Floor Plan with windows and doors

Representing windows and doors on floor plans is relatively simple.

The connector doors will be placed as shown on the floor plan. No magic there. While we're talking about the connector, we need to select and place the windows there as well. In the front of the house, we have a laundry room. Keeping with a balanced look, we ought to place a 3/0 3/2 window about 4' off the floor in the center of that space. This will place the window about where the laundry tub is and works well on the inside and looks good on the outside. On the rear elevation, we will not get a balance because of the way the room lays out. When a toilet is backed up to a wall, the window is typically placed above it. When it is on the side of a wall in a typical two-piece powder room, the window is usually placed between the toilet and the sink, as we'll do in this example.

Garage doors are usually no brainers. They usually are self-determined by balance and the amount of room left. Obviously, there has to be enough framing on the sides and between them (when two are used) to attach the frame of the door. They should be centered. Again, they are typically 7' tall and either 8'–9' wide.

Representing windows and doors on floor plans is relatively simple. Windows are shown exactly where they would be in the wall by darkening the perimeter walls at their location. Doors are shown as they are represented inside the house, showing door swing and typically a threshold. Windows are typically labeled on the floor plan, though not always on the elevations. ■

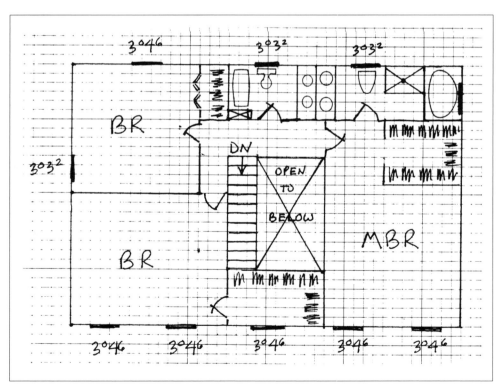

Second Floor Plan with windows and doors

14

What Do You Need
To Get Going?

Get Off the Pot!

You've got your plans where you want them in either ⅛" or ¼" scale. What's the next step? Whatever it is, you're at the stage where you've got to get off the pot and spend some money. No more putzing around. If you're serious, get out your checkbook.

You have two immediate tasks. First, see what the government says about your house plans. What do they want? Second, what does the bank want? Unless you've found a way to avoid paying for this (you're rich) or you don't want to take advantage of mortgage tax credits (you're stupid), you're going to get up close and personal with a banker real soon. And, oh yeah, it would help if you already have first dibs on some land.

Most people want to get all their ducks in a row before they spend the first cent. While not a bad idea, the ducks are going to be a moving target until you spend some money. Interest rates move all the time. Codes, covenants, and zoning change as well. The price of materials and the availability of subcontractors is extremely seasonal. Sometimes a housing slump doesn't give you better access to sub—they go out of business or move like gypsies. A hot market brings in more subs, thus remedying a shortage of subs. But nothing is going to happen until you spend some money.

We'll assume that you've already purchased your land and have a set of plans that fit the topography of your lot. The reason that is such an amazing thing to me is that so many people buy or develop house plans long before they own the land. While all kinds of wonderful things can happen prior to getting your land, you're going nowhere until you buy it. Many people try to get all their questions answered before they spend a cent. They get house plans and construction estimates. They talk to bankers and code officials. They also wonder why these guys act so dumb. They get angry because their builder won't talk in complete sentences. Their banker is being real precise about being imprecise. The problem is that the land ties it all together and nothing is firm until the land is purchased. People in the profession of building have little time or patience for hypothetical cases.

I once heard a builder tell a potential customer who wanted a ballpark estimate for a house that ballparks are for ballplayers. I thought this was a pretty good answer since I get this same question almost every day (although I don't use this retort—I still need the business). The other side of spending money is doing some work—often some very hard work. You might have thought that agreeing on *Design by Lists* was hard; now you have to zero in on what your house is going to cost. You can't do that until you determine what's going into your house. Even if you have a builder do almost all the work for you, you still have to make dozens of decisions before you can start your house. And once you've decided on what you want (or made allowances for things you can't decide on), you still need to give the builder time to come up with an estimate.

While you need to own the land and have settled on a builder and a plan of some specification, you still have work to do at the bank. You'll be amazed at how smart they've become since you got the land, the plans, the builder and the cost estimate. Now what you're looking for is all the answers and maybe even a permit. You've got a better chance of hitting your first major league pitch. What you're going to get is a lot of questions, not answers. The bankers and the code officials are much better than you at this and it makes their day quite pleasant to load you up with things to do. Still, you can't do anything until you spend some money and make up your mind. It's the beginning of a long trip but at least you're on your way. ■

15

Financing

How Much House Can You Afford?

Usually a lot more than you think or are willing to spend. When I was selling homes, part of my job was to pre-qualify potential customers. I had a number of charts and tables that told me how much home a person could afford. People would tell me their income and how much debt they had and I could tell them which house they could buy. It seemed like everyone who would let me pre-qualify them could afford a house.

All that I sold to also qualified at our mortgage company, proving that I had done a good job in pre-qualifying them. Since this was my first sales job, I wasn't sure if I was a good salesman or if the company just had a good formula for selling. It did seem that I was able to sell to more than half of those I pre-qualified. I also was meeting quota, which was about one to two homes sold a week. I never went more than two weeks without a sale. My best week was four sales.

After my first three months in sales, I had a performance review from my sales manager. He started by telling me that I had the highest mortgage approval rating in the company (100%). I was expecting a pat on the back, but instead got told that was not good enough and that I needed to take more chances. He said that while the guidelines were fairly stringent, we might get some borderline customers if they just missed the guidelines. I told him that buying a house was very emotional and that I didn't want to get people excited about a house if it looked like they couldn't afford it. We left that conversation at an impasse. Since I made salesman of the quarter during the next three months (with a 100% qualification rate), he left me alone on this issue. After a few years as a sales manager myself, I realized his point and did try to take more risks in sales. I still realize the toll this can take and advise that you fully understand how well you qualify for a loan before you get too financially or emotionally wrapped up into it. Salesmen want to sell you a house!

In This Chapter . . .

▲ Ratios banks use to qualify you for a loan

▲ Normal sources of loans

▲ Abnormal sources of loans

In qualifying for a loan, the bank looks at three things:

1. What percentage of your gross income will be going towards the loan;

2. What percentage of your gross income plus any long-term debt that will be consumed from your gross income; and

3. How good a risk are you?

As I mentioned, most people are surprised at how much a bank will lend them to buy a house. Home loans are relatively risk free, especially those with a decent down payment. If the loan goes bad, the down payment goes to the bank as fees to liquidate the loan. You can be assured that enough costs will be applied to the defaulting of the loan to leave you with next to nothing.

The first item, a percentage of gross income alone, is usually limited to 25–28%. For example, if you make (before taxes) $4,000 per month, you can obtain a loan for about $1,000 a month. What this will purchase will depend on the current interest rate, but generally will support a $100,000-plus loan.

The second item the bank looks at is long-term debt, which is loosely defined as any recurring (monthly) debt that will take over one year to payoff. Usually this is a car payment, but could be a college loan, a furniture payment, average credit card minimum payments (if you have a history of not paying these off every month), etc. The bank typically lets you have a ratio percentage of 33–36% of your gross monthly income. This percentage takes the house payment and adds to it your long-term debt. In the case of a $100,000 loan with $4,000 a month gross pay, a maximum of a $300 car payment and a $100 credit card payment, or a total of $400 would qualify you for a loan. More debt than this puts you out of the running.

The third thing the bank looks at is your credit history. Credit checks are a routine part of business today and easy to obtain. You, as a consumer, never know for sure what is on your credit report because there is no requirement for you to be notified if you are being reported for bad credit. You could be placed on the list for something as simple as a late payment as you would be for outright fraud. This doesn't mean that a late payment will deny you the loan nor that every late payment is placed on your credit report. As we all know, sometimes bills don't get paid on time because we forget or lose the bill. Most companies will let you slide for one payment, others will not. All will report you soon enough, although you can delay or avoid that by working out a better payment schedule. The worst thing you can do is to ignore the bill and not pay.

It is hard but not impossible to repair a bad credit rating. Time usually solves it by reestablishing a longer period of time of paying bills on time. Sometimes increasing your down payment can get you over the hurdle of a bad credit report. Small infractions can usually just be explained away, if done in good faith.

A few hints: If you are planing to get a mortgage loan, pay off as many long-term bills as you can before you apply for the loan. Also, delay the purchase of a new car or other major items until after you are approved. This will help you with the second ratio. In addition, if you suspect you have a credit history problem, get a recent credit report and see what it looks like. If there are some things you've overlooked, take care of them and make sure you keep receipts of paying these off. While many companies are quick to report you, few are in any hurry to clear your name. You best defense is to not be surprised and to show good faith. Bring your receipts that show that you've paid these off because it is going to be a while before your records are cleared.

What Are Some Choices?

Each bank will have a slightly different program. Many will want to combine the construction loan with the permanent financing. The advantage is that you only have one closing. The disadvantage is that it takes longer to get this loan and the rates might change, not necessarily in your favor. Other banks want to keep the loans separate and thus involve a second closing once the house is finished. While it is possible that you might have greater difficulty getting a permanent loan doing this, you could reap the benefits of a lower interest rate plus a better appraisal on the finished house. There are enough pros and cons of each for you to make your own decision. The bottom line is to shop around for mortgages and do what serves you best.

In shopping around, you will find enough variations of these terms to find no one loan able to meet all of these needs. Many people focus only on the lowest interest rate. Others look only at upfront fees. Some need special terms, such as payment upon delivery of a packaged home. It can be a frustrating adventure with banks being unwilling to change any of their rules for you. An approach you can take in *shopping* for financing might be to tell the bank exactly what you are looking for before they tell you their terms. Again, this is especially true if you are purchasing a packaged home. Bring the bank a copy of your contract with the supplier. The issue here is usually payment terms, i.e., when the supplier expects to be paid. The short answer is "upon delivery." The bank's short answer typically is "after we've inspected and all the parts are permanently attached to the foundation." Since this is often a conflict, let it be known that this will be a factor in which bank you select to finance your home.

Again, with packaged homes, you might find it hard to get a bank to finance your home according to their schedule. The supplier should be able to help you if they have local service. While some packaged home manufacturers have financing, it is increasingly rare and usually not at the best rates. The best thing to do is to shop around and try to negotiate a solution that works for you, your supplier and the bank. It is possible, but will require some legwork and some compromises for all parties. ■

You might find difficulty in getting the loan with the terms you need. The terms of the loan could include:

▲ Interest rate

▲ Number of points

▲ Amount of down payment

▲ Closing costs

▲ Payment schedule

▲ Services you desire

There is one fairly new advance in the financing of package homes. This is the mortgage companies that are now specializing in package or kit homes. Some companies currently doing this are:

First Financial Services Mortgage Co., Inc.
6797 N. High Street · Suite 330
Worthington, OH 43085-2533
(614) 888-6797

Home Builders Finance, Inc.
13801 Reese Blvd. · Suite 320
Huntersville, NC 28078
(704) 875-0551

Waterfield Mortgage Company
7500 W. Jefferson Blvd.
Ft. Wayne, IN 46804
(800)-444-9847

Normal sources of mortgages include the following:

▲ **Commercial banks** – not their main business but they do lend money for home mortgages

▲ **Credit Unions** – you have to be a member though

▲ **Mortgage Companies** – these guys do mostly FHA and VA loans

▲ **Savings and Loans** – the one in Bedford Falls went under when George Bailey was sent to prison, the few that remain do mostly conventional loans

▲ **Mortgage Brokers** – new guys on the block doing almost half the home loans now

▲ **U.S. Government** – look in the phone book—they're still in business!

Notes and Sketches

16

Permits

$50,000 Napkins

Permits can range in price from less than $25 to over $50,000 depending on where you live. The most expensive places to build in the lower 48 states are New York and California.

The two biggest factors in the cost of a permit are external environmental costs and the size and aggressiveness of your local government. Permit hell is best exemplified in Los Angeles. The environmental factors are earthquakes, forest fires, bad soil conditions and the ocean. Government factors include the "save the whales" attitude, a bad history with inept builders, an overwhelming building boom, and the oversupply of lawyers.

The environmental factors are very real. Earthquakes are quite common and buildings have to be built to resist earthquakes. What typically happens to a house in an earthquake is that it is shaken off its foundation. The solution is actually quite simple. The wooden members of the house are strapped or bolted down to the masonry part of the house. However, the folks in California want you to hire an engineer to "do the math" on your particular house. The solution (strap or bolt it down) is almost always the same, but you must still hire an engineer "because your house is special" and they must certify that you're using the right amount of connection devices.

The next environmental factor is fires. Fires are very common in California, especially in the southern half of the state which receives very little rain and is vegetated with very flammable plants, grass and trees. These fires always make the news because they are attracted to movie stars' houses and provide good plots for made-for-TV movies. The problem is that people are building houses in fire prone areas. I think God is trying to tell something to people in California (don't live here or it's the brimstone thing) and they're not home to receive the message. The solutions are interesting. They include the restriction of certain building materials, e.g., no cedar shake roofs or the requirement for providing your own water supply to fight the fire with. It also could include fire retardant roofing materials and the installation of a fire sprinkler system within the house (like is required in commercial structures). While these are pretty neat ideas, they are expensive and none of these solutions improve the appearance of your home unless its' style is "early industrial."

Soil conditions in California are also not the best. The soil is dry and unstable. Soil near the ocean (where people like to build) is prone to giving way and taking the house with it. This condition is most useful to late night talk show hosts who like to joke about how the latest waterfront properties in California will be in Arizona. Engineers will help you out here with test borings and "do the math" for you to ensure your house will be on a solid foundation. They will design a foundation "just for you" and only charge what an entire house costs in Arkansas.

Being on the ocean is one of the greatest appeals of California. It made the Beach Boys famous and provided an excuse to never grow up for thousands of surfers and beach bums. The ocean does, however, have an effect on housing. While earthquakes normally shake houses off their foundations, the ocean and its hurricane force winds blow their roofs off. What is amazing is that these conditions rarely happen at the same time. And that hurricanes last for hours while earthquakes last only seconds and minutes. The solution to dealing with hurricane forces on a house is to hire an engineer to "do the math" and come up with a solution for your personal house. The answer is to strap or bolt the roof system to the walls. Since you are dealing with both earthquakes and hurricanes, why not just run straps from the foundation, through the walls and into the roof? Golly, that is just what they do in California. Although every house has the same system and uses the same connection parts, you still have to hire your own special engineer to do your own personal house. Just for you. The combination of parts, labor and "engineering services" can easily exceed $10,000. Throw in the occasional "soil condition" problem and you can exceed $20,000 or more dollars with extra foundation work. Add the fire problem and you're looking at more than $25,000 in extra materials, labor and fees. Just because you missed God's message about building in California.

The next part of the higher cost of permits in California is best seen in Los Angeles. The next most popular sport in L.A., after drive by shootings, is suing people. People in L.A. love to sue each other. Lawyers get very rich in L.A. You can only sue a builder until he goes out of business. You can't sue God. Let's see, who's left? The government! The government, however, doesn't like to be sued. The leaders of the government, the politicians, realize that they cannot get re-elected if their government gets sued all the time. Since most politicians get elected by pointing out the faults of their predecessors, they have to be careful that their ducks are in order when they're in charge. A common election theme is to clean up the corruption and ineptitude of the current government. Remember all those movie star houses that burned up or fell into the ocean? The made-for-TV movies? Great stuff for election campaigns.

What is a politician to do? First, they are going to make sure that it is near impossible for the next house to be built without some protection for the citizenry. Tremendous sums of money will be spent to enlarge and increase the building inspection departments throughout the state. In L.A., the building inspection department is the largest in the country. It is staffed with engineers and scientists. They are going to make sure that your house will not bounce off its foundation in an earthquake, its roof will not blow off in a hurricane, it will not fall into the ocean or not burn up in a canyon fire. And if it does (and probably will), they've added a special treat just for you. They are going to make sure that when the lawyers hit their front door, there will be plenty of grief to pass around.

A little history about the building of California. California was devoid of people until 1849 (unless you count the Indians). The Spanish owned it a little while before then and built a few missions and other adobe and tile structures. They kept away from the edge of the ocean (they knew you could fall in), they built using fireproof materials (they knew about fire and brimstone from the Bible) and they left all the lawyers in Spain. In 1849, gold was discovered near Sacramento. The "gold rush" exploded the growth of California and a building boom occurred that built the predominant cities of California, including San Francisco and Los Angeles.

God sent a pretty strong message to California in 1906 (with an earthquake centered around San Francisco), but all they did was make a movie about it (starring Clark Gable) and built their houses a little bit better as well as making firemen a nobler profession. The next big boom in California came around and after World War II and was seen predominantly in L.A. The automobile made the greatest impact there and created the sprawling freeways of L.A. This building boom, like most building booms, attracted builders to, like Jed Clampett, "come to Californie, that's the place you oughta be." They came in droves and built a magnificent city. At that time, California did not have a strong tradition of building. There were few unions that could teach the trades correctly, using apprenticeships or passing down skills from father to son. The politicians of the time responded to their constituents. They wanted houses, lots of them and did not want the government to slow the process up. Rigorous inspections and small details like methods that would make houses safe and long lasting were not important. Skilled labor and honest tradesmen was in short supply. Eventually, it became obvious that there was a problem. A lot of bad houses got built.

Another factor was seen during the 1960s. Colleges were booming. The parents who suffered through the Depression and fought WWII were being rewarded with a period of prosperity. While they enjoyed its' rewards, they were also able to give their kids everything and sent them to the best colleges in the country. These lucky kids rewarded their hard-working and long-suffering parents by becoming hippies, flower children and lovers of the earth. When they finally had to grow up, they became enlightened consumers, lawyers, and building inspectors. They saw evil and they wanted to do something about it. What better way than to become involved with one of man's greatest emotional involvement—their home?

The hippie generation learned that nothing was ever their fault. They also believed that while sometimes things just happen (like the Depression, world wars, etc.), they don't have to take it. They developed a plan. First was to protect the earth at all costs. Second was to make sure that as few people as possible gum up their freeways (by moving to L. A). Third was to devise ways to become rich the old fashioned way—to sue someone. College had taught them how governments worked, especially bureaucracies. They learned how to enact non-funded mandates. Who cares of the problems this caused because they already had their home. They would actually prefer that you not get yours because you're taking up too much of their "space."

They realized that they couldn't keep everyone out so they would at least protect the earth. This cost money. How much clean air and water can you afford (98%, 99%, 99.98%)?

Again, they didn't care because they didn't have to pay for it. They enacted laws that made the new guy in town pay for their environmental concerns. It's not that improving the environment is bad, it is just that it is not free and people need to understand and agree to the costs of doing so. Having a burned-up hippie unilaterally make those decisions just isn't right.

The suing part is the most interesting and the most costly. America wouldn't have been built without banks and the insurance companies. As distasteful as that sounds, it is the truth. People would not take the risk of building and expanding businesses without taking out insurance. Banks wouldn't lend money without insurance. Even housing loans are insured. The government has a hard time getting all the insurance it needs from insurance companies. It isn't free. Since the informed consumer learned the great benefits of their proactive legal system (getting rich from normal misfortune), the government needed a better insurance policy. Juries would be made of these hippies who were taught that big business and big government are bad and had lots of money to give away to the downtrodden masses. They knew that if misfortune came, someone had to pay and why not those with the deep pockets. You never know what a jury is going to decide in California and eventually the government and the politicians figured this out. The insurance policy they worked out was to make sure that the blame would be spread around as far as possible and that the premiums would be paid by those trying to build a new house.

The methodology was simple. Every house to be built would be individually reviewed, designed, certified and insured by an engineer and an architect. If something went wrong, they would be part of the suit. The engineers and architects were no fools. A large part of their fee would be insurance that, in the rare case, something went wrong or God had a particularly hard day, they wouldn't be sued out of existence. So every plan was certified by very expensive players in the game. Next, the process would take a very long time. This was done for two reasons. First was to discourage anyone from ever building. Second was that the plans had to go through a very long and complicated review process. Since very smart engineers and architects had to design and "do the math" on these projects, someone equally smart in the building department had to review these plans.[9]

To complicate matters and to make sure that the architects and engineers had plenty of work to do, the inspection department in L.A. required that all house plans are drawn in the greatest detail possible. Every possible thing has to be

War Story

#9: I was first indoctrinated to L.A. permits with a post and beam house my company had shipped to Hollywood, California. It was an amazing ride. First, for those of you that didn't know, there is no such place as Hollywood. The Hollywood sign was the name of a subdivision in the hills above L.A. Hollywood is really L.A. city. The post and beam house we supplied was made of Eastern White Pine and was joined using mortise and tenon joinery, secured with oak pegs. The company, was based in New Hampshire, had been in business since 1974 and had produced thousands of homes that were built around the country.

Post and beam is a building method that came to America from Europe and was over 500 years old. Many of the homes built in America that used this method of building still stand today, surviving for over 350 years. It is a beautiful way to build, with massive timbers of the home exposed to the inside of the house. It is also somewhat expensive and this particular house was being built for a movie producer and was across the street from movie actress Loretta (the original hot lips in "M*A*S*H") Swit's house. It was being built on a vacant lot that was once a dump site. The first problem we had was with the wood. Eastern White Pine, as the name implies, comes from "back East." It doesn't grow in California. The code people had a book that listed all the wood that exists in California and this species was not in the book. Logically (to the California mindset), it did not exist.

The next problem was that the joinery was something they had not seen before. Therefore, it too did not exist. They requested tests and certification of the joinery. We did a little research and asked one of the preeminent building systems engineering firms in the country what it would cost and how long it would take to certify the system to California's liking. The answer was at least $100,000, one to three years, maybe. Things were not looking good. I decided to talk to the inspector directly. I was going to appeal to his intellect and hippie good nature. I was going to tell him that this method of building and this species of trees has been successfully done for hundreds of years. It pre-dates the oldest houses in California. He didn't care. It wasn't in his book and he would not allow it.

We did find a solution. We ignored the frame, the wood and the connections. We used huge metal plates to reinforce every wooden connection in the house (there were hundreds). Since all these joints were exposed to the inside of the house and the major feature of the house, we hid as many as we could from the outside and laughed about the others. Then we used a new product called stress skin panels and covered the outside side walls and roof with this newly approved building system. The strength of the stress skin panels actually made the post and beam frame superfluous and provided all the structure the house needed to pass L.A. code. The frame was, in their mind, decorative. The house was transformed from early Colonial to early industrial with the flick of a bureaucrat's pen.

The rest of the story, as Paul Harvey puts it, is that the house was finally finished. During the owner's housewarming party, he was offered $100,000 more than it cost him to build. It seemed that very few homes were being built in the Hollywood hills (I wonder why?) and was truly a marvelous house in spite of the L.A. building department. The other rest of the story was that my company gave up on L.A. and spent most of its marketing effort and time in Oregon and Washington.

In the process of getting this house approved and built (two years to do a six-month job), I learned a lot about building hell in L.A. While I mentioned some of the requirement for details in drawing, an example of the extremes that this could go was the planter box detail. Apparently, years ago, a planter box fell off a house and hit someone. The ensuing lawsuit cost the city over a million dollars. The result was that all future planter boxes had to be drawn by a board certified architect and engineered by a board certified engineer. A planter box is normally part of Shop 101. It's what moms get for Mother's Day from their ninth-grade sons. Not in L.A. It is a work of art and engineering marvel and costs hundreds of dollars.

drawn. Every connection. Every component. If it contains parts from another manufacturer, it has to have complete certification and test data supplied. If it is from "back east," it must also be certified for California. Just because the part has been used millions of times elsewhere in the country doesn't mean that it is good enough for California. Remember the EPA standards for cars in California?

The next interesting thing required in L.A. was part of the security code. All houses had to have dead bolts and doors and windows of a certain capacity to resist burglars. The choice was no longer yours. Another part of this code was that you could not violate city ordinances with your home. One of the city ordinances was that you could not back out of your driveway into the street. I did happen to know that this was not unique. I had backed out of my driveway in Charlotte, North Carolina once and hit a parked car. In the process of dealing with the police on this (my point was that the parked car was opposite my driveway and shouldn't have parked there), I learned that it was illegal to back onto a public street. I'll bet that if you checked your local laws, you would find this to also be true. However, no one enforces this and you'll also find that 90% of all driveways in subdivisions in America are built so you have to back out of them. However, L.A. and its legions of hippie building inspectors know about this ordinance and have decided to do something about it. So, among the many plans you have to submit to get a permit in L.A. is a site plan that shows your driveway. If it shows that you would have to back out of it to get out, your permit will be rejected. You have to design it so that it has a turnaround. Not only does this cost more (more driveway material), it also consumes more of your lot. In a small lot situation, it could consume almost all the lot. Not too bad if you don't want to cut the grass, but it could be awfully ugly or require an expensive landscaping job to make it look decent again.

Another thing that happened to the house in War Story #9 was that someone tried to steal the building materials, (in broad daylight) in front of the owner and builder. With a car, not a truck. Someone had driven into the lot (less than a quarter acre) and started loading up their trunk with expensive siding and trim. The builder ran out of the house and started yelling at the thief who yelled back and said it was his stuff (it wasn't). When he saw he was getting nowhere, the thief got into his car and drove off, spilling the wood out of his trunk onto the street. Only in L.A.

While this is L.A., it could be your town next. The biggest problem is that most people only build one house in their lifetime. They don't care about housing codes and costs until it directly affects them. However, as you can see, it can get out of control. The ones who care are the builders and the developers. In L.A., most of the construction done there is by building giants (like Kaufman and Broad), multimillion dollar houses for the very rich and persistent, and re-modelers. In fact, outside of the huge tract house developments, the majority of the building done in California is remodeling. It is just too hard to build new houses. Some people will demolish all but a room (sometimes only one wall) of an existing house just to permit it as a remodel rather than a new home. There are three times the number of re-modelers (compared to new house builders) in California as there are anywhere else in the country. The government is trying to catch up with them too and throws a lot of laws at them as well. One is that if a house is being remodeled, the outside improvements have to meet current codes. In this case, if new homes have to have sidewalks, street lights and fireplugs, a remodeled house has to add a sidewalk, street light and fireplug, adding thousands of dollars to the cost of the job. Often there are no adjoining sidewalks or street lights to tie into until someone else remodels nearby.

The big developers know they can't fight city hall, so they just plan ahead. They know that they must be at least two years out to get a subdivision with its housing permits approved.

This helps explain why when housing slows down, the big guys take it in the shorts with excess inventory on hand. They've been there long enough to put this extra cost into the price of their homes. Since the rules change all the time, often houses are sold through a lottery system where you get the right to purchase the house at whatever price it happens to be once it is completed. At contract, you're given an approximate price. Another solution to the slow permit process in L.A. is firms that specialize in getting permits approved. I know of one firm that hires very attractive women to take permits into the building department and sweet talk them through the process. You better believe it works.

The building department has its problems, too. Every time a new series of ordinances is passed, they have to gear up to meet demand. When their resources are exhausted, it just takes longer to get permits approved. They are too scared of lawsuits to let things slide and often are unable to hire new staff to take care of the work-load. What they do is to sub out the work, usually to engineers, often foreign born who cannot get work elsewhere. I found this out once when a building inspector offered to fulfill his requirement for extra engineering on a house. I told him that I thought that was a conflict of interest for him to require something and then offer to do it for a fee. That is when I found out that he was not an inspector at all but that the permit was subbed out to him. What a racket.

From Building Hell to Good Old Boys

Now that I've shown you building hell, I'll show you what is more normal in most places. The other end of the spectrum starts with house plans sketched on napkins. Well, it's not that simple but permits can be had for less than $25.

Often, all that is required is a septic permit. In some cases, not even that. It depends primarily on how many houses are built a year in your county and what kind of government services are provided. If your county builds only a handful of houses a year, there is no need for a permit or inspections department. Whatever requirements they might dream up are usually incorporated into another department. The most common in these situations is the health department might want to look at your septic or well conditions.

The health/septic department is, like all government, "only there to help you." They certainly have your best interests at heart, but can also be a nuisance. If a septic permit is required, they will come out to your site and determine where your tank and drain fields will go and how much of a house you can build. The frustration is how the rules are interpreted. One method is the number of bed-

Remember, there is no such thing as a perfect house. They will find a violation and make you fix it, often at great expense. Get a permit.

rooms, the other the number of bathrooms. I'm not sure why some counties use bedrooms and some bathrooms. However, the number of bedrooms can be modified by renaming them as dens and studios if your permit only allows three bedrooms and you want four. (I'm not supposed to tell you this. Shhh.)

Another problem with septic systems is that the inspector might want to put it where you don't want it or it might take too much room on the lot. Often, they will require room for not only the current drain field but also another one for future use, thus taking twice the land needed. They might also require you to install a system that costs more than the routine system. There is more than one system, the more expensive ones being used for less conducive soil conditions. In either case, you should not fight the inspector because they do have your best interest in heart. If their solution is a killer, you might want to look into an engineer coming up with another solution. You should check with the inspector to see if they would accept an independent engineer's findings and system. You can also approach the seller of your property to see if they can deed you some more land or trade lots that would be better suited to your needs. All they can say is "No."

Most inspectors will require that you install the septic system before you start the house. Don't fight this either. The tank and drain field has to be lower than the house for it to work using gravity. It is possible for you to mistakenly build the house lower than the septic system, especially one with a basement. This is a major problem you really want to avoid. Follow the rules or you'll be up to your elbows in . . .

The next level of permits is one that involves house plans. Here's where the napkin comes in because you can draw and submit your own plans in some areas. Often, they can be very rough. In other areas, you can submit plans cut out of plan books. While the requirement can be quite lax, eventually an accurate set of plans is almost always used to build the house. However, these plans might not be finished at the time you want to pull a permit and therefore you would just submit whatever you have available or what would satisfy the inspector.

Having been in the "kit" home business for a number of years, I do know that many people will submit stock plans that will be modified later. If time is of the essence, this often works just fine. In situations where financing is involved, a fairly complete set of plans have already been submitted to the bank for their needs and therefore, these plans are already available. The point is, many places only require very basic plans.

Another requirement you might see either by itself or in conjunction with a set of plans is a plot plan that shows the house plan, in scale, as it will be positioned on the lot. This is often required so that zoning officials can ensure that your house does not violate setback or side yard requirements. You usually do not need to have a professional draw this on the plot plan, but you should be as accurate as you can be.

If you are building under "normal" conditions, the most common requirements are a set of plans, a plot plan and a listing of who is building the house and their license number. Many times you will need to have already selected your major licensed subcontractors and provide their names and license numbers. These include plumbers, electricians, and heating contractors. In many states, you can be your own contractor but there might be other requirements, such as attendance at a building class or a waiver of responsibility.

Since so many owner-builders get in trouble with their homes and can be a nuisance with their many questions and mistakes, many building departments really discourage owner-builders. While there are plenty of rules that should be followed in the permit and building process, building officials often will force the owner-builder through every single hoop while letting well-known contractors slide. Expect to be "hassled" if you're on your own.

Another thing to look for is how long it will take to get the permit. This can range from getting it while you wait to many months like in L.A. You should call ahead and ask what they want and have it ready. If there is a process you have to go through, get an estimate on how long it will take. Waiting for permits can drive you nuts. Remember, you're dealing with a government entity and they are always (ask them, they'll tell you) behind, overworked, understaffed (underpaid, unappreciated, etc.).

While I have been showing you some typical conditions and the state of the art, every county will be different. The short answer is to go down there and see what they want. Determine the fees and the procedures. You really don't have a choice and I strongly urge you to not start building without a permit. They can shut your job down, fine you, make you take the building apart, and start over. Plus, they are going to be very upset with you and look for reasons to turn down every inspection you ever ask for. Remember, there is no such thing as a perfect house. They will find a violation and make you fix it, often at great expense. Get a permit. ■

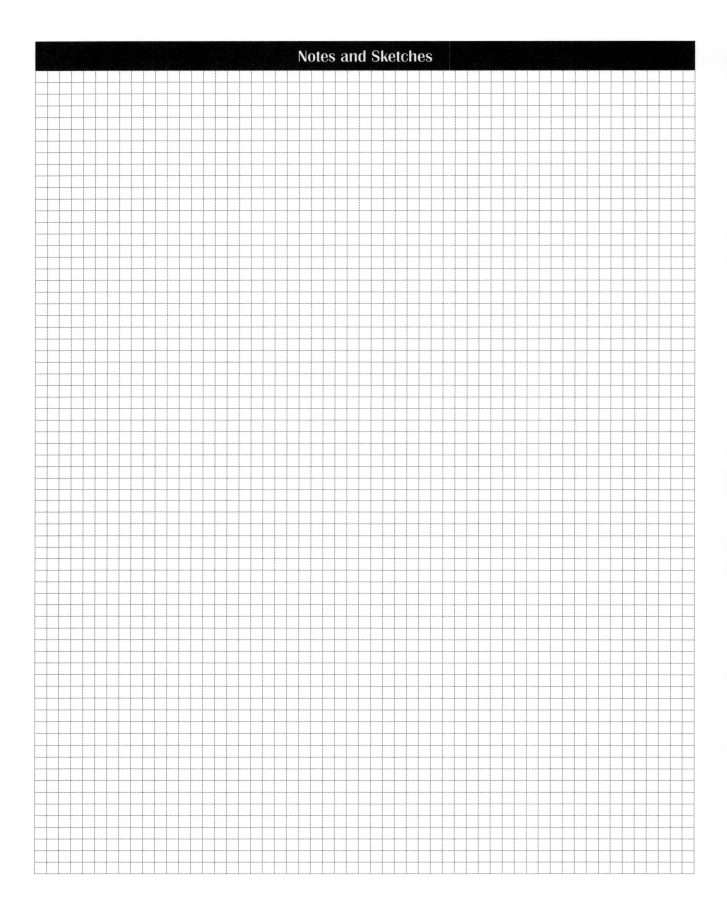

17

Land Regulations

Your Strongest Heritage

The right to own land and property is one of America's greatest freedom. It is an absolute ingredient to our democratic system of government. In this country and others, areas where land ownership is low are also areas where government does not work well. It is only when land is owned by many that people care about the laws of the land. There are plenty of laws that deal with property. In fact, most laws deal with property.

Yet these laws are a two-way street. Individuals have rights and the government has rights (although government public relations people call these rights "duties"). Conflicts are resolved in court and through arbitration. Jurisdictions range from subdivision covenants to the federal government. Villages, towns, cities, counties, regions, and states also have their own slice of the pie.

Land regulations start right at the top with the federal level. The federal government reaches right into your home with regulations on what goes into it and what affect it has on the land around it. Most of the components in your home have been tested and approved by some government regulatory office. FHA, EPA, DOE, etc., want to ensure that your home is safe and not harmful to you or the environment. Environmental concerns have increased dramatically over the past few years. These concerns have caused a number of changes in how house components are used and developed. An example of product changes is seen with the paint industry and oil based paints, which are almost a thing of the past now. Oil based paints are hazardous because of flammability, toxic vapors and the difficulty of disposing of not only the paint in the field but also the by-products of paint manufacture. Fortunately, water based acrylic paints have improved to such a degree that they are suitable replacements for most oil based paints.

The EPA has had a great impact on where homes can be built and on the precautions that must be taken when building homes. Spotted owls and wet lands (a nice word for swamp) protection have directed developments away from the

> ### In This Chapter . . .
>
> ▲ How the government is here to help you
>
> ▲ Using the laws to solve problems
>
> ▲ Real laws made by busy-bodies and fools-covenants

areas where these entities are present. One of the major concerns of land development is keeping silt, which is eroded dirt, from washing into and clogging up streams. Where before developers did whatever they wanted in clearing land, they must now take precautions to prevent debris and silt from leaving a job site and affecting adjacent areas. The EPA wants to ensure that streams stay clean and that endangered fish like snail darters are not pushed out of their natural environment by the effects of you wanting to build a dream home.

Other products used in construction have to meet federal standards, especially when burning. Carpet is especially prone to producing toxic gases when aflame. Some products can cause allergic reaction to their presence. Asbestos was used in year's past in roofing and siding as well as in insulation and ceiling tiles. Poisonous liquids were used in the production of plywood and pressed board. All these products were then trapped in your home, making you sick.

The oil crisis of the 1970s created the Department of Energy (DOE) and vastly improved the energy efficiency of homes. A side effect of this energy improvement and "tighter houses" was the trapping of noxious chemicals in homes, making many people ill. Tight houses not only trap noxious gases but also moisture which can cause a build up of mold and mildew.[10]

War Story

#10: I was building homes in Charlotte, when EPA set up an office there. One of their first concerns was the county landfill and what was being placed in it. They looked, didn't like what they saw and closed it down. It didn't matter that Charlotte was undergoing a housing boom at that time and used the landfills to their maximum capacity. The problem wasn't just debris from construction, but also trees and stumps from clearing lots. The city had earlier made it illegal to burn trees and stumps. This debris was either hauled to the dump or buried somewhere on each lot. With the landfills closed and burning illegal, the last choice was to bury the debris on site. EPA got wind of this and ruled that it didn't want anything buried on site until they had a chance to inspect it. The builders in town thought that was nuts and started to fight the EPA. Meanwhile, they could not haul off, burn or bury the trees or construction debris. They also, for some reason, could not get the EPA inspectors to inspect the holes in a timely manner. Rather than hold up a $60 an hour machine, builders stacked up the debris on vacant lots in each neighborhood until they could get some resolve for the issue. What they got was big ugly piles of trash, several stories high in each new subdivision. It was getting to be a mess. Finally, the builders had their showdown with the EPA. Research had showed that an estimated 400 holes were dug a day in the county. EPA's earlier mandate was that all holes dug were to be inspected prior to covering them up. At least now the builders knew why the inspectors were having a hard time getting to their jobs to inspect the holes.

You could have heard a pin drop when EPA admitted that they had but three inspectors to inspect the holes that were opened each day. Three people to look at 400 holes a day. Talk about unfunded mandates. The EPA compromised and let builders certify that all they would put into their holes would be trees and no construction waste. Builders were to mark on plot plans where these holes were and what was in them. The EPA tripled the cost of using the landfills for the other debris (this had worked before with fuel shortages) and every one was happy except the homeowner who had the price of their homes raised by about $1,000.

At the state and local level, regulations are fine tuned to meet specific needs of the community. Local regulations often pass on all state regulation and then add their own. Sometimes local municipalities are too small or under equipped to enforce the state laws and thus enforce only the ones they can inspect. While it would be nice that they take a stab at making sure your home is built to code, they are often only able to make sure that your water is safe to drink and your septic system works properly.

If your local municipality is large enough, they might try to enact and enforce some zoning ordinances. These include things like setbacks and side yard restriction as well as public right of ways. These terms are important to know because most properties have them. A brief discussion of these follows:

Setback: This is how far your house should be set back from the road in front. If this is an exact concern (you're pushing the limits of this), you often would go to the center of the road and measure back to the gutters of where the house will be. You should measure to the gutters (rather than the foundation) because that is usually the part of your house that sticks out the furthest. A surveyor might be needed to determine the center of the road.

Side yard restrictions: This is how far your house should be from your neighbor's property line. Twenty to 30' between houses is a common side yard restriction in a development. Some will use eight and six or a total of 14', giving the developer the flexibility to determine who gets the 8'.[11]

Public Right of Way: Actually I have found this restriction to be useful. A public right of way is a portion of your property that you own but the government has the right to do certain things with. This usually includes running utility lines and adding sidewalks or eventually widening the street.[12]

War Stories

#11: I once was building a house in a tight neighborhood and a customer asked if I could add a fireplace to their home. I told them that I could and instructed the footing and masonry contractor to do so. I didn't think about it again until near completion when the surveyor told me that the fireplace violated the distance between houses and that it wasn't his fault. He had placed the house tight to that side and he didn't know about the fireplace. He was right and I was in trouble. As we say in our business, "Let no good deed go unpunished." Through some finagling, we were able to work it out, but I certainly learned a lesson. Here again is where an innocuous change caused a major problem.

#12: I once was building in a tight neighborhood with 14 feet between houses, utility boxes in the front yard and a fairly hilly terrain. These conditions made it difficult to get driveways to houses, especially in cul de sacs. I had one case where I could not get a driveway into two houses—there was not enough room at the curb to give each person their 10 feet of driveway starting at the curb. I asked for help and my boss suggested that I look at what point there was room for both driveways. I saw that it wasn't until 8 feet into the lot that the each driveways had their own 10 feet. He then told me to join the driveways at the street and keep them together until I reached beyond the public right of way, a point 10 feet from the curb. Since I had the right to do whatever I wanted in the right of way, I was able to get the two drives in and satisfy the law and the contract. I also made the customers happy because they now had wider (a total of 18 feet) approach to their driveway.

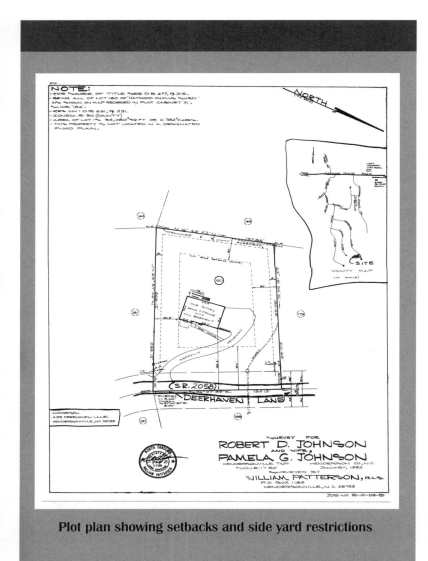

Plot plan showing setbacks and side yard restrictions

While these most often are at the front of the house next to the street, they can also be along your side or rear yard property line. You should never fence over a public right of way. If you must, recognize that the fence could be taken down and probably not be put back up very well. The utility companies are usually the ones who want to get on your right of way to install or repair lines or just to read your meter. They can even require you to maintain (cut) the grass in the right of way.

Flood lines: One thing the federal government does for you at the local level is determine when the next flood is going to be. They use the U.S. Army Corps of Engineers to do this and, through magic, can predict when the next flood will be (within a 100 years). These 100-year floodlines tell you where you can build safely. They are broken down into two subcategories. One is where you can build but have to keep the finished (carpeted) floor of the house above a certain elevation above sea level. The next is where you cannot build at all. Often a lot will have both lines on them. Since this is critical information, a surveyor often becomes involved and certifies that the finished floor is above the flood line. Usually property with flood lines require flood insurance, but since there are literally millions of homes built on property with flood lines, it is not a problem, especially if you want to live near a river or lake.

Eminent Domain: You probably do not have to worry about this but you should realize that the government has the right to take your house away. It's called *eminent domain*. This is usually done when building roads, dams and other public projects. You are supposed to receive fair market value for your home though most people probably don't agree with this. However, you usually don't see newly constructed mansions being torn down and paid for by the government. Eminent domain is usually used where a 50-year-old house was built too close to a road that is being widened.

Covenants

Land use regulations usually start with a subdivision covenant. These covenants, or one sided agreements, most often deal with minimum sizes of houses, distances between structures, etc. These criteria are intended to protect and preserve the value of the entire subdivision. In their simplest state, they work pretty well. Given to a lawyer, they can become a nightmare. Most covenants are given to a lawyer. When this happens, they are often called "restrictive" covenants.[13]

Some important things to look for in covenants are:

Minimum size of house: Look for tricks like how many square feet *per floor* or the words *heated space* or *under roof*. A 1,800-square-foot ranch (all footage on one level) is a lot more restrictive (expensive) than 900' per floor two-story (which also gives you 1,800 square feet overall). What you'll probably find is the single level square footage to be larger than the first story of a two-story. For example, the requirement might be 1,200' for a one level building or 1,400 for a two-level building. *Heated* space is different from *under roof* in that *under roof* includes porches and the garage, which are not normally heated. There is a lot more *under roof* space in most homes. Heated space also costs a lot more than *under roof* space. Most covenants spell out *heated space,* but you have to look for it.

Two issues come up in the interpretation of square footage. First is where you measure from—the inside of the house or the outside. That 6"–10" difference in the thickness of the walls can add some serious numbers to the square footage of a house. The other issue is how much square footage can you count in a Cape Cod style or story and a half house. Most people allow all floor plans that has a 4'–5' tall side wall to count as heated space. Space below this is storage and doesn't count in determining square footage. However, if you're close to meeting a minimum, you need to clarify how this is defined.

War Story

#13: I once worked in a sub-division where we only sold land. It was an expensive development with lot prices reaching over $100,000. Our "restrictive" covenants were almost three quarters of an inch thick. They were based on the covenants used at Hilton Head Island, South Carolina, one of America's first modern day planned developments. Hilton Head is a beautiful development that is well known for its restriction of neon and other garish signs typically used in commercial developments. You can still find the golden arches. However, their sign is made of painted wood and is about six feet above sea level. The covenants at Hilton Head are a master stroke. However, Hilton Head has thousands of homes and, while protected, the island begins to look very much alike. This is not a bad thing—it is just different.

The major difference is that these covenants were intended to greatly restrict individual's property to the betterment of the island as a whole. You have to buy into this and might not realize the long lasting impact. In the development where I worked, the "restricted" covenants were used as a sales tool. We showed our prospective clients this oversized tome, trying to impress them with how "protected" they would be and how well thought out the development was. The amazing thing was that most people could care less about the "restrictive" covenants and just assumed that they were "good" because there were so many of them and that they were based on Hilton Head. Sometimes they would buy without reading them. Other times they would (with their lawyer) and the fireworks began. The point is that you need to understand the covenants of the place that you are buying. Their size and where they came from are mostly irrelevant. How they meet your needs is what is most important.

Distance between structure: This is becoming more important today because many developments are making their lots smaller and smaller. While many people want to be as far away from their neighbors as possible, the freedom to move the house site on the lot can make all the difference in the world. People alter the house site primarily for two reasons. First is to get the best view available on the lot. The second reason is to build the home economically. You probably never noticed before but most homes are placed on the lot with one side of the house tight to one of the property set back lines. If your property has a lot of slope, a high tide or flood zone requirement, or a "best" view characteristic, you need to pay particular attention to how close you can place your house to a boundary.

Restricted or prescribed material: This is an interesting requirements that I have seen work against the seller. Some developers have a bias towards certain materials, usually siding and roofing. I've seen it both ways. One neighborhood I know of in Dallas required that all houses had to be at least 60% brick. Another development in North Carolina banned brick altogether. Some areas require a certain grade or type of roof shingle, while others exclude cedar shakes. While these requirements might make sense in preserving the "look" of the development, they can get expensive and make you awful unhappy if you didn't realize they were a requirement before you bought the land.

Restriction from view: This is where you have to keep certain things hidden from view. It could be air conditioners (no window units, hedge or fence off central units), clothes lines (get a dryer), motor homes or boats (build a bigger garage or store off site) or garage doors visible from the street (face garage doors to the side of the house). Also, big on this list is satellite dishes and antennas. Probably the toughest one here is the motor home because they are hard to hide. If the motor home or boat is part of your lifestyle, you might not want to live in that neighborhood.

Commercial activity: This one is common but can get tricky and even go overboard. With a trend towards home offices, you have to be on the look out for ways to get trapped here. An example that I know of is dealers for packaged homes use their homes as their models. While they often don't use a sign, they might want to have periodic open houses and covenants could ban this as a violation of commercial activity. If you're planning on building a home and using it for show, get this issue cleared up front.

Type of structure: Some neighborhoods only want certain types of structures. Homes typically banned are log and dome homes as well as modular homes. Some neighborhood might require a certain type of home, i.e., log homes. The modular issue is new and leads to another war story.[14]

If you're planning to build something other than a stick built house, look at the covenants for this condition. If it's there, it probably is not worth fighting. Look elsewhere.

Architectural plan review: This is a killer. It can also get very expensive. Many developments will form architectural review boards. These boards are typically a nosy bunch of busy bodies who feel that they are God's gift to architecture. The board usually includes the developer, his wife, a former monarch and some sort of washed up or retired design professional. They are there to pass judgment on your personal taste They also want you to spend a lot of money and jump through a number of hoops for their enjoyment. Among the things they might require is that you use only an architect to develop your house plans, hopefully one they recommend. While an architect can be very useful to your home, here you are forced to spend at least $5,000 that might not be necessary.

Another common requirement is a site plan that not only shows the topography of your lot but also the exact location of every tree on your lot. The board wants this done so that you only take out the trees they want you to take out. They might compromise and let you replace trees that you want out and they do not. You are looking at about $1,000 for this topo/arbor plan. The board might also want a rendering of your finished house, including the trees you are leaving to show how your new home will look on the lot. Another $1,000.

Now that the board has spent at least $7,000 of your money, it is ready to pass judgment on your house design. They probably gave you some guidelines, like their favorite house styles, to ensure that you design a house to their liking. If you do this, you're probably home free. (Well, almost, because many have added a plan review fee to pay for *their* valuable time.) If they don't like your plan, hopefully they will give you a hint on what they didn't like and send you back to the drawing board with an opportunity to spend more money. Beyond the costs of extra drafting, these changes will also increase the cost of your house to meet their needs and taste in design.

The good news here is that everyone has to go through this process (except probably the developer and his wife) and the neighborhood will be protected by its "restrictive" covenants. If your covenants have a review committee, just be prepared for this drill. The best test of this is to see how the other homes in the development look, especially the developer's. If they look appropriate and you really want other people to spend your money, go for it.

Completion clause, camping, etc.: If you are going to build your own home,

War Story

#14: I was working for one of the state-of-the art modular companies based in the mid-Atlantic. Modulars were doing quite well there and the company was trying to break into the Carolina market. We had sold one of our two story Colonial houses in a development near Greensboro, North Carolina to a builder. He had purchased a few odd lots in a 10 year old development and wanted to build some spec homes. Everything was going fine until the house showed up and was assembled in one day. One day, a typical foundation, the next day, a 2,000 square foot house. The neighbors went ballistic. Big meetings, lawyers (and law suits), zoning and building inspectors. It was the Civil War all over again. The problem was made worse by the fact that the modular home was better looking, better built and used better materials than any existing house in the neighborhood. It had already been appraised at a higher level than any house there, thus raising everyone's property values. However, it was a "modular" house and was not to be tolerated. Someone found a copy of the "restrictive" covenants and it clearly stated that "no mobile homes" were to be built in the development. A small technicality in semantics, but since when did reality make any difference when it came to someone's home place. The furor lasted for weeks but was finally settled by the builder agreeing to not build any more modular homes in the neighborhood and the homeowners agreeing to not burn down the one that he already built.

you probably are going to take extra time to do it. You might even want to live on the land for a few nights a year to test it out or just dream closer to you dream home. If this is the case, make sure that the covenants don't preclude that. Camping might not be allowed. Also, your timed schedule of completion might not coincide with the covenants as well.

Many developments want homes to be completed in a set amount of time, i.e., one year. Others might restrict this requirement to the outside only, thus giving you extra time to finish up inside. You might have to finish the yard (to a minimal degree) and keep construction debris and noise to a minimum. Many neighborhoods only allow construction to occur from 8 a.m. to 5 p.m., Monday through Friday. This could be a real problem if you are planning to do the work yourself at night and on weekends.

Homeowner associations and dues: You better read this one closely. Especially if the development you're planning to live in has plenty of amenities. Often these fees are kept low in the beginning of a project to keep this devil at bay. Future costs, such as gate guards and the repainting or reroofing of the clubhouse might not be obvious. Look to see who will be running the association and how they are elected/selected. While homeowner fees might look small in the beginning, they can wallop you later on. A quadrupling of these fees are not unheard of. If your house is a second home, you might be unfairly paying for services you don't want or need, i.e., snow removable at your summer home. Realize too that some developers keep association dues artificially low at first to get people to buy the lots and then let them rise to their natural levels after the development is sold out. Also, some of the wealthier year-round lot owners might want to raise the fees to cover future amenities that you might not be interested in.

Boilerplate: You might need a lawyer here but most likely you can gut it out and read this stuff. You'll probably find that you can't raise goats or pigs. You won't be able to rent your house out to four families of refugees. You might see all sorts of things copied out of Hilton Head or Aspen. There might be some hidden jewels like a fee to sell your property paid to the developer regardless of who sells your home. I've seen this one in the Hilton Head model. Often the seller might back off of strange and grossly unfair sections of a covenant if you say you won't buy unless it is changed. Here is where your friendly lawyers earn their keep. ■

18

Basic Common Sense Codes

A Dead Body or a Crashed House for Each Code

The first known building codes are found in the Bible at Deuteronomy 22:8. I quote, "Every new house must have a guardrail around the edge of the flat rooftop to prevent anyone from falling off and bring guilt to both the house and its owner." It looks like people were falling off their roofs and God wanted to do something about it. I just found this out recently and wonder why this Bible verse isn't on the wall in every code office in the nation. Probably something to do with mixing church and state. It does help explain the "Godlike" attitude many building inspectors have about their work, though.

Codes come from many sources, starting at the national level. Residential building codes, however, do not have a single, universal standard. There is no national building code. There is a national HUD code, but it pertains only to manufactured mobile homes. Mobile, not modular, which has to deal with local, state and regional codes. There is a National Electrical code, but it is amended at the regional, state and sometimes local level. Actual residential building codes are regionalized. Sometimes the names of the code agency changes and often there is talk of a national building code, but it's not going to happen anytime soon. There's too much turf to protect. Remember also that some trees don't grow everywhere in this country (and therefore don't exist) so there must be different codes.

Each state will model their own codes on their regional codes. They might accept them almost in their entirety (and thus save their taxpayers a fortune by not setting up departments to reinvent the wheel) or they might set up their own departments and use what they want. They often add their own ideas. Some will be easy to read and actually give you the answers. Others are written so only an engineer or lawyer can understand them. ICBO, which governs Western states, likes you to use math and convert technical data to get answers.

For example, if you want to know how far you can span a 2x10 under a 40-pound load, ICBO gives you a table that tells you that the deflection is 3.45 and modulus of elasticity is 1.21 and expects you to figure it out. BOCA, which covers Eastern states, will tell you that it is 11'6". Both regional code agencies like you to use some brain power when figuring out R-values, which tell you how good insulation is. Instead of just telling you what the R value is, they give the requirement to you in U-values. Nowhere do they tell you that the formula you use is $1/U=R$, but that is the way you figure it out. Simple stuff, but don't expect any help. If they make it too simple, they'll be out of a job.

Codes change all the time. Most states are not very good at letting you know when the change is going into effect and often are introducing code changes throughout the year. You often find out when you get turned down for some work. Codes are also not uniformly enforced. Some officials just don't care or simply don't agree. While working with building systems, we often found some counties would turn down the way we assembled a building system and some had no problem. I would question the local guy for their concern and they would quote some part of the code. Obviously, it would not be clear cut and thus be the reason for the problem. I would call the state office for clarification. Most times it would go my way.

However, I have found that some coequal managers at the state office disagreed on the interpretation and we would go round and round until we could reach some common ground. One company I worked for shipped about 200 houses a year nationwide. About 25 of these went to North Carolina, which has 100 counties and building departments. Each county would interpret the code their own way. We'd have a problem in one county and not the next. Often it was personal, not towards my company, but towards my product (log homes). There are over 400 manufacturers of log homes and a whole range of quality levels. If the last log home into that county by another company became a problem, all log homes in the future would be suspect. It's not fair, but that's life.

Most of the codes on the books are common sense. They are based on physical properties of materials. Wood can carry only so much weight for only so much of a span. A nail can properly connect two pieces of wood of certain dimensions and under so much load. Codes are full of test data and technical information. Most of the code is undisputed and fully expected.

The other part of codes is from experience and screw-ups. Like in California, if a planter box falls off and kills someone, the next code book has a planter box code. If a deck falls off a house (like what happened in Raleigh, N.C., with 50 people on it) the next code book will have stronger connection details and requirements for decks. Another example is where North Carolina increased the load requirements for second floors from 30 to 40 pounds. This was done primarily because of the increased use of waterbeds and the resulting problems of sagging floors. Before there were waterbeds, this was not a problem and North Carolina got along just fine with 30-pound loads on the second floor. It's always interesting to see the changes in the code book each year and try to find out why the change was made. I guess you would hope that it wasn't because of something you did.

As I mentioned, code changes often come from extraordinary events that are not from misuse or misapplication of components, but the component itself. There have been some legendary screw-ups in components. Along with the aluminum wire debacle was the problems with fire-retardant plywood. This product was used mostly in apartment buildings. For some reason, apartments seem to be involved with more fires than single-family houses. A fire retardant plywood for the roof made sense. Was it a fire hazard? No, it did just fine. However, it rotted. Real quick. A major screw-up. And since it was on the roof, it involved other components like shingles and expensive labor.

Another part of the code that was changed had to do with smoke detectors. Smoke detectors are great and have saved hundreds of lives. The code said that new homes had to have them and it was a routine part of home building. People were still dying from fire, however. What was the problem? Well, the first smoke detectors were battery powered and the batteries wore out. People would not take the time to replace them. So they made them with a safety device that beeped when the batteries got low. These are still available and you might have heard these before.

However, there was another problem. It just so happened that the batteries that ran the smoke detectors were also the same size as ones used for transistor radios. When junior's batteries ran low on his "boom box," he'd just open up the smoke detector and take it—no more protection. The code was changed to require that a smoke detector be wired directly into the main current of the house. The next question is: what happens when the power goes out? You're right, there is no protection, but the problem is greatly reduced from before.

Reading a code book is not many people's favorite pastimes. There is a lot of stuff in there you really don't need to know. There are, however, some things that can help preserve your investment and prevent problems in the future. There are also things that the inspector might miss or it just needs to be done right the first time. Therefore, here is an overview of important codes. While this list is not all inclusive, it will highlight some of the most important aspects of building a code-complying, properly built house. These are based primarily on the codes of North Carolina, where my license is. Since we are looking at basic common sense codes, these will either apply where you are building or give you something to think about. Remember, in their purest form, codes are derived from good building practices, experience and technical data.

The Very Basics

Minimum room sizes — Not every state will have minimums but these might be useful to your planning. "Living or primary rooms will be at least 150 square feet; the first bedroom at least 100 square feet; the kitchen/dining room 100 square feet; all other bedrooms and principal rooms at least 70 square feet." For example, this code requires that a one-bedroom house with one bath would be at least 390 square feet. This, by the way, is a very small house.

Light and ventilation — Windows must represent at least eight percent of the floor space. For example, a 150-square foot living room should have a window 12 square feet or a 3'x4' window. Half of the window has to open. In bathrooms, windows have to be at least 3 square feet, half of which can be opened.

An alternative to an opening window in a bathroom (as seen in interior bathrooms) is proper ventilation that is achieved by mechanical exhaust fans that vent the air to the outside.

Ceiling Heights — Ceilings should be at least 7½' tall. This is typical of mobile homes. Ceilings of 7'9" are common on the second floor of lower cost homes. Eight-foot ceilings are the norm.

Excavation: Solid, undisturbed, virgin soil — Foundations have to be excavated to sit on solid ground. This is probably the most important requirement of a home. Solid ground is also defined as "virgin, undisturbed soil" that can bear the weight of the house. Exceptions include houses that are built on pilings and those built on engineered "fill." These conditions are rare but not unheard of. If disturbed soil is found while excavating a lot, there are two common remedies. First is to reposition the house so that it is not built on disturbed soil. When this is not possible, you must dig through the disturbed soil down to virgin soil. Sometimes this might be a few feet for one section of the house or it could represent the entire house site. Judgment calls come into play here. The following are some examples where soil conditions were less than ideal and how these conditions were dealt with:

Case 1: The house that was mentioned earlier in Hollywood was built on a shallow trash dump. It covered the entire lot and was too deep to dig through. The solution was to drive pilings 20' into the ground and, with an engineer, develop a foundation that would carry the weight of the house (and deal with earthquakes). While this solution cost over $40,000, there were no comparably-priced lots left in Hollywood and the homeowner really wanted to live there.

Case 2: I was working on a house that was to be built in San Francisco. The foundation, which had to be built on piling and also had earthquake considerations, was estimated to cost $270,000. This was more than the cost of the rest of the house. The design and expensive building system (timberframe) was abandoned for that project.

Case 3: I was building a house in Charlotte when we discovered tree stumps and limbs in the building site. It was a fall away lot and no excavation was required. The trees were discovered while digging footings with a back hoe. I told the operator to dig through the trees and see if he could find solid ground below them. He did, at an average depth of 6'. I first went back to the developer and told him of the problem. He said that he had buried trees on the back side of all the lots on that street and that he must have gotten into the home site on that particular lot.

The spec for the development allowed for burying the trees on the lot, which was a common practice. He said he would pay for the extra cost involved. I next spoke with the mason, who said he would not go into a trench 6' deep to lay block. A utility worker had been killed earlier in the month in a trench cave-in and everyone was very concerned about this. The acceptable solution was to dig through the trees to solid ground, fill the trench with concrete and start the block from there. The developer paid the extra cost and the house was built.

Case 4: I was not involved with this house, but knew about it. A common condition in a development is that some lots are not sold while the subdivision is active. This was the case here. Unfortunately, the leftover lot was too close to a common dump site and debris got into the home site. As I had mentioned before in Charlotte, it was often difficult to get rid of trees and stump holes were dug on the back or side property line. This was a case where a number of different superintendents managed the subdivision over a period of time. The exact location of the stump hole was lost and the lot was never sold, probably because an active stump hole was next door. Often, when a stump hole is covered up, you would never know that it was there.

A customer wanted to build in that particular neighborhood and the lot was sold. Like in my case, debris was found in the home site. However, rather than 6' deep, it had no bottom, or at least a bottom that a back hoe could reach. An engineer was consulted and a plan was devised. Like in Hollywood, pilings were to be driven through the debris and a foundation was designed. Unlike Hollywood, the cost was less than $10,000, the approximate cost of the lot. While the profit for the lot sale was lost, profit was still to be made on the building of the house and the customer was happy.

Case 5: This did not involve footings, but fill (loose dirt) placed under a slab. Slab homes, where the main floor is concrete rather than wood, are less expensive than crawl space homes. It is a common building method, particularly in flat terrain like Texas and Florida. A block perimeter is built and dirt (fill) is brought in, leveled and concrete is poured on top to serve as the floor. It works pretty well as long as the foundation wall is not too tall and the fill dirt is placed in solidly and tamped. Where it becomes a problem is when the fill dirt is too deep and/or it is not tamped. Tamping is done with a hand-held machine that vibrates the dirt, compacting it. It is not a pleasant job and is often done haphazardly. Sometimes it is not done at all. What happens is the dirt settles on its own and the concrete, which was poured directly on top of it, gives way.

Fortunately, this was not a house that I built, but all the superintendents had to view the effects of not tamping a slab. Concrete, while it does crack, also has some elastic properties. In this case, the slab of the house sagged. This particular house had a trussed roof, which rested totally on the perimeter wall. The foundation wall and perimeter framing was just fine and held up as designed. The center of the house was the problem. As the slab settled (because the fill settled), it brought down the interior partition walls. They were nailed to the trusses, but pulled loose as the floor gave way. The drywall tape ripped at the intersection of the walls and the ceiling. It was a mess.

This was one of those occasions where a structural warranty was worth its weight in gold. The customer was moved into a motel for two months. The entire house was gutted. The cabinets, doors, bi-folds, appliances, and fixtures were stored and all the partition walls were removed. The slab was ripped out with pneumatic hammers, new fill dirt was added and tamped (correctly this time) plumbing was reinstalled, and the slab was re-poured. The house was rebuilt from the inside, the partition walls, cabinets, doors and fixtures reinstalled and the customer moved back in. Total cost was over $20,000, but made the customer happy, preserved the company's reputation and saved a lawsuit. From the inside, the customer got a brand new house and warranty along with new carpet and vinyl and whatever they didn't want from the old house. The company got some good press, some terrified but wiser superintendents and I got a good war story.

Case 6: This was my biggest mistake in building. No one got hurt and it didn't cost that much, but it had reconfirmed the importance of building on solid, undisturbed dirt. I once built a house in 30 days. That was remarkable, but came as the result of a screw-up with the city. The house was being built on a leftover lot, the exact condition as Case 4. Rather than being built on fill, the house was downhill from the street and the sewer lateral couldn't be found. Since it was downhill, I could not start the house until I located the sewer. The city stalled, delayed, had broken equipment and, to make a long story short, ate up two months of my building time locating the sewer. What had happened was that the street had been widened and the city had paved over the sewer lateral. It was not on their maps and their TV camera was in the shop. When sewer laterals (pipes that come from the main sewer to the lot) couldn't be found, they put a special TV camera in the sewer to find the lateral connection.

When I first got the job, I looked at the lot and noticed that a deck had been purchased to be placed on the back of the house. Since this was a fall away lot (and it kept falling), I knew that the deck was going to be a problem. I asked that the deck be eliminated because it would be too high off the ground. Since I didn't know where the sewer was, I didn't want to deal with a deck that could be 25' in the air. The sales department said it had to be there and I let it go as they told me of one more problem. The buyer had a capital gains problem. He had to close on that house within 90 days or the deal wouldn't go through. It was in the contract and the heat was on. Not only couldn't I find the sewer, I had little time to build the house and or to figure out how to put a deck on it.

To make a long story short, by the time the sewer was found and the foundation was built, I had 30 days to build a 2,200-square-foot, four-level house. I practically lived at that house, but got it done with one day to spare. One of the last things I did was put the deck on. Obviously, I had to put footings under the porch posts. However, my footing man would not take his back hoe down the steep incline to dig to solid ground. The backyard had been filled with tons of dirt and was steep and slippery. He was afraid of flipping over, a very real fear. The footing man hired two men to dig, with hand shovels, as deep as the handles of their shovels and install an oversized footing. I was in a corner and decided that it might work. The diggers said the dirt felt solid so I went on and built the deck.

I won all kinds of accolades and warm feelings from the homeowner and the company for doing an impossible task. One year later, the deck started to sink.

It was obvious that the footings were not on solid ground. A crane was hired and the deck was lifted off the house from the street. We hired heavy machinery and built a path down to the back of the house. Solid ground was found 10 more feet below the footing I had placed. Longer porch posts were installed and the deck rebuilt. The cost was about $1,500 and my embarrassment. No one was really mad because they knew of the problem of building the house (including my problem and objection to the deck). Nevertheless, it was a good lesson.

While most of these stories deal with subdivision houses, you can easily encounter disturbed soil on the 40 acres you just bought. In excavating, you might run into ancient trees, Indian artifacts or an old Model-T. If the ground has been disturbed any time since Moses, you either have to dig through it, get an engineer involved or move your home site. You must build on solid soil or your house is going to fall down.

Frost line protection: Almost all ground is subject to freezing. When ground freezes, then thaws, it moves in an upward thrust. If your excavation does not go deep enough into the ground to be below the *frost line,* the footing will move (break) and ruin your house. This condition is especially evident in northern climates where the frost line is much deeper than the South.

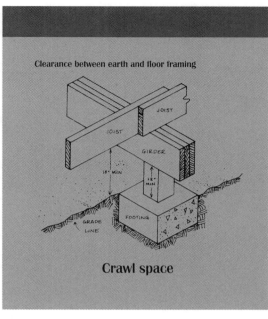

Clearance between earth and floor framing

Crawl space

COURTESY OF AMERICAN FOREST & PAPER
ASSOCIATION, WASHINGTON, D.C.

Charlotte has a frost line of only 12". This means that the *bottom* of the footing has to be 12" into the ground. In Northern climates, the frost line could be 48" or deeper. This extra, required depth is one reason why Northern homes almost always have basements and Southern houses usually don't. If you have to dig down 4' (or more) anyway, why not go all the way and get a full basement. You should check with your local code to see what the frost line is. Be aware that it can vary from county to county within a state. As an example, 100 miles west of Charlotte, in the North Carolina mountains, the frost line is 6" deeper than Charlotte.

Crawl spaces: Houses without basements have crawl spaces, which literally have space below the house to crawl around. Since the framing members of the house are closest to the ground here, a number of precautions should be taken. First, the floor joists, the wooden members that support the floor, need to be a minimum of 18" above ground level. In addition, the main girder, a large beam that the floor joist rests on in the center of the house, should be a minimum of 12" above ground level.

You should double check with your local code people to ensure that these measurements are correct or current for your particular area, as things can change without notice.

Often mechanical devices, like a furnace, are located in the crawl space. If this is the case, ground level should far enough below the bottom of the floor joist for this device to fit in the crawl space. Code also requires that there should be an access door of a particular size, i.e., 18"x24" (or large enough to remove the mechanical device) into the crawl space. Determining how tall to make the crawl space is somewhat of a debate. A taller crawl space is easier to work in. However, it costs more money and thus becomes a compromise beyond meeting minimum code. Realize too that raising the crawl space could add more steps into the house.

The crawl space floor is more important than most people realize. Since it is an area that is dark, full of spiders (and snakes), and is hard to get into and around in, most people never look at or inspect their crawl space. There are a number of very good reasons to inspect your crawl space. Codes have one requirement and that is that the floor of the crawl space be smooth and provides adequate drainage at all times. This includes the installation of a drain pipe at the

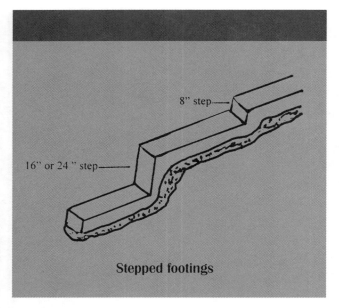

Stepped footings

8" step

16" or 24" step

lowest corner. In addition, debris, such as stumps, tree limbs and construction waste should be removed from the crawl space.

There are two primary reasons for the height of the crawl space. First is to allow adequate circulation of air under the house. Less than the minimum could cause wood rot, damaging your house. Second, also related to wood rot, is that insects, like termites, are less prone to invade wood if they are kept away from it. This prescribed distance also affects contact with the earth. Houses that have wooden framing members closer to the earth are more prone to damage.

Debris left under the house is also an open invitation to insects and termites. Once they've eaten the leftovers, they'll be looking for something else to eat nearby—your house! The positive drainage aspect of the crawl space is also important because water will normally get into and pass through your crawl space. This is not normally a problem, provided it has a way out. If water gets trapped in your crawl space, it will provide a nice environment for insects and animals that you probably don't want living there as well as introducing excess moisture into the framing members, causing wood rot and other damage.[15]

Footings: Footings are the first part of your house. Many people never realize that they are there because they are always covered up. We already know that they are very important and must be placed below the frost line and on solid ground. There are a number of equally important aspects of footings as well. They can be placed right into the ground with the sides of the trench serving as a natural form. Where the earth won't hold the concrete (or it makes sense to not trench footings), form boards can also be used to form footings. These form boards are removed after the concrete has set up. Since home sites are almost never perfectly level, footings will need to be stepped. This should be done in increments of 8", since that is the standard size of block. Each step typically should run for at least 2' before the next step.

The prescribed thickness of the footing will vary from state to state and should be confirmed before digging the footing. In North Carolina, footings for one-story houses are a minimum of 6" thick, with 8" required for two-story houses. If this is being contracted out, the contractor already knows the state requirements. The footing also has to be wider than the block wall going on top of it. In North Carolina, the footing must be 3" wider (on each side) than the foundation wall.

War Story

#15: I was told of a story where a house had a problem where a piece of furniture with metal feet was rusting and staining the carpet. An investigation into the crawl space showed that a vapor barrier had not been installed and moisture was coming directly into the house through the floor and rusting the feet of the table. Replacing the vapor barrier and installing a drain solved the problem.

Simple math will tell you that the footing must be 14" for an 8" block foundation (8+3+3). Reality of the workplace tells you that most footings are at least 16" wide. This is primarily because the standard bucket size of a back hoe is 16". Another standard size backhoe bucket is 24", which would be used if the block were 12". This is a little overkill. I would be careful that a 16" bucket (versus a 24") be used if the house had a standard 8" thick foundation wall.

The slightly oversized footing is not the end of the world as installing footings is not rocket science or that accurate. However, a larger than needed footing will cost more.

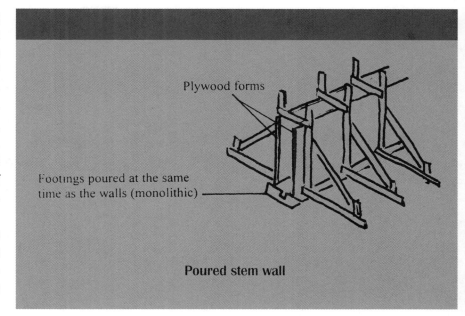

Plywood forms

Footings poured at the same time as the walls (monolithic)

Poured stem wall

Concrete: There are a number of things that you should know about concrete. First is that is should not normally be placed (poured) when it is below freezing. This also applies to installing masonry (laying bricks). There are chemicals you can add to concrete that allows you to place it in freezing weather, but it costs more and is a second choice. If you are building where freezing weather is short lived, you should wait until it gets above freezing to work. Your contractor knows this, so you should be prepared for delays in freezing weather.

What typically happens when placing concrete during colder months is that the contractor will wait until later in the day (when it is warmer) to install concrete. They will, however, stay with that job, sometimes late into the night, until it sets up properly. They might also take precautions, like laying straw on the concrete or using some external source of heat to protect the job. In areas where it stays below freezing for weeks and months at a time, foundations and houses are built first and then concrete floors are poured later after the house can be sealed up from the weather. Often a basement window or door is left out so that the chute from the concrete truck can be placed inside the house to pour the concrete.

Concrete comes in various compressive strength, measured in psi or pounds per square inch. There is a slight cost difference in a higher psi mix. Your contractor knows what to use, but if you are ordering the material, you should check with your local code for the correct materials. The two most common psi's are 2500 and 3000. Another interesting thing about concrete is that it's strength (hardness) is measured after 28 days, not when it is hard enough to work on, which usually is the next day or so.

In the summertime, it is not uncommon for framing to begin the day after a slab has been poured. In the winter time, it might be several days. Working on a "green" slab can cause damage to the slab (chipping and gouges) that might need to be repaired, especially in an area where vinyl flooring is to be installed

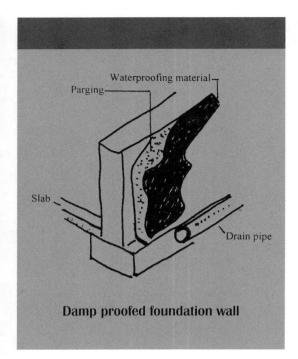

Damp proofed foundation wall

directly on top of the concrete. It is best to wait until the concrete is cured (several days, not 28).

Foundation walls: These are sometimes called stem walls. Foundations are usually either made of concrete block or poured concrete. Both are adequate and the choice between the two are often limited to the availability of the contractors to do the work. In many areas, one of the two of these methods are not readily available. When a poured wall is used, the footing and the stem wall are often poured at the same time. This is called a monolithic pour. Monolithic means "one stone." Foundation walls are usually 8" thick and extend above finish grade 8".

Basement walls: Basement foundation walls have other requirements. First, if they are more than 4' under ground, they need to be 12" thick rather than 8". This is to handle the pressure the earth places against the wall. It is not uncommon for a wall to "blow out" during construction. Therefore, care must be taken while back filling against a tall basement wall.

Another consideration in a basement wall is keeping it dry on the inside. This is accomplished in a number of different ways. First, the outside wall must be waterproofed with a material that will keep moisture from penetrating the wall. This could be as simple as tar placed on the wall or the use of a material made especially for this purpose. The key is to install it properly, leaving no holes or spaces for water to penetrate. Since this is usually a messy job (especially with tar), the homeowner should get involved with this. The person who usually does it is the lowest paid member of the building crew. It is unpleasant, but important work. Make sure that this is done properly and with care, even if you have to do it yourself.

The next thing to keep the basement dry is to install a drain at the bottom of the wall near the footing. This drain is usually covered with gravel to filter silt (fine sand) that could clog the drain. The drain should go completely around the outside of the foundation and then, using gravity, be directed to the lowest point in the yard. This drain should not be placed into a storm drain, as it is illegal to do this in most areas. In some areas where the terrain is very flat, mechanical pumps, called sump pumps, are used to get rid of the water that naturally enters a basement. I do not recommend this as a primary system unless it cannot be avoided. Pumps and electricity can fail while gravity never does.

Crawl space foundations: While we discussed crawl spaces earlier, there are a few other items that pertain to the construction of the crawl space walls. This has to do with installing foundation vents in the wall. Local codes will prescribe the size and nature of these vents. A typical formula for determining the number and size of vents is as follows: Two square feet of vents for each 100 linear feet of wall plus 1/3 square feet of each 100 square feet of floor footage. For a 28'x40' house, this works out to 136 linear feet of wall space and 1,120 square feet. The linear wall figure is 2.6 square feet. The square footage of floor space figure is 3.7. Foundation vents usually come in a standard size of 6"x9" or .375 square feet. The math works out to the requirement for 17 vents. However, if a plastic vapor barrier is used, the number of vents required can be reduced in half. Almost all houses with crawl spaces use a 6 mil plastic vapor barrier. The lack of this is what caused the house with the rusting furniture feet mentioned earlier. Installation of vapor barrier solved the problem.

Fireplaces: Almost everyone loves a fireplace. Code officials also know that fireplaces (along with faulty wiring) typically are the leading source of house fires and are thus very concerned with their construction. While most homeowners do not build their own fireplaces, they sometimes get involved in the design of the hearth and mantel.

Codes will vary from area to area and are subject to change. A typical requirement is for the hearth to extend at least 16" in front of the fireplace and 8" to each side of the fireplace opening. Fireplaces with an opening greater than 6 square feet should have hearths that extend at least 20" and 12" on the side. In both cases, mantels or wooden fireplace surrounds should be a least 6" away from the opening of the fireplace. If the wood member project is more than 1½" beyond the face of the fireplace, they should be at least 12" away from the opening. The short answer is to keep the fireplace surround or mantel 12" away from the fireplace opening.

Protection against decay and termites: Next to fires, termites and decay destroy the most houses. A protection against this is using pressure treated wood where it comes in contact with masonry or concrete. The most common place this occurs is in slab homes where the bottom plate of the interior partition walls rests directly on the concrete. Pressure treated wood is also used for the first piece of wood to come in contact with the perimeter stem wall. This piece of wood is often called the mud sill. The reason for using treated wood is that concrete and block is still very wet and its contact with wood can cause it to rot.

We had mentioned that a stem wall has to be at least 8" above finish grade. If siding is used, this must be at least 6" above finish grade. Usually, siding will cover the mud sill and continue on another inch or so over the block or veneer. While the top of the wall is 8" above grade, siding can come to within 6" of grade.

Most houses are treated for insect resistance during construction. This is a typical bank and FHA/VA requirement. However, this is not the case everywhere. In addition, this treatment seldom lasts more than one year. If you are concerned with termites, you should buy a treatment program from a local company and be thinking in terms of annual treatments.

General framing: There are a number of things you should know about framing a house that are critical. First is the spacing of lumber. Stud spacing is typically 16 or 24" on center (or o.c.). Sixteen on center is typical for outside and load bearing walls and 24" o.c. is allowable for partition walls in most instances. Many carpenters build everything at 16 o.c. through habit though. Closer spacing might be required under unusual loads. Girders, which are usually three 2x10s or 2x12s nailed together, can span only a limited distance, usually 8'–9' depending on the load and the state code. This might become critical in house design so it must be determined what the code is and how far apart posts or columns can be to support a main girder. Floor joist spacing is determined on the load they will carry, the spacing between joists and the size of the joist. Most joists are 2x10s

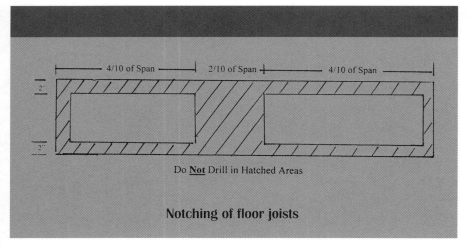

—— 4/10 of Span —— 2/10 of Span —— 4/10 of Span ——

Do **Not** Drill in Hatched Areas

Notching of floor joists

and 2x12s, but these can vary depending on the requirements shown on a span table. To determine the span, you need to know the weight to be carried. Typically, floors are designed to carry a 40-pound load, though some states allow 30 pounds on the second floor. Other conditions (like a water bed or pool table) might require 45 or 50 pound loads.

A critical matter in floor joists is cutting them to accommodate pipes and wires. Cutting them in the wrong place will weaken them. No cutting should take place in the center third of the joist nor should they be notched more than one-sixth ($\frac{1}{6}$) of their depth.

You should look at your specific code for the requirements. Hopefully, it will include a diagram of where to cut so that you do not cut too much. This is a critical thing to check, so don't guess on this one.

Access holes in a house are predetermined to be a minimum size. Access to the crawl space has already been mentioned in that section. Access must also be provided to attic space. Two things are at play. First, if a furnace or some other device is in an attic, the access hole must be large enough to remove it. The second is that fires sometimes start in attics and firemen have to get up there to fight the fire. Adequate room must be provided. Not only does the hole have to be large enough to get into, there has to be adequate headroom for the fireman to maneuver around in. Placing an access hole (also called a "scuttle" hole) near an outside wall of a house with a shallow pitched roof will not work. The most common location of a scuttle hole is in a center hallway or in a large walk-in closet near the center of the house. A typical prescribed size is 14" by 24", but this should be checked against any equipment in the attic as well as local code. I imagine there is at least one town in America where this size was increased because a fat fireman got stuck in one of these holes.

Stairs: Codes relating to stairs are strictly enforced. This is because most home accidents involve falls, usually around stairs. Like the ergonomics of design, people have a natural feeling for how much they can step up and across and stair design is determined by these factors. States vary greatly on how high a stair is and how much room there is on each step. How high you go up is called the rise; how wide the step is called the run. A typical rise is 8", a typical run is 10". These vary from state to state in fractions of an inch.

A regional code authority recently tried to change the rise and run to a 7" rise and an 11" run. This was requested because this is a safe, easy climb. However, its affect on other elements of the house caused a furor seldom seen in the industry. This rise and run would require houses to be deeper, thus causing more cost and also affecting the size of lumber, waste, handrails, etc. It did not get changed. North Carolina is a strict enforcer of its rise and run (8¼" rise, 10¼" run) and is fairly much alone in its requirement. The 10¼" run is a problem because a 2x10, which is actually 9½", cannot be used as a tread. You have to go up to a 2x12 or two 2x6s.

Another aspect of stairs is the circular stair or winder stair. The problem here is that a winder or circular stair has a portion of it that is less than 10¼" wide. North Carolina code requires that the winder or circular stair tread be no less than 4" wide and that 12" from the narrowest part (the 4" part), it is at least 9" wide and get wider from that point, usually to 14" wide. What usually happens is that few houses in North Carolina have winder or circular stairs.

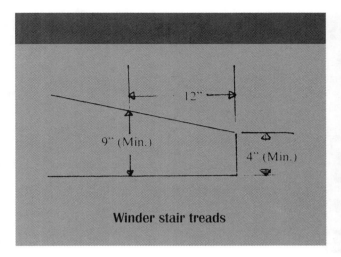

Winder stair treads

Another important aspect of stairs is that they must be uniform in rise throughout the entire stair system. This only makes sense since we get into a rhythm when climbing stairs and a slight variation can trip us. In fact, it usually does. This often occurs at the beginning or the end of a stair due to sloppy carpentry or math. Determining and cutting a set of stairs that meet this requirement is one of the few complicated math skills required of carpenters. Getting it wrong is expensive since usually 2x10s or 2x12s are used to make stairs and mistakes are unforgiving and expensive.

Egress: This means a way out of a house. Codes are absolute here because many fire deaths are caused by people being trapped in their houses. Code generally require at least two ways out of a house. North Carolina code requires that at least one of these ways be side hinged, meaning a swinging door. This becomes a problem if you want all your doors to be sliding doors. The width of the exit doors vary from state to state, but the most common size is 3' wide and every door manufacturer makes a standard 3' door. The second door might be less wide, usually 2/8. However, you should check with your local department because they won't let you slide on this one. Speaking of sliding, the most common second door in a house is a sliding door. Some state require that *all* exit doors (you might have three or more) be of a prescribed size, other states only require that *two* doors meet their prescribed requirements.

Egress out of a bedroom is especially critical because fires often occur at night when people are asleep in their bedrooms. The fireman comes into play here as well. They have to have a way in to rescue you during a fire. The window has to be big enough and close enough to the floor to get them in and you out. A typical size of a double hung window that meets egress code is either 3/0 4/6 or 2/8 5/2. Other sizes and types of windows will work (including roof windows), but these two sizes are the most common and every window manufacturer makes these sizes. The window also has to be close enough to the floor to get you out of the building. A typical requirement is for the sill to be no more than 44" from the floor. If you recall, this becomes critical in the design of the house as it is sometimes difficult to design egress windows for a house. Nevertheless, it is a design problem that has to be solved.

Stairs and hallways have to be wide enough for easy egress and for just getting around. Hallways and stairways have to be 3' wide. Stairways also have to be 2'8" clear of the handrail. Since handrails typically extend out 4" from the wall, this is usually not a problem unless you make you handrails thicker than normal. Landings typically have to be 3' square and must have an adequate handrail if they are over 32" above the ground or floor. This requirement is the main reason builders try to build houses with only three steps (or fewer) into the house. Handrails can get expensive and are difficult to make sturdy and often are at the root of a lawsuit if they give way.

Energy efficiency: The oil crisis of the 1970s made an impact on all aspects of American life including the housing industry. Many states prescribe the energy values of their homes either through strict codes or through discounts and tax credits for building an energy efficient home. The common measuring tool is called the R-value. R-value is a measurement of the resistance to heat transfer and is readily available for each building component. A lot of math goes into determining the R-value of a house wall. Each component is assigned its own value and the whole wall as a unit gets extra points for being a part of the whole.

For example, the air around and the air within a wall gets points as either air "film" or "dead" air trapped between layers. This air usually gives at least an R-value of R-1. Insulation usually gives the most R-value, ranging from 2–6 R-values per inch. Rigid foam insulation has the most R value per inch, while fiberglass batts the least (as an insulation material). Solid brick and block usually gives less than one R-value per brick or block with wood itself being valued at little over one R-value per inch. A log cabin with solid 6" walls, for example, has an R-value of a little over R-7.

With the typical home today requiring an R-value of at least 13 for an exterior wall, log homes have had difficulty getting approved by code. Two elements help the case of log homes. One is scientifically proven, the other is known but no adequate measurement device has been determined. Log walls retain heat better than most materials, which are judged only on their ability to resist heat transfer. Log homes have lower energy bills and are easier to heat because of this property.

However, codes only look at R-value and not heat retention. Therefore, states that strictly enforce energy codes require that log homes be reviewed as total homes or "envelopes." These *envelope* reports (required by many states for building systems that do not normally meet code compliance) are typically developed by engineers and can cost over $500 to produce. They take the entire value of the house including walls, floor and roof. Since the walls are typically R-7, extra insulation is placed in the roof and floor to give the house a total value that meets the same values as a standard stick built house. While expensive, the log home is now within compliance and usually quite warm and easy to heat.

Each state will prescribe what their standards for R-values are. North Carolina typically wants a roof of at least R-30, with side walls R-13 to R-19 and floors at R-19. These codes are different throughout the state and within regions. Usually R-values in excess of R-30 are superfluous, but still might be required anyway. This is because an R-value of R-19 is 97% efficient and one of R-30 is 98% efficient. Don't tell anyone I told you this and don't try to fight the code. Just realize the cost versus benefit value of extra insulation.

Another aspect of R-value is seen in the latest technology found in window insulation. Glass is a terrible insulator, less than one R-value. However, double pane windows, often filled with argon gas can bring their efficiency to over an R-4, greatly improving the efficiency of a house.

Insulation of basements provide an interesting phenomena. This is because about 4' under the ground, the temperature stabilizes and insulation is no longer required. Some states will give you a break on this while others ignore it, requiring you to insulate the entire wall. Some people just don't trust this fact and insulate the entire wall anyway. However, insulating an underground wall 4' below grade is a waste of money.

Miscellaneous codes — Not everything fits under neat categories. Here are a few more codes that you need to be aware of:

Smoke detectors: Must be permanently attached to the power of a house, we discussed this earlier in the evolution of building codes.

Chimney height: Chimneys should be at least 2' higher than the ridge of a house or 2' taller than the closest ridge 10' away. This is primarily to help the fireplace draw and to get the smoke away from the house.

Glass: Glass that is near a door or close to the floor should be tempered to prevent it from breaking. A rule of thumb is glass that is closer than 2' to a door or the floor but check with your local codes for an exact requirement.

Railings: Railing around decks and at steps should be placed a prescribed distance apart so that small children cannot fall through or trapped between the railing. Each area will have a prescribed distance apart that usually follows common sense, i.e., the typical width of a toddler's head. I have also heard this described as the width of a soccer ball, which is about 6 inches.

Nailing schedule: Sometimes called fastening schedule. This is a chart that tells you what size, type and distance apart nails should be in every application. This fits well in the saying of there is no such thing as a perfect house. The nailing schedule will never be perfect, at least in the spacing of the nails. The size and type is generally correct, but people seldom get the spacing totally right. If you upset an inspector and he wants to fail you for something, he'll get you on the nailing schedule.

Codes are primarily there to help you, protect your property and to keep you safe.

Constantly Changing, Constantly Moving

Please note that these are only a sampling of codes. Most of them will apply to your house, at least in prescription. The details might change and therefore must be confirmed for your particular area. Many of the problems of codes are never seen or heard of because the contractor takes care of them. This chapter lets you be aware of them and should put you in a mind set of why they are there and what to look for. You should not panic if you fail an inspection based on a code violation. People make mistakes and the states have a hard time getting changes out to the field. Often they are never adequately announced but told to contractors when they are out of compliance.

Code changes are the source of much small talk among builders and tradesmen and they spread the word pretty well. In states like California, where so much detail must be put on a set of plans, code violations are discovered in the plan review stage. In other areas where plans are not required or are not reviewed in detail, changes are only made in the field. While expensive to change something, it is a trade-off to having to draw every aspect of the house at great expense as is done in California. Nevertheless, codes are primarily there to help you, protect your property and to keep you safe. If you're living in an area where it has not turned to building hell like California, count your blessings and don't be the cause of a new code by doing something stupid. Remember, most codes come from a dead body or a fallen down house. ■

19

How To Work With Building Inspectors

Bribes or K.A.

K.A. could mean kick or kiss. Kiss is almost always appropriate. These guys hold your dreams in their hand and can keep you from reaching them. Most inspectors are helpful civil servants, truly there to help you. While bribes are not unheard of, especially in big cities, they are probably not going to be a problem. A few of the inspectors I knew were arrogant, self-centered, opinionated, and thought they were God's gift to the construction industry, but they were not dishonest. If you encounter what appears to be a bald-faced bribe request, you need to look into the situation in much more detail before you respond. If your local department has some bad eggs, how bad are they going to hurt you? No one wants to wake up with a horse's head in their bed. Fighting "city hall" might not be worth the misery an inspector can bring to your job. It might not be a bribe at all but a favor.

I had one building inspector ask me for a component one time. It was slightly damaged and of no use. I had been working with him for more than two years and he was fair and competent. I gave him the part (rather than throw it away) and he never made another request. Nothing. I know some superintendents give inspectors Christmas gifts and deer meat (a Southern thing). It doesn't hurt, but certainly is not a bribe.

While I was in Charlotte, the local TV station did an exposé on building inspectors. One of those they followed around was one of mine (not the same one mentioned earlier, but a decent guy; I had lots of different building inspectors). The upshot of the investigation was that my inspector was not very busy. The reporters followed him around when he went to the bank, the grocery store, etc. He never held up any of my jobs and I thought the exposé was fluff and mostly unfair. He was not the only one followed around, but none featured in the week-long series was found to be incompetent or taking bribes. They just didn't have much to do that week and it made them look bad. My guy received a week's suspension, a lot of embarrassment and that was about it. His 15 minutes of fame will certainly keep his name off a promotion list for a while but the matter died down.

In some communities, the building inspection position becomes political. There is a lot of pressure on an inspector. Sometimes people want to cut corners. The inspector is virtually the law. They can cause the job to take much longer and cost thousands more. People get very mad when their jobs are turned down because it gets into their pocketbook. A common practice is to not pay a sub until the job passes inspection. This is not at all a bad idea for the customer, but can be tough on the tradesmen who often live week to week. Since a building inspector's job is not going to make anyone rich, the temptation is there to pay a bribe (rather than for the inspector to ask for one).

In many communities, the building inspector is the only one on the side of the consumer. If a bad tradesman comes into town, the inspector can fulfill their charter and protect the citizens from the bad guys. Many are treated like heroes. They can also help train a novice and make sure they do the job right. If they can get a young tradesman to perform their work well, they can help this person make a living in a small town. People often ask an inspector for recommendations of who does good work. A good recommendation can bring the tradesman more work. If the tradesman is truly good and dependable, the inspector's job is much easier.

On the other hand, if someone new comes to town, the building inspector can make it hard for them to make a living. Margins on much of the work they do is so slim that it can be totally eaten up by having to do something over. Often the spec is a fixed fee for work that passes inspection. If it takes one or two retries to get it right, the tradesman can go broke. Inspectors can drive people out of town or out of work by being too picky.

Not only do new tradesmen have a hard time in small towns, so do new products. I had mentioned things like aluminum wire and fireproof plywood. Even though these fiascoes were not the inspector's fault, serious damage was done to the inspector's reputation. They are resistant to allow new products and techniques. Often the supplier has to appeal to the state to force the product in. While this often will work for a legitimate product, the inspector can develop a bad attitude towards the project as a whole.

Building homes is part of America's culture and is also a part of a community's culture. New, less expensive products and building systems can hurt a local community. One of the main objectives of innovation in building is to make things cheaper and faster. This is often harmful to local tradesmen. These lower prices usually force the tradesmen to lower their fees, which often are not out of line to begin with. Sometimes they are lowered so much that they go out of business. While this might be good for the consumer, it is terrible for the community and the building inspector is right in the middle of it. The building inspector is almost always a part of the community and has coffee in the same cafe as the tradesmen. His hours and workplace is the same as theirs. When innovation comes along, like new, unpopular laws, he has to allow them. If he makes a mistake and something goes wrong, the town is going to scream at him.

Manufacturers of new products and building systems are on the other end of this. They want to sell their wares and feel that they are leading the wave of the future. Their customers want the product because it is new, cheaper and faster. These manufacturers are generally big enough to have test data and pull with state and regional code departments. They fight back hard to get their products in and often embarrass the inspector with the technical data. A good old boy who grew up in that town doesn't care much for a smart aleck from out of town. Plus, the new product is putting people out of work. You can see the conflict. Building inspector's are walking a tightrope and they're not paid the circus performer's high wages.

The result is often a person who has seen it all. They have been burned more times than they care to talk about. They've been threatened with guns by "poor mountaineers trying to keep their families fed" and by their bosses back in the capitol for not keeping up with progress. It's a tough life. They probably have been in the trades themselves and things didn't work out. In big cities, they might have engineering or technical degrees. Whatever their background and wherever they work, they share common ground. It's a tough way to make a living and you just entered their lives with your hopes and dreams.

Building inspectors have tremendous power. They can enter your (unlocked, under construction) house anytime they want to. While common sense says that they will do this during normal working hours, they can come whenever they can. If you haven't pulled a permit and they find out about your project, they can cite you for not getting a permit. The laws will vary around the country, but you've done three bad things.

First, you have broken the law. Enforcement type people don't like for the law to be broken. Second, you are probably endangering yourself, your neighbors or future inhabitants of your house. Third, and probably the worst thing you've done is not paid much needed fees to the city/county and are taking work away from the building inspector. You can be assured that someone is counting the number of permits pulled a year and every number counts. Bad dog.

The least that could happen is that they make you pull a permit and pay the required amount. The inspector might be tougher on you than normal or just might be happy that you've been counted, fees paid and his job justified. They probably have been placed in a tough situation, especially if you've covered something up like wiring. They have to make a judgment of whether you should tear out something. This can be disheartening as well as expensive. You, however, put them in this situation and are causing them grief. Do what they say. You messed up and it can only get worse if you fight it. The worse that could happen is that you have to pay a fine and take everything out. Your attitude has a direct part in whether it goes to this extreme.

Many people don't pull permits because they don't think they are necessary, especially if they are remodeling a house and the work cannot be seen from outside the house. How can you get caught? It is not too hard, although the building department probably doesn't have a surveillance team in black fatigues and night vision goggles looking for you. I know of one person who was caught because they threw the boxes for bathtubs, sinks and skylights in front of their house for trash pickup. The building inspector just happened to be driving by and saw it. It is kind of hard to be buying that stuff and not installing it. It invited a question, a fine and a permit.

You might also get caught picking up building supplies or having them delivered to your house. Let's say you've had a number of estimates made for a remodel or the house itself. It has taken time and effort for builders to do this. While you might have found their prices high, you were probably quoted the going rate and the price included the cost of a permit and building to meet code.

Your thoughts might be to save yourself the cost of the permit and to build below the code. While this could be done, you might run into someone at the lumberyard who lost the bid. They usually don't get upset if some competitor gets the business. They do if you're doing it yourself illegally. If they see you, they might turn you in. It's a small world with many eyes. Some people are vicious enough to turn you in when you're almost finished and pass strong hints on to the building inspector that you cheated them out of legitimate work.

It would be difficult for an inspector to let you off easily if the legitimate builders in the county knew about the problem. The inspector has to deal with these people every day and you are the one who is wrong, not them. Get a permit. Call the building office and confirm what exactly is required. It is not worth the risk and the cost is minimal.

Now just imagine that your first meeting with a building inspector follows one of the problems mentioned earlier. They might not be in a good mood. Most inspectors are easy to work with and want the house to be built right. When houses burn or fall down, inspection records are reviewed by the insurance and fire departments. In North Carolina, for example, all residential construction is actually under the North Carolina Department of Insurance. Houses are insured and houses are damaged by fire and/or through bad building practices. It is a logical link. The inspector signs their name on your house stating that it has been built safely and in compliance to current codes. When something goes wrong, it's their neck on the line. A common cause of death in America is house fires and house fires usually are caused by faulty wiring or defects in fireplaces. It all goes back to the building inspector and is the essence of their livelihood.

You should approach the building inspector as one who wants to help you and ensure your house is built properly and safe. They do. In doing so, however, it is probably going to cost you extra money and take extra time. A turn down means something has to be redone and it takes at least two days to correct and re-inspect the problem. In a rural area, it might take more than a week. Many trades are paid only after the work has passed inspection. This is definitely in your favor because it ensures that the tradesman comes back quickly. If this was not part of your contract or the problem involves something else, it can take quite a bit longer.

When I was building, I was never concerned if a licensed trade failed inspections. They always came back quickly and fixed the problem. When it involved framing or something else, it was a different matter. This had a lot to do with how houses are built. Framers usually want to be paid within a week of completing their work. However, frames are usually not inspected until the wiring and

Most inspectors are easy to work with and want the house to be built right.

plumbing has been installed. Inspectors want to make sure that parts of the frame, especially the floor joists, have not been improperly cut while installing wiring and plumbing. Time to do this as well as scheduling this work can take weeks. The framers are long gone and often are difficult to get back in a timely manner or at all. If it is simple problem, i.e., adding blocking, you can probably fix it yourself.

Sometimes it's difficult to assign blame or several people are involved. You can stick to your guns and get justice or you can just solve the problem and get the house going again. Justice might take weeks. In seeking justice, you need to take into account the interest payment on your construction loan plus the fact that some future sub might not be available because of the delay. A law professor once told me that a common concern of seeking justice is how much justice you can afford. Sometimes it's best to solve the problem and move on.

Sometimes the inspector is wrong in what they are asking you. They have opinions, like everyone else, and might not agree with the current code and want you to exceed it. Most times, this involves extra expense and time. If you question what they are asking, the best way to handle it is to ask them to show you where in the book it says to do this. I would caution you that you are treading on thin ice here. If you don't feel you can request this without upsetting the inspector, it might not be worth it. I have done it in the past after a few years of experience and in a case where they were clearly wrong. I also became very familiar with the code book and knew the answer before I asked the question. I usually pulled it off, but occasionally I was wrong.[16]

I had an occasion where I had flunked an insulation inspection. We had used batt insulation that was covered with plastic as a vapor barrier. Other times we used insulation that was attached to paper that had the R-values printed on it. I had built dozens of houses this way and never had a problem. The first house of mine this new inspector did was turned down for insulation. I called him up and he said that the insulation had to be marked with its R-value. Since it was just insulation (without the paper), there was nowhere to mark it. I thought he was nuts and asked him to show me. He was right, it was right there in the book. I called the supplier and asked him what to do. He was amazed too, but knew the answer. I had not ever paid attention to the three stripes that were imbedded into

each batt of insulation. I always thought that the stripes were part of the manufacturing process. They were there to tell the R-value of the insulation. I got a technical data sheet that explained this, gave it to the inspector and he passed the job. You learn something new every day.

The point is that you have to question your inspector with great care. You could be wrong. If right, you could still be wrong if you embarrassed them or made them look bad. If they are injecting personal opinion, they usually will back off. Even so, you need to see their point and could win brownie points if you follow their advice. I can't imagine their advice being wrong, though it could be expensive.

If you are running the job yourself and it's your first and probably last house, the inspector can be very helpful to you. Make a point to be there when they inspect. They usually do not make appointments, but you could ask them about when they will be there. You should plan your day to be doing something else at the site so that you can meet the inspector and find out what might be wrong with the house. I always met the inspector if I could. This proved to be very beneficial.[17]

Inspectors sometimes give builders a break when it is a minor matter and the builder fixes the problem as promised. I got to this stage when I was building with some inspectors. I knew, however, that if the repair slipped my mind, there would be serious reciprocations. Because of that, I rarely asked for a break.

If things get really out of hand with an inspector, they do have a boss at the local or state level. You need to make sure that the problem cannot be solved and you are willing to risk trouble from thereon. Examples where help might be needed are requests for bribes, incompetence or an unwarranted or disrespectful attitude. Some inspectors are just jerks and need to be fired. Enough complaints from the citizenry will do this. ■

War Story

#17: I made a point of having a good relationship with my inspectors. While you don't want to name your children after them, you should be courteous and respectful. Try not to be too friendly and bring them expensive gifts because they might think you're covering something up. You don't want them to be suspicious of you. They truly do not want to be placed in a compromising position. However, if you baked some cookies or your beans just came in, giving them a small amount wouldn't hurt. A lot of things that can be turned down on an inspection are easily remedied.

I remember one occasion when the electrical inspector came in. I saw him drive up from across the street and joined up with him as he was completing his inspection. He said he was going to have to turn the house down because a ground wire connection was too loose. He said he couldn't do anything about it, but I could. He handed me some pliers, I made a few turns and it passed. Had I not been there, he would have turned it down. I talked to him about this later and he told me that he could not fix anything, by policy, even though a few turns of a wrench would solve the problem as was the case here. The point is that they will work with you if you are there when they inspect. Plus, by human nature, it was always harder to turn you down when you are standing there, weepy eyed. Always try to be there.

20

Building Systems or Stick?

What's Available

You can build your house from scratch (stick) or you can get some help using a building system. Stick, or conventional houses can be built on site (site built) or they can be partially built in a factory and transported to the site. The end result is essentially the same house. Some conventional factory built houses are totally indistinguishable from site built while others have a few clues. Choices here include panelized homes, modular homes and pre-cut packaged homes.

Another choice is a non-conventional house using either an antique system or an advanced system. Antique systems include log and timberframe (also called heavy timber) homes while advanced systems include dome and structural insulated panel (SIP) homes (also called stress skin panel and foam core panel.)

There are a variety of reasons to build using a building system. These include cost savings, time savings, work savings and to obtain a home not readily available, like a log or timberframe home. Sometimes a building system offers a quality of design and materials that are not available in a market. Some building systems even have snob appeal through effective marketing by the manufacturer. The reasons are many and best reviewed on a case by case basis.

Modular or Barely Building

We'll start our review with a system that is almost complete from the factory. This system, modular, is probably the least understood of all building systems. The state of the art has far surpassed public preconceptions. Modular homes are not trailers or mobile homes. They are built to the same code as site built homes and often far exceed the quality and specifications of site built homes. Still, the perception persists and this industry is still struggling, with slow but steady progress.

The biggest advantage of modular is speed of construction. If you're in a hurry, you can't get it done any faster than modular. Another advantage is that, once the foundation is in, you've pretty much locked in the cost of the house.

Modular homes are built up to 90 percent complete in a factory. They are built in 12' or 14' wide sections up to 60' long. They can be single or multistory homes. Each section is shipped to the job site on a flatbed truck and lifted onto the foundation with a crane. They can be assembled back-to-back or side-to-side. Since the maximum width that can be routinely shipped down the road is 14', houses assembled back-to-back are 28' deep, an adequate depth of a home. If a deeper home is desired, it can be designed to be assembled side-to-side and thus be 60' deep by however many sections are used. With multiple stories, these homes can exceed 4,000 square-feet in size, hardly a trailer.

What is not completed in a modular home has mostly to do with where the sections join. This affects some of the siding, roofing and drywall, as well as the painting, carpeting, wiring, heating and plumbing. Some of the rooms of a modular home are totally complete including floor coverings, switch plates and light fixtures, paint and wallpaper.

What is done on site is the construction of a conventional foundation and connecting the house sections to each other and then to utilities such as power, water and sewer/septic. Other work on site most likely would include completing the shingles on the roof, finishing siding and trim, seaming a carpet, and installing and painting some drywall. This work usually takes a few days. The house is almost always dried in from the weather on the day of shipment to the site.

The biggest advantage of modular is speed of construction. If you're in a hurry, you can't get it done any faster than modular. Another advantage is that, once the foundation is in, you've pretty much locked in the cost of the house. There is little room for cost overruns, if for no other reason than there is so little to do. Sometimes modular homes quality exceeds the craftsmanship available in a certain area. If you're building in a remote area or one where builders become arrogant or sloppy, the quality can far exceed the norm. Even where quality is good, a building boom can make it hard to get builders to do your house in a timely or economical manner. Modular fits the bill quite nicely.

There are a number of disadvantages of modular homes. Some are very real, some have to do with perception. We'll deal with perception first. Modulars, because of the similarities to mobile homes, still carry a stigma to them. While they can cost less than site built houses, the price differential is minimal, especially when comparing houses with similar specifications. Modular homes are not cheap houses built cheaply but are typically thought of as such.

Therefore, many people shy away from these homes or, if they buy them, keep waiting for the "catch." Still, you might get snide comments about your new home that might not make you feel good about the house. Nevertheless, this stigma is going away and has virtually disappeared in some areas of the country.

The second disadvantage of a modular home is that there are some design limitations. One of the greatest innovations in modular housing in the past 10 years has been the hinged roof system. Prior to this, roofs had to be permanently attached to each section and kept at a low roof pitch to be shipped down the road. When assembled, these 2/12 pitched roofs let everyone know that your house was modular. They were just plain ugly. This innovation, the hinged roof, allowed the roof to be at least a 5/12 roof pitch with 6/12, 9/12, and in some cases, 12/12 roofs available. Since lower cost site built houses typically had 4/12 roof pitches, modulars with 5/12 and steeper roofs actually looked better than many site built homes.

Another limitation is reduced opportunities for customization of the plans. You still start with a maximum of a 14x60' box for house design. Most companies allow a remarkable amount of customization as to placement of partition walls (sometimes to their regret because some of the layouts are absolutely horrible). While a number of innovations can be done to a modular house, such as bay windows and imitation of unusual styles (like Victorian), you cannot get everything you want. Nevertheless, the choices you do have are certainly viable and can meet most people's needs.[18]

Another problem with modular homes is financing or lack there of. The industry as a whole is still not fully ready to have a house built in a few weeks or to pay single invoices for tens of thousands of dollars all at once. Manufacturers

War Story

#18: I was in the modular home business for a while and the finance issue was the greatest problem we had. We did not sell directly to consumers, but through builders. Still, ours was a cash business and we had no receivables. It was cash upon delivery. A company only has to be burned once to establish a strict policy on when the money changed hands. In our case, it was before the house left our trailer. Legally, at the moment the house rests on someone else's foundation, property rights take a sharp left turn. While the company would probably get its money eventually, it could take months and years to get paid. While it was still on the trailer, it can be brought back to the factory and sold to someone else. The reality of the business world was that some unscrupulous person would take delivery and not pay as agreed. While we took tremendous precautions for this not to happen, it did occasionally and we did, what we called "the drill."

If a check wasn't there and the builder was backing away from their agreement, we would drive off with the house. Our contracts were vicious and had all kinds of clauses for damages and rights if this occurred. This included triple transportation charges (first trip out, return trip, second trip out) and no guarantee for damages of the house after the first delivery attempt. Since the buyer had a substantial deposit (usually 10 or more percent), they had a stake in the house as well. The sight of the house driving away was an excellent motivator and usually got the builder to quit monkeying around and come up with the money as agreed. Rather than take the house all the way back to the factory, it was usually taken to a place a few miles down the road to let the buyer rethink their plan. This almost always worked and the house was delivered later that same day. In cases where it didn't work, the house was brought back to the plant and resold at a discounted price (usually reduced by the amount of the forfeited deposit.)

It was a high tension day, but where I worked the owners seemed to enjoy their hardball tactics. However, in companies where non-payment on delivery was a problem, it usually took the company into bankruptcy. This was the case where I worked because they had bought out a company with that exact problem. A house that was not accepted and paid for upon delivery was called a "stocker." When my company took over the bankrupt company, they had 23 "stockers" as testament to the problem. It took a while to clear these out. I was amazed at the number of calls I continued to get from builders asking if we had any "stockers" they could buy at a discount. It was a common industry problem.

Modular house—hardly a trailer

have built you a fairly complete house worth $30,000 to $80,000 as it sits on the truck and want to be paid before they put it on your foundation. The bank doesn't want to pay that much money at once, especially if it can be driven away. It can become a Mexican stand-off or just a matter of you having that kind of money in hand, in cash (or certified check).

Modular homes today are remarkable homes and are virtually indistinguishable from custom homes. If fact, the only way to tell if a home is a modular home is by looking to see if the interior walls in the center of the house are thicker than 4". These walls, called "mating walls," are usually three or more inches thick and thus become 6" thick when the house was assembled. Often doors and cased openings are part of the mating walls and have thicker trim and moldings. The only other way to tell is quite subtle and that is by the location of the electrical breaker panel. In most conventional homes, these are placed in garages or utility/laundry rooms. In modular homes, they sometimes wind up in other rooms like dining and living rooms. This was because they were located in the most economical and workable location for a house that had two sections that joined with the wiring already in place. Aesthetically, this is not a problem because they can easily be hidden by a picture or wall hanging.

When I first went into the modular business, I saw that these panel boxes were left exposed in our model homes and suggested that they be covered up. I was told that this could not be done because it would be a deceptive business practice to not show the customer where the panel box would be. I did instruct my salesmen to make sure everyone knew that these could be covered up in their personal homes so that people didn't think that they had to be left exposed. I do know that in many cases people just got used to seeing them there and often painted or wall papered them to match the room.

Panelized Housing

There are two general types of panelized houses, open wall and closed wall. Open wall panels are essentially just a section of framing, with sheathing installed on outside walls. Closed wall goes a few steps further and could include installation of windows, siding, wiring, and insulation. In addition, closed wall construction could also include "wet" cores, where kitchens and baths are finished almost to the state of modular homes. These "wet" cores are lifted onto the foundation first and the walls are built around them. Closed wall panelized houses are becoming more rare now as they really were an evolutionary step towards modular.[19]

War Story

#19: I was involved with various aspects of closed wall panelized houses two times in my construction career. First was as a "gorilla" on a framing crew while in college. To say that I was unskilled was being kind. A good day was when I could use a hammer. Most days my skillful tool was a shovel or my strong back. The company was in Hampton, Virginia, where I worked during the summers of 1971 and 1972. The first summer I worked on homes that were mostly open wall panels. I started by digging monolithic footings, by hand, that were formed into three long piers that the house rested on. The house was brought to the site on a truck and we used a large forklift to move the sections in place. The floor was made in sections with the plywood already nailed to the floor joists. A typical house might have eight or 10 sections that made up the entire floor. The walls were just framed panels covered with sheathing. Each piece was marked where it went, with the foreman using the framing plan to tell us where to put each section. Once the outside walls were in place, trusses were lifted onto the top of the wall panels. They were brought over about six at a time and placed upside down on the top plate. Since I was the tallest in the crew, it was my job to–using a stick that I rigged up–flip them over and slide them over to two co-workers who sat on top of the outside walls. Once these were in place, we sheathed the roof (I got to use a real hammer at this point–joy!). The homes were pretty simple and proceeded on like a stick built house.

The next summer I got rehired and came back to some technology changes. That year, wet cores were introduced as well as the roofs were pre-assembled with four roof trusses already attached to the plywood. These roof sections were placed on top of the house with the forklift so that there was no more flipping of trusses. The wet cores were also put in place with the forklift. I thought the system was pretty nifty. I never went back to that company since I went into the service the next summer and was away from construction for the next 10 years.

My next encounter with panelized construction was with a top 10 builder in Charlotte. They built homes in more than 30 markets, all of which were open wall panelized and manufactured in four regional plants. Charlotte's plant was in Georgia, about 100 miles away. The plant built sheathed wall panels and roof trusses. The panels were loaded on flatbed trucks and brought to the home site where the foundation had already been built. The trailer had a pneumatic lift that raised up and, as the truck drove away, the house package rolled off the back of the truck. It was a pretty neat sight to see these house packages come rolling off these trucks.

Windows and doors and some miscellaneous materials were also on the back of the truck. These items were unloaded by hand prior to dropping the package. Framing crews would take the trusses off the top of the load and then bring each piece over to the foundation. The first-floor deck was framed using conventional methods. Panels were then nailed into place and the trusses handed into place on top of the walls. Some other poor gorilla was flipping those trusses. Small single-story houses were usually framed in a day while larger two-story homes might take two to three days. The end result of the framing carpenter's efforts was a house with felt paper on the roof, windows in place, stairs installed, and the front door locked.

Into my third year with this company, they decided that they wanted to take the evolution of building a step further. They went to the "wet" core closed wall system with wall panels already insulated, sided, windows installed, and wiring and boxes in place. The wiring was not placed into the boxes because code required that a local electrician do that. Drywall was delivered with the package but was installed by local labor. The cores were complete like modular. All the finish items including baseboards and casings, interior doors, light fixtures, and even light bulbs were all delivered at the same time as the main house.

While I was not the first person in Charlotte to start a house with this system, I was the first to turn a house over to a customer. The first house was a spec house that was sold later. I finished that house as well, but did not start it. To say that this method of construction was a disaster is an understatement. I knew this the first day I built my first closed wall house. I remember the moment, when a rough framing carpenter dropped a sledgehammer from the roof into the kitchen core. The hammer bounced and hit the door to the dishwasher, putting a huge dent into it. I also knew when we were finishing the house and the lights bulbs had all been stolen. I knew when critical finish parts had been either damaged, stolen or thrown away.

At first, they tried to side the house in the factory. Where sections joined, they devised what we called zippers, where siding from each section joined into a molding at the center of the gable end. Not only did it look horrible, by the time the house was finished, the siding was so damaged that most of it had to be replaced. The company also tried to build these houses on slabs, leaving a small hole under the wet core to hook the plumbing up. The masons could never get the hole in the right place and there would usually be gaps of up to two inches between the core and the slab floor. Even though this was inside the house and this gap could be covered and filled in, it just didn't seem right. Fortunately, they gave up after a few homes and built the rest on crawl spaces.

Another aspect of these closed wall houses was that a considerable amount of work was taken away from our normal vendors. The rough carpentry crews were hurt the least but still had a learning curve to go through. The houses were assembled using cranes and they seemed to take the same amount of time although the crews received less because of the pre-assembly of some parts. The heating and air conditioning, plumbing, and wiring only needed connections and there was no opportunity to put a mark up on materials since they were already supplied. Drywall labor was mostly the same (except the cores were already finished). Trim labor was reduced as was paint and floor coverings. The end result was that there was less for everyone to do and the subs were not very happy. Even the building inspector had less to do since the core were inspected in the factory.

While improvements were made, it remained a disaster. The expected savings never materialized. While houses were done somewhat faster, they still were subject to weather damage as it was difficult to get the houses buttoned up in one day because of all the intricate parts and sophisticated operations that had to be done on the first day. Damage, theft and loss of critical parts, especially finish components ate up any potential profits. Building inspectors were not at all happy and looked for excuses to turn us down. It really bothered them that they could not inspect key components hidden behind drywall. They also did not trust factory inspectors.

In closing the first house in Charlotte, I almost didn't get it done in time because of an end cap of a cabinet. It was the side of the cabinet that faced the refrigerator and was thus never seen. A fiberboard panel had long since disappeared. I ordered the part but also painted the sub panel so that its absence was not prominent. I would install the piece when it came in (a one-minute job), but did not want to hold the house up waiting for such a superfluous item. The piece was placed on back order (these new homes had numerous extra pieces, many hand fabricated) and thus was not going to be there in time for the final inspection. As I have mentioned before, there is no such thing as a perfect house and the inspector zeroed in on this panel. I tried to talk my way out of it.

My solution (painting it) was certainly viable and not uncommon in many instances. The panel would never be seen. I had told the customer about it and he had no problem waiting for the piece. He wanted to get in the house. The inspector said that the plans showed this piece and it should be here in this "trailer" house. I knew I was doomed. Frantic calls to the factory and up the chain of command made this panel everyone's priority. This was, by the way, the first house of its kind in Charlotte and the company bet its future on it. The piece was located, the inspector satisfied, the customer in their new home, and history was made.

As Paul Harvey says, there was a "rest of the story." The end result was that the company stopped building using this method and by passed open wall panels, which it had done for years successfully and went all the way back to stick building their homes. Along the way, they went bankrupt. While this might have been for other reasons, I think the closed wall debacle played a major role. Among the lessons I learned here was that you cannot mix rough and finish crews and components. If a house is in a rough phase, you have to keep the finish materials out. You also should not use rough crews to do finish work. While they might be capable of doing the work, their mindset is totally different and it can mostly lead to disaster. Another broader lesson is don't do things halfway–open wall panel or modular. Let the evolution stay part of the history, not the future. Both systems work very well.

With the war story out of the way, why would you consider panels as a way to build a home? There are a number of good reasons. One is that it takes some skill in building framed walls. Panelized homes have already done that for you. You don't need to know where to put in jacks and headers and built up corners. You don't have to measure carefully and locate window and door openings. In fact, you don't have to do anything. All the framing is done for you according to your plan. It's a no-brainer.

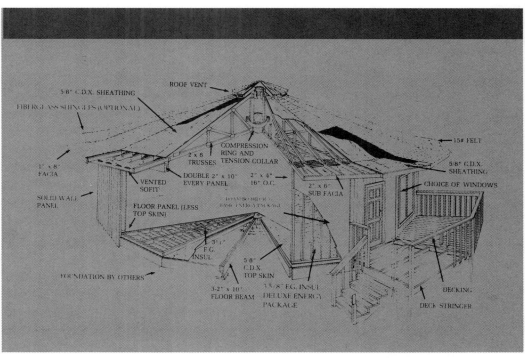

COURTESY OF DELTEC HOMES

A panelized, packaged home

The second advantage is speed of construction. Panelized houses go up very fast. You and a few buddies can put up your house over the weekend. Speed is the number one reason why professional builders use panels. The other reason could be a lack of skilled crews, which should fit well in your case.

Money savings are probably not there. Wood costs what wood costs. While the panel plant might get better prices for lumber because of quantity buying, they are not going to pass those on to you. They've got lots of expenses you don't, plus their plant costs at least half a million dollars. I hear potential customers tell me that they can build it themselves cheaper than panels cost. Well, of course, you can. But building it correctly, skillfully and quickly more than makes up for the cost saving you might be seeing.

Disadvantages of panelized building include some possible reduction in design flexibility, though most companies are very flexible. Some companies might want you to stick close to standard models. Another disadvantage is that these companies want to be paid upon delivery. Since some of the labor of the framing is already included in the panels, this might not fit into a pay out schedule or to your pay-as-you-go budget. For example, you might be able to afford $6,000 for the lumber to frame your house but not the $9,000 a panelized package might cost. The ultimate cost might be the same, but the lumber yard might give you 30 day terms while the panel company wants a check at delivery.

Another disadvantage might be shipping costs to the site or a plant that is too far away. It might appear that the lumberyard has no shipping costs. It does. It is in the price of the materials. There are no free lunches. Shipping costs for panelized homes can be extraordinary if they are far away. These companies might be hard to work with if they are a distance away and this might be a reason to not use them.

Packaged Homes

The differences here are subtle. This type of home is more one of convenience. These homes can most probably be built on site. However, companies have taken advantage of design, estimating, specification, engineering, and financing needs and put them into a program that makes it easier to build a house. In some cases, this also includes materials that are not readily available in most lumberyards.

A packaged home is, as the name implies, a package or grouping of materials and services that make it easier to build. Necessary materials have been predetermined and are assembled into a truckload that is sent to your home site. This is little different than if you had determined how many trusses, 2x10s and squares of roofing you need on your own. These companies do this for you based on all the materials needed for a complete house or just for parts of a home. It is rare that everything will be supplied, but some companies will sell you as many materials as possible. Sometimes materials are pre-cut or sent in the most economical sizes for field cutting. Basic panelization might be included.

In some cases, the packaged home is supplying materials that are hard to find in local markets, such as heavy timber or higher grades of cedar and fir. Special components like glu-lams, with inherent special connecting plates and gussets, might be part of the plan. Some of these companies might even make their own windows and doors. These companies are usually more expensive than the average home because of the use of premium materials and superior services in design, engineering and salesmanship. Often, these packages have exclusive brand names, like luxury automobiles, and appeal to those who want to make a statement with their home.

At the lower end of the scale, financing is the broad appeal. Jim Walter's Homes is the undisputed leader in this and their appeal is affordability. A Jim Walter home is essentially a stick built house that you can take at various levels of completion. Often the ownership of a lot is all that is necessary to get the ball rolling with a Jim Walter home. Disadvantages to this include some limitation in design and quality levels and you might be able to find better deals on some component of the sale, like interest rates.

The other end of the spectrum could be companies like Lindal Cedar Homes and Deck House/Acorn. These premium homes are also mostly stick built or panelized, but include premium materials and services. They usually have the disadvantage of self financing and often require deposits and payments that are not a routine part of a construction loan. They also suffer from the shipping issue since Lindal Cedar is in Washington state and Deck House/Acorn is in Massachusetts. There are a number of other similar quality homes scattered about, with the majority based in New England. Cost and difficulty in financing is a common problem with these homes. However, a large percentage of people who build these prestigious homes do so out of pocket, which should give you an indication of whether they are right for you.

These premium house packages have the advantage of superior materials and superior design, most of which is very custom. They also provide excellent services, from well-trained salesmen to excellent customer service. Disadvantages include higher costs, shipping costs, difficulty in getting like minded and experienced subcontractors, and some limitation in design and workmanship at the state of the art level. These companies will provide houses that are safe and do not stretch the envelope in design and engineering that the wealthy and adventurous might want. This is not to say that these houses are not stunning.

Antique Heavy Timber Housing

Log Homes

This type of housing is probably the most interesting and exciting. These homes can be breathtaking and have strong emotional ties. There are two distinct types of heavy timber structures, log and timberframe. Timberframe is also known as post and beam. Since these two systems are so different, they will be discussed separately.

Log homes are built in two basic ways. First is as "log on log" or "stacked logs." The other method is called "Appalachian" style with a chink space or simply "chinked logs." *Log on log* are logs that are milled with an interlocking tongue and groove, with each log resting directly on top of the one below. Caulk and foam tapes are typically installed between each row of logs and each log is spiked or lag screwed into the log below.

Appalachian style are connected at the corners, but there is a 2" to 4" gap between each log. This gap if typically filled with insulation and then covered with a cement-like substance called "chinking." This style of logs is typically squared off and usually uses 6"x12" or larger logs. Dove tail corners and hand-hewed surfaces are common with this style of log. Either system is fine, although suppliers might want to wrestle you to the ground over the merits of one over the other. It really is a matter of personal taste.

The original homes built in America were mostly log homes. These were intended as temporary shelter, often for animals and most of these rustic homes did not survive long. The first permanent homes were actually timberframe or post and beam homes.

The original settlers got out of log homes as soon as they could. These pioneers had no love for these homes and certainly didn't brag back to their relatives in Europe or back East about their log homes. They viewed them as we view trailers. The majority of the last authentic log homes were built around the turn of the century. Log homes built after that were in remote areas and as novelties. They have always been a part of the history and romance of the country and, at one time, seemed to be a prerequisite to run for president.

Nevertheless, it was not until after WWII that any significant resurgence of interest in log homes began. While a few existing companies predate WWII, most log home companies started in the 1960s and '70s. Probably the biggest influence on the growth of the log home industry was the TV show "Bonanza," which was set in a log cabin near Reno, Nevada. The set for this program is now a tourist attraction. Later programs like "Little House on the Prairie," plus all the Westerns shot in the 1940s, '50s and '60s, contributed to this desire of people to own log cabins. For many, it is an American dream.

It can also be a nightmare. There are over 400 companies producing log homes today, many of which make less than 25 homes a year. It is an industry that is easy to get into and easy to get out of, often by bankruptcy. Many a fortune in deposits have been lost in this craze. For some reason, the log home industry can be a den of snakes.

There are a lot of unscrupulous people in that business and they know a sucker when they see one. The companies that I worked for were leaders in the field and had a strong, well-deserved reputation for quality, integrity and well built and engineered houses. They also were among the more expensive log homes on the market. You get what you pay for.

The biggest problem with log homes is that the logs, when laid horizontally, naturally twist, warp and settle. It takes a while but within the first year or so, the house will shrink about one to three inches. It is the only building system with this problem. It is not the end of the world and reputable companies, like one that I worked for, made allowances for this settling and essentially solved a good bit of the problem. They did this with settling systems, which included crank down screws jacks, sliding jambs and through bolts with compression springs. Although expensive, the use of these systems is better than just letting the logs settle naturally, which is an inexact science.

Another aspect of log home settling has to do with how dry the logs are. The drier the logs, the more stable the log home. In line with this is cost. Again, the drier the log, the more it costs. Many people compare log companies on cost alone. This would range from a saw mill that sells green lumber to a larger, more established company that kiln dries their logs and grades them in accordance with a nationally recognized standard. The sawmill logs will cost less. However, they will be more prone to twist, split, warp, and settle much more than a properly graded and dried log home. Saw mill logs might have up to a 40% moisture content.

Most log home companies acknowledge the benefits of using kiln dried logs and make a point of it in their sales literature and specifications. Most log customers quickly become aware of this and buy only kiln dried logs. However, there is a trick wrapped up in this kiln dried business. This is that saying that a log is kiln dried doesn't mean anything unless you know "to what standard." Within the log industry, a heavy timber log, which is defined as a piece of wood at least 5"x5", has to be dried to less than 23% to officially be listed as "kiln dried" or KD. As a frame of reference, 2x4s, 2x10s, etc., used in conventional framing is dried to 15% to 19% moisture content. It will be stamped right on the piece of wood, i.e., KD 19. Still, many suppliers call their logs kiln dried because it might have spent a few hours in a kiln. It is a play on words or trick that most people don't know about.

Another aspect of this dried wood game is air drying the logs. Here the logs sit in a yard for some period of time (who knows how long) and dry out. While better than building with green logs, it typically still does not conform to any standard. You can get into wrestling matches with the various manufacturers of log homes to debate these issues. Still, you are best off to know "to what standard" their individual claims are made to. A major inspection agency for heavy timber lumber is Timber Products, Inc. (TPI). You will find that the bigger, longer

Log homes, along with modular homes, are the most misunderstood building system available.

8"x6" "D"   **8"x8" "D"**   **8"x6" Ship lap**   **8"x8" Ship lap**   **8"x8" Round**

Laminated Logs

serving players in the log industry conform to their standards. Your low cost producers and saw mills have probably never heard of these folks.

A recent innovation in log home manufacture is the use of "laminated" logs, which are glu-lams that are molded into log shapes. Laminated logs are actually drier than framing lumber and are stronger, straighter and more stable than conventional logs. Their moisture content ranges from 12% to 15%, making for a very stable log. It is one log system that has solved the age old settling problem of log homes and is worth looking into. Many log builders who have used laminated logs never go back. A straighter, more stable log that doesn't have settling, warping, twisting, and cracking problems (as well as no call backs) is very appealing to a log home builder.

Another aspect to log homes is that they are not cheap. Log homes, along with modular homes, are the most misunderstood building system available. Log homes are generally more expensive than typical stick built houses. Some people's conception is that they are an alternative to a double wide. This is not true. This is frustrating to the potential buyer and to the ethical seller, who gets numerous calls from people who can't even afford a double wide, much less a log home. Most log homes have to be built to state and regional code. Banks will not finance a home that is not built to code. It is not just a matter of cutting down the trees on your lot and building your own home.

While not cheap, log homes are also not extraordinary in costs. It is just that their typical features, like wood paneled, cathedral ceilings with heavy timber beams, extensive porches and intricate, labor intensive details cost more. Compared to a similarly detailed custom stick built house, log homes actually cost about the same.

Log homes also require a degree of maintenance, while similar to every house, is critical to a log home. Improperly cared for log homes can leak through the walls and are susceptible to insect damage. Properly maintained log homes will not have these problems. Insects are a prime concern for many who purchase log homes. There are two very real reasons for this concern. First is that using insect infested wood in building a log home is not unheard of. If the company doesn't know what it's doing (with 400 companies, many of which are mom and pop operations, what do you think?), it is quite possible. Lawsuits over insect damage have brought more than one log company into bankruptcy. It can and does happen.

The other aspect is that people see these great big logs and imagine a huge feast for insects. It is not necessarily so. The reality is that a log home that is built to code is no more susceptible to insect problems than any other type of home. The insect problem has more to do with an improperly constructed foundation, improper grading and not using normal insecticides. Regardless of building system, violating codes and good building practices is going to promote insect problems rather than the fact that it is a log home.

There are a number of things to look for if you want a log home. These points are not intended to make the product look bad. People who own log homes are generally very happy with their homes and would have no other. However, a number of people don't know what they're getting into and there are plenty of vendors who will tell you anything to sell you a home.

First is energy efficiency. The walls of a log home are made of wood, which has an R-value of a little over 1 per inch, making a typical log home's wall R-7. Most stick built homes range from R-11 to R-19. There is a curve thrown here, though. R-value is the only universally accepted way to determine energy efficiency today. However, heat retention or "thermal sink" is another aspect of log homes that has merit. Essentially, the log walls absorb and retain heat, staying warmer longer and performing as well as a stick built home with higher R-values. Nevertheless, you might have trouble getting your house to pass a strict code, because that is all code people have to look.

A recent development in log home energy code compliance is what is called an "envelope report." While code officials won't give credit for "thermal sink," they will accept an alternate method of determining energy efficiency. Here they look at the total surface of the house and require you to super insulate the ceiling, gables and crawl space. In addition, they give you credit for high performance, low "E" glass. As an example, local code might require R-13 walls, R-19 crawl spaces and R-30 roofs on conventional construction. With a log wall of only R-7, you could still come into compliance by increasing the crawl space to R-30, the roof to R-36 and use low "E" windows. An engineer would compute the surface of the entire house, come up with a number comparable to a conventional house and meet the same overall energy requirements.

While this still ignores "thermal sink" and actual performance, it does allow you to build your home in areas that are actively enforcing energy codes. Engineers typically charge about $500 for this *envelope report* and there is the extra cost of the additional insulation and upgraded windows. In some areas, the power company will do these reports for free or at a nominal fee. In addition, some code offices also accept reports done by non-engineers or a HVAC contractor that will cost less. The extra cost of the upgraded insulation and windows will have its' own pay back with even lower energy bills.

As was mentioned, log homes (except laminated logs) settle. Try to look at homes that are five or more years old. See how they have held up. Talk to a homeowner (in private) and discuss the whole aspect of buying, building and living in a log home.

Look at the reputation of the company. Some of the older companies were founded in the 1960s and '70s. You can't stay in business that long with too many screwups. Look closely at estimates of cost. Each company is different. They all have specification sheets that tell you what they are providing and the quality and size levels of the components. A quick review of this will narrow down proposals of different companies. A wide variation after that doesn't necessarily mean that the higher priced company is gouging you. It usually means that there are subtle, but important differences that cannot be put to paper. Many companies can match specs. What they cannot do is match quality of manufacture, engineering, code compliance and most important, ability to respond when things go wrong.

Distance from the manufacturer can make a difference, not only in shipping costs but also in service. Since there are over 400 choices, you should see some commonalities among suppliers and might lean towards the closer vendor, all other things being equal.

I have found that many people who buy log homes do so through the love of the

A modern log home

product and what, in their mind, the product does for them. You have to love the product. You can't be buying it to save money. Unfortunately, there are a lot of people who buy the "kit" at a very low price (you get what you pay for) only to find out the real cost of the house after the logs are up. This is harmful not only to those who bought a house they cannot afford to finish or live in, but also to the industry as a whole. This is because people will find out about your folly and make it difficult for others to enjoy log homes in the future. This is quite typical when a bank has lent money for a home that goes sour. It makes it difficult for the next guy to get a loan.

You also have to love the house because of the many hoops you have to jump through to get it. Financing is one that stands out. Manufacturers want deposits and partial payment up front and complete payment upon delivery. Banks and especially appraisers are going to make the going tough. While log homes typically cost more to build, appraisers have a hard time giving them their full value. Often you have to come up with additional money to finish the house because the bank will only lend on the appraised value that doesn't give credit for the inherent features of a log home.

Some subcontractors are going to charge extra to build your house because it is a different or unusual building system. Since so much of the house's floor, ceiling and walls are exposed, it is difficult to conceal the plumbing, wiring and heating systems. Contractors often will charge extra to install these components due to real extra costs or because they aren't familiar with the system. Others might decline to work on your home at all, thus reducing the chance for fair or timely bids.

Come reselling time, you're faced with the same problem as before with realtors, bankers and appraisers. You will have to find someone as emotionally involved as you are to buy the house. Usually, people do not build log homes with the expectation of ever selling them. Often, this is because they truly love their homes but this makes it hard to find comparable sales, the basics of an appraisal.

You just gotta love it. And people do. They love their log homes, but you need to know the inherent drawbacks. Look carefully, study thoroughly, and remember, you're a different person building a home with your heart.

Timberframe Homes

Timberframes are also antique houses. I personally like timberframes because of their beauty. They have many of the same inherent problems of log homes. These include extra expense, realtor resistance, sub-trade problems, and general misunderstanding of the product. Problems they typically do not share with log homes are unscrupulous sellers, settling problems and energy efficiency concerns. Timberframe homes are typically super-insulated. This is because they are usually covered with a rigid foam insulated panel which usually exceeds standard stick framing R-values. This insulation, with R-values of up to R-4 per inch totally covers the frame, making the house extremely tight.

The industry itself is much smaller than the log industry with the largest player making less than 100 frames a year. The average player makes less than 20 and many do only several a year. It is a labor of love and the frame can be very ornate and quite complicated. A close relationship usually develops between the manufacturer and the customer. While it is not hard to get into the business, it takes considerably more skill to make timberframes than log homes. This is probably why this industry seems to be less trouble prone than the log industry. The homes also do not settle, but some species of wood can twist or shrink. This is usually not a problem to the structure, but might be an aesthetic problem if you're not aware of it. It is also a good idea to look at a five-year-old frame of the same species of wood as the one you're considering.

There are some distinctions in the timberframe industry. First is how the wood is connected. Most timberframes are joined using mortise and tenon joinery, secured with oak pegs. This is an intricate, highly detailed way to join wood and is a great part of the appeal. Another way to join the wood is with metal connectors. This method is usually done when mortise and tenon joinery is not available or solid timbers are not used. Laminated or other advanced methods of manufacturing beams and large timbers typically do not use mortise and tenon joinery and thus metal connectors are used. Other reasons metal connectors are used include lower cost and personal taste.

There is a subtle distinction between timberframing and post and beam. Often both words are used interchangeably. The look, to the untrained eye, is quite similar. Timberframing uses an entire wall section as a building unit, called a "bent." This *bent* includes the wall timbers and the rafters, all joined as one piece and erected as one unit. *Bents* are connected at the rafters to other bents with timbers called purlins. A typical house would have three to five bents.

Post and beam homes are built piece by piece, very similar to platform framing. While the weight of a timberframed *bent* requires a crane to erect, post and beam homes can often be built without any extra lifting devices. They are most

If you want a truly remarkable home and can stretch your budget, you should consider making at least some part of your home a timberframe.

often assembled by a four-man crew. Post and beam homes typically use mortise and tenon joinery but usually are not as intricate as timberframing.

Since the systems both use heavy timbers with mortise and tenon joinery, the words post and beam and timberframing are interchangeable (to all but the purist.) Timberframe homes can be built from a variety of woods. However, White pine, Douglas fir and White oak are the three most common species of wood used. All three are excellent woods for timberframing though they have their own advantages and disadvantages. These are looked at with several criteria. These include cost, appearance, strength, and stability of the wood. For example, White pine is the least expensive, can be stained a variety of colors and is very stable. However, it is the weakest of all common species and thus requires posts to be closer together, which could interfere with house design. Oak is a bit more expensive, has great strength and looks good but has limited ability to accept stains. Because of that, most oak frames are typically only finished with linseed oil. Oak is very hard and heavy, thus hard to work with. Also, oak is not a very stable wood and is prone to shrinkage and twisting. Oak frames tend to separate and crack more deeply than other species. This is usually not a structural problem but is bothersome to some people who want the joinery to remain as tight as it was the day the frame was assembled.

COURTESY OF MILL CREEK POST & BEAM COMPANY

**Timberframing . . .
a.k.a. post and beam**

Douglas fir has the advantage of strength and relative stability. It is easier to work with and lighter in weight than oak and less prone to twist and shrink. Its natural red color makes it hard to stain and thus it is usually just oiled or stained with a dark color. It is the most expensive of all materials and is increasingly harder to obtain in larger sizes due to limited supply and environmental issues. Fir is a good compromise between oak and pine except for the extra cost and limited availability. Purists seem to prefer Douglas fir as well. I personally like White pine for its lower cost, appearance, ease of manufacturer and erection and stainability. The best advice on selecting species of wood is that you look at older frames and see if their natural aging is what you like.

One neat aspect of a timberframe home is that you cannot tell from the outside that it is a timberframe home. Obviously, a log home is distinguished by the logs wall. Timberframe homes can be sided with any material, including brick and stucco, making them no different than conventional houses. Most, however, are sided with horizontal cedar clapboard siding, primarily because the original timberframe homes used this material.

Another aspect of a timberframe home is that the entire home does not have to be built using a timberframe. Often, only one room, or a center core of rooms are built using a timberframe. This method is often called hybrid homes, because of the blending of two or more building systems. Typically, what occurs is that the timberframe is used for the public rooms, usually a great room that encompasses the living room, dining room, entry hall and kitchen. Other rooms, like bedrooms, utility rooms and the garage are made of conventional materials. Reasons for this is cost savings and personal taste (some people don't want timberframing in every room of their house.)

The greatest disadvantage of timberframing is cost. It is probably the most expensive way to build. Sometimes it is difficult to find proper tradesmen to erect the frame or build in conjunction with a timberframe. Timberframes are also typically so energy efficient and tight that accumulated moisture from heating and cooling systems trap air inside. The solution is easily achieved through the professional sizing and installation of these systems and sometimes, the use of an air-to-air heat exchanger. While these extra efforts will cost more money, they should pay for themselves over time through lower energy bills.

While timberframing is an antique system of building, it was primarily dropped because cheaper and less skillful ways of construction were found in the middle of the 19th century. The system is still viable and can be breathtaking when used in a residential application. If you want a truly remarkable home and can stretch your budget, you should consider making at least some part of your home a timberframe.

State of the Art, Weird and Advanced Systems

Geniuses and crackpots are always looking for better mousetraps. This occurs in the housing industry as well. While there are new products being developed daily, consumers and builders alike are fairly resistant towards new building systems. Modular housing, for example, makes tremendous sense for the consumer and the builder. While this is an expanding system, it still lags far behind stick building, a well-known wasteful and inefficient system. Nevertheless, modular and other systems will continue to lag behind for no other reason than habit and the extreme emotional nature of building and buying a home.

There are three fairly new building systems available on the market. These are geodesic domes, structural insulated panel homes and homes made with steel components.

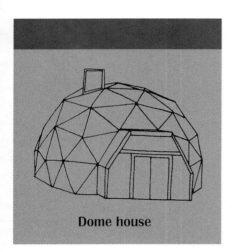

Dome house

Dome homes are based on a geometric theory that a partial sphere encloses the greatest amount of volume with the least amount of surface area. Domes are also stronger than conventional methods of building homes and can be economical to build. The other side of the coin is that it looks strange. This type of home is probably one that is most dependent on personal taste. There are only a handful of manufacturers, most of which advertise in the back of science and mechanics magazines.

Homes built using this building system are seen mostly on the West Coast where, coincidentally, most of the manufacturers are. Buckminster Fuller's name is most associated with building homes and commercial structures using geodesic domes. These homes are built on a short riser wall, require minimal technical knowledge or special tools and usually can be constructed in one to three days. The speed of construction and relative ease of assembly make this building system ideal for the do-it-yourselfer.

Structural insulated panel homes, called SIPs for short, are also known as foam core panel or stress skin panel homes. The basic building block of this system is a panel of rigid insulation that is glued between two sheets of OSB or plywood. The rigid insulation is usually either polystyrene (what coffee cups are made of) or polyisocyanurate, a denser, rigid foam. The panels typically range in size from a 4x8' panel to a 8x24' panel. They range in thickness from four inches to over 12, with the polystyrene panels being thicker because their R-value per inch is less than the polyisocyanurate panels.

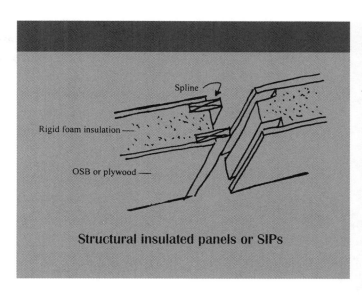

Structural insulated panels or SIPs

This system has the twin advantages of higher and better performing insulation values and a faster rate of construction. Their main disadvantage is higher initial costs and the fact that it is a relatively new building system. They also require special tools and the use of a crane as well as some expertise, usually picked up on the first house.

SIPs are exceptionally strong and insulate better because there is no internal framing in the panel to reduce R-values with "thermal breaks." In stud construction, every stud typically has one third the R-value of the wall insulation. These "interruptions" in the wall dilute the energy efficiency of the wall, causing *breaks.* SIPs avoid this problem because the insulation is continuous and thus not interrupted.

SIPs are fairly new to residential construction but have been used in commercial building prior to WWII, especially in buildings used for refrigeration. SIPs crossed over into residential construction concurrent to the resurgence of interest in timberframing. Here, SIPs are used as closure walls and roofs. They were ideal because they could span the greater distances between framing members of a timberframe. They also added greatly to the strength of timberframe structures and solved a number of engineering concerns in California where meeting earthquake codes were a problem.

Used as an independent building system, SIPs are combined with floor trusses (on two-story structures) and either roof trusses or laminated beams. Where laminated beams are used, these beams serve as purlins to support the SIPs used on the roof. When used with roof trusses, conventional insulation is used on the roof. SIPs that are used on roofs sometimes are bonded with either drywall or pine paneling on the inside, thus providing a finished ceiling surface. It is expected that this product will continue to grow in use in the future.

Steel homes have become more popular recently as a result of sharp increases in the price of lumber. Lumber prices fluctuated so much in the late 1980s and early '90s that prices almost doubled in the course of a normal building cycle. Steel had been used in the past, especially in conjunction with fire walls in apartments but was not considered a normal framing material. While lumber prices have settled down, it did give entrée to a small, but growing market in steel homes. Steel homes have number of advantages. This includes studs that are perfectly straight, absolutely resistant to insects and termites as well as fireproof. The disadvantages includes the requirement for special tools and training and a general hesitancy for builders and homeowners to try anything new. The end result of a steel house would be indistinguishable from a conventionally framed home.

Other systems, such as Styrofoam blocks filled with concrete, are constantly coming on the market. Each is trying to address a different issue, such as a shortage of materials or increased efficiencies in insulation, labor or costs. Each is worth a look. Often these systems are limited by the availability of trained craftsmen. If a new system comes to your town, you should give them a shot and hear them out. It is important that these systems meet local, regional and national codes. For the most part they will, since it would make no sense to manufacture something that doesn't meet code. It goes back to the question of how much of a pioneer do you want to be? Some systems are great advancements with savings in cost and energy efficiency. Other are flops. It's your money and your home. ■

21

Why Not Just Stick It?

The Pros of a Building System

There are many excellent reasons to use a building system. In fact, chances are that some part of your house is going to have a pre-assembled/pre-built component in it. For example, many houses are now using roof trusses instead of rafters. Stairs often come pre-built as a total unit or, at least, some part of the stair system, is pre-manufactured. An example would be the railing, finish treads and balusters. Almost all doors come pre-hung. Windows typically come with pre-cut moldings. Cabinets are typically pre-built or what they call "KD." KD means "knocked down," which means it comes in a box and has to be assembled on site. Lower cost bathroom vanities are often KD vanities. Whether you like it or not, you're going to have some parts of a building system in your home. There is no such thing as a pure stick built, site built house today.

However, a building system, in its' purest sense, is quite different from a site built/stick built house. For definition, we will call a building system house a home where the basic structural framing of the house is pre-determined, pre-cut, pre-assembled and/or pre-manufactured off site and then brought to the house site for erection and assembly. What are the advantages of this system and what are the trends? We'll address the trends first since the answer is as simple as it is obvious. More and more houses are built each year using a building system and fewer homes are purely stick built. It is a trend that is not going away.

While there are many reasons for this trend, they focus primarily on cost. Building system houses cost less than site built houses. This does not mean that they are cheaper or inexpensive. Many building system homes costs well above the average cost of a site built home. Antique heavy timber structures are very expensive. Some package homes like Lindal Cedar, Deck House and Acorn are also very expensive. They are not, however, expensive because they are building systems but rather because of the use of high quality materials, engineering and services. The key difference is that if you were to totally replicate a heavy timber or premium package house without using a building system, it would cost considerably more than if you were using a system.

The cost savings is not only in the cost of the package or system but also in the speed of construction. Time is money. A typical stick built house will take from 90 to 150 days to build. All the while this house is being built, money disbursed to build it is being charged interest, hundreds and thousands of dollars of interest. Any time saved in building is money saved in interest. The fastest system of building modular can sometimes turn a house in less than 30 days. This period also matches sometimes terms of most suppliers, making modular housing a way to almost avoid all finance charges as well as reduce cash flow requirements. While things like weather can delay jobs past 30 days and some contractors want payment at completion rather than after 30 days, modular housing can certainly reduce finance charges considerably.

Another element of time is how quickly you can get into the house. Most people who build a home have a period of time between when they are displaced from their old home and when they can move into their new one. This can range from a few days to a few months. It is always an unpleasant time of living in inadequate housing and discomfort. This happens because you often have to sell your current home to get the money to build your new one. In many areas, rental houses are hard to find, are expensive, and it is difficult to find rental property with leases shorter than six months. A building system can reduce this "nomad" time and greatly reduce the stress of building a new home.

Another advantage of a building system is that it allows you to build your own home with fewer skills. Many people who want to build their own homes might not be able to do so because of the complexity of the home. Building systems make it easier, doing all the hard work for you. While a panelized system is just barely a step above stick building, an owner-builder does not need to know how to frame a wall or partitions. While doing this is not terribly hard, you have to have skill, knowledge and patience to locate and frame window and door opening, build corners, square and plumb walls, etc. A panelized system reduces this to a tinker toy level where you just match up numbered panels to the floor and each other.

Building with heavy timber systems is simpler with a building system as well. Could you image the time it would take to cut all the tenons and mortises in a timberframe house? Mistakes would be costly. Rather than reaching for another $2.50 stud, you would be looking for a $300 timber. Heavy timber systems are easy to assemble, often done in a few days with only strong backs.

Since many building systems are developed for unusual methods of building, they are often the only practical way to get what you want. Here again, log and

War Story

#20: I have worked for four different building system manufacturers over a 12-year period. I have been asked by hundreds of customers how quickly I could get a house to them. I always told them "faster than you can get ready." I didn't even have to look at the production schedule because I knew that they never could get ready as fast as I could. It was always their concern that I wouldn't be ready. It was also always, in every case (dozens of actual houses), me waiting on them to get some final detail straightened out. I also know from this experience that when I first met a customer, we always picked a target delivery date. One hundred percent of the time it was not met, always because they could not get ready as fast as I could produce a house. Now, to be fair, most times plans had to be prepared and these took at least a month. Even so, there seemed to always be something else that slowed the process down. Bottom line is that you will not be held up by a building system manufacturer.

timberframe homes comes to mind. A building system is virtually the only way you are going to get these type of houses. While there are some craftsmen who specialize in these methods of construction, they are hard to find and have very limited capacity to build, usually only one or two homes a year. Building system manufacturers would have no trouble getting your home produced.[20]

In line with the special skills and work that building systems houses can provide is the special materials that are available. Many package homes come with materials that are rarely available in most areas. Some of the materials are specially milled for that particular manufacturer or application. For example, many heavy timber roof systems use six by eights as rafters, spaced four feet apart. They often sheath this roof with 2x6 or 2x8 tongue-and-groove planking. This size is needed to span this distance and to carry the roof and floor load. You are not going to find this material in any lumberyard. Another example is the grade of materials, especially in cedar products. While many lumberyards will carry cedar siding, it will be in only one or two grades. Most premium packages use a grade that is far superior to the standard grade used by local builders. Most people are unaware that cedar comes in the high grade and quality levels used in premium house packages.

While pre-cut or pre-assembled packages make it easier for the owner-builder to build themselves, they also provide another service. This is pre-estimated and supplied materials. A package home typically has all the components, in the right size and lengths, already determined. This is a major service, as most owner-builders have no idea what is necessary to build a house. Estimating materials is an art and a science. It is also a profession, a job that people do all day long. In major firms, estimators are paid salaries approaching $100,000 a year. While anyone can estimate materials (including you), packaged homes already have this done for you. It is a valuable service.

Another benefit of a packaged home is that it is pre-engineered. Many people call the building system or package homes industry the pre-engineered industry. What this means is that routine engineered requirements for the home are already done. The beams, rafters and joists have been sized to carry the load prescribed. Wind loads, snow loads, dead loads and live loads, etc., have all been pre-determined. If you were stick building the house, you would have to determine the size and spacing of the floor joists. While there are charts that show you how to do this, there are a number of elements that you would most likely be unable to determine with ease. Carpenters who stick build usually know this. Designers, draftsman and architects often figure this out for you as well. It works pretty well with stick building. However, if you are using an unusual system or heavy timber, it would be difficult and costly to determine the span capability of a large timber or how notching can affect its strength.

It is also advantageous to have the majority of the main components of the house arrive in one bundle or package. There is no need to keep going to the lumberyard. One delivery to meet, one check-off sheet to verify. One check to sign. Everything is there, can be secured and ensured that you will not have to wait. If there is a backordered part, you have time for it to come in rather than stop the job waiting.

The Cons of a Building System

As wonderful as building systems are, they are not for everyone. Not every house can be built using a building system due to limitations in what can be done. A primary limitation is what can be shipped down the road. Some sites are so far back up into the woods that a large truck cannot reach them. Some designs are so far off the wall that pre-fabrication makes no sense. Some areas limit what can be pre-fabricated by code or covenant. In some areas, shipping costs would be prohibitive. While there are good arguments to counter this problems, they are very real and not easily overcome.

Reluctance to use a building system often starts with you, the customer. Building systems do not have a good name. The questions people ask are, "Why don't you build a 'real' house?" or "Are you going to build a 'kit' house?" If these comments would bother you (and it does some people), you probably should not build a "kit" home.

Another problem with a building system is that some trades might not want to finish them for you. Structural Insulated Panel (SIP) houses require special tools for installing wiring. While the tools don't cost that much and the skills to be learned are not that hard, some sub-contractors will not work on your house. You might run into resistance with modular houses because so much of the plumbing and wiring is already hooked up. Not only is there less work to do and hence a smaller job profit, the question of who is responsible for problems is a concern as well.[21]

In line with this is a tendency for materials to run short on packaged houses. There are three basic reasons this happens. First, materials are stolen from the job, not common but it does happen. Second is that it is damaged on site or is misapplied. This is the number one culprit. The best illustration of this is with siding. Wood siding is usually sent out in various lengths, ranging from eight to 16 feet.[22]

The third possibility is that you were not shipped enough material for one of two reasons. First was that the company misestimated what it would take to do the job. This is not uncommon and is easily remedied if you did your job right. The second thing that could happen is that you got what you paid for, but it wasn't enough to do the job. This is also common and deals with the question of what you are buying. Is it enough material to do the job or is it the amount your contract says and it is not enough to do the job? This is a subtle point but many companies use this point to keep themselves out of trouble. You would need to ask the question. If the policy is that it is enough to do the house, someone will re-estimate and see if a mistake was made. If there was, you will get the rest of the material. If no mistake was made, you are on thin ice. If the policy is that you get what you paid for, the same estimate would be made. In this case, if you are short of materials to finish the job but the amount you paid for was sent, you are out of luck. If you did not get what you paid for, you will be made whole.

If your position is weak in either case, it could be made stronger by you doing something that most people do not do, even though they are told to. That is to inventory the materials as they are delivered. Count every piece, every board and every window. People do not do this because it takes time and effort. Often these materials are crowded into a room or scattered around the lot. You will be told to make these inventories. Most of you won't; weak position and high probability for heartache and hard feelings. Doing this inventory in a timely manner (usually within hours or days of delivery) will point out mistakes and shortages that can be taken care of with ease. Since siding and roofing are sometimes parts of packaged houses, they become a problem later on. First, since they are often left out in the open, they are often stolen or damaged. Also, since they are installed weeks and months later, no one can tell if they were short at the day of arrival or stolen weeks and months later. Weak position. Count the material.

An advantage to a package home can also be a disadvantage. This is also related closely to the problem of damage and theft as well as not counting or miscounting. Getting all that stuff on one day can be a problem if you don't have adequate or secure storage room for all these parts. They are all there for your convenience. They are also there to be looted and destroyed. Stick builders only take delivery on parts as they are needed. You might not have this luxury in a package home.

In line with this is cash flow, which is also a problem with building systems. The supplier wants payment upon delivery. This usually does not fit anyone's cash flow position, especially the bank. They typically only want to come out to

War Stories

#21: When I was involved in building the first closed wall house in Charlotte, the sub-contractor base we had developed over many years was understandably upset. We had either eliminated or greatly reduced the need for these subs. Overnight, we became a much smaller contract for them. Over time, some subs left for builders with more work. The ones that remained were not as responsive as before. Another area where it might be hard to get subs is where the house structure itself has to be put up. While many companies have trained crews to do this, many do not. Customers are either supplied with a construction manual or a factory rep comes to teach them or their builder how to assemble the house. Many people are nervous about this and shy away from building systems as well. I have heard on more than one occasion where the customer just did not think a local crew was capable, skilled or sensitive enough to build a premium home package. Therefore, the lack of trained crews often is the reason people don't use building systems. I also know of more than a few occasions where customers brought in their own crews from out-of-state to build their homes. The reality is that, while packaged homes are well within the scope of any professional builder, there are a number of bad, unskilled or uncaring builders who give building with a system a bad name. In addition, if you are planning to build the house yourself, you still need some basic skills and desire for quality and the best use of materials.

#22: I have had more than one frantic call from a customer that said they were short siding and only discovered this on the last side of the house. I have gone to the job site and found huge stacks of two and four foot pieces of cut siding. I asked them where they started and they would show me. Beautiful work, with few joints. In fact, the whole house looks good with very few joints, until they get to the last side. What happened is that they used up all their 16 foot boards at the beginning and by the time they got to the last side, all that was left over was short boards and scrap. The board count was right. The square foot of coverage was right. The application was wrong. An experienced crew would have known where to use the long boards. The crew they used did not and hence a "shortage" that the customer wanted to blame on the manufacturer. The real tragedy here is that the materials are premium in cost and quality and they were wasted.

the site a few times. What they want to see is work completed and pieces in place. What they don't want to see is a truck driver with a bundle of lumber and a request for a $50,000 cashier's check before he breaks the bands on his load. This requirement, more than any other, is what is holding back the building systems industry. It is an industry at all because this is a solvable problem. It is also a slowly growing industry because it is so hard to solve. While you most likely will be able to deal with this cash flow issue, it is a reason why many people do not use systems.

Another reason that systems are a potential problem has to do with the subs themselves and their resistance to anything pre-cut. The problem is that the house itself is most likely to be made exactly like the plans say that it will be. However, the foundation might be a wee bit off. While this is not uncommon and typically easy to fix through adjustments in framing, it is a problem with a house that was cut perfectly square, plumb and level like a system built house.

Builders are often afraid to use a system because of the adjustments they like to make in the field. If something is wrong with the foundation, it is hard for them to fix something in the framed part of the house. Also, there is a learning curve to deal with. Building systems are a bit different and can be challenging to learn. It also becomes a problem in pricing since a builder might not know how to charge you for the work if they've never done it before. A common problem with building systems is that a builder will overcharge or double charge because he does not know what he is getting into. Double charging occurs when he doesn't realize that something already comes with the package and he thought he had to supply and/or install it. Extra charges also come about just because of the unknown. If the builder or sub-contractor has never worked with your system, he might pad his bill to protect himself.

Sometimes the building system company makes mistakes in manufacturing and this causes problems for you. Miscuts and short pieces are common. The manufacturer is responsible for correcting these problems, but they are going to limit themselves to correcting the problem, not for any inconvenience or downtime their mistake caused. This will not make you happy and can be further negotiated, but usually is the nature of the beast and is hidden in the contract somewhere. The vast majority of the companies will be more than fair about this, but they are not going to open their treasuries up to you.

It is not uncommon for a customer to get upset with a problem and try to solve it themselves without notifying the manufacturer. This is an absolute mistake. Your position is weak because most companies reserve the right *and method* of solution to themselves. What happens is that they will do it the proper, but least expensive, way. Their solutions are almost always the best for all concerned and lets you get on with your house. People who fight companies over small, easily remedied errors create their own nightmares. If you live in a world where mistakes cannot be tolerated, you are going to be very unhappy with a building system. Building systems, like the people who design and build them, are not perfect. Neither are stick-built houses. ■

22

Should Your Subs Drive Trucks or Harleys?

What Do You Think?

Selecting the subcontractors for your home is probably the most important decision you will make. Subs will make or break a job. It is not only a matter of their skills and cost, but also how you get along with the subs and their method of work. Some people always go for the lowest price, regardless of other factors.

If the crew comes to work on "Harleys," it is a good clue that they have another agenda. You need to be seeing trucks, not motorcycles. However, if the crew leader drives up on a Harley and the rest come in trucks, that might not be so bad. Harleys are expensive and a sign of success provided it isn't the only asset they have. Jay Leno makes a pretty decent wage and he drives a Harley.

The point is that you need to not prejudge the crew. Gut feelings would tell you that the Harley is a sign of one of two things. It could be a successful sub who likes his toys. His working equipment is coming in a new truck that will arrive shortly. On the other hand, it could be that he's just gotten out of jail and his truck was sold to pay his bail. Chances are that he's just gotten out of jail, but, hey, subs are hard to get and you need to take a few minutes to hear him out.

<table>
<tr><td>**In This Chapter . . .**</td></tr>
<tr><td>▲ Signs of a good sub</td></tr>
<tr><td>▲ Signs of a bad sub</td></tr>
<tr><td>▲ How to find a sub</td></tr>
</table>

Where To Find Good Subs

Finding subs is not all that hard. There are a number of sources to check out. The obvious place is the "Yellow Pages." The pros are listed there. They have probably been there for at least a year as the phonebook is published annually. Stability is a useful trait in a sub. The Yellow Pages are not inexpensive, but also not an end all in stability. They do show that the sub has some sense of marketing and thinks of himself as a professional. He has a phone and thinks he is going to be there for at least a year.

The biggest problem with using the Yellow Pages is that not all subs are listed there. While there are a number of bad reasons for them not to be listed there

SIGNS OF A GOOD SUB

1. You like the sub.

2. The sub is currently doing the work.

3. The sub lives in your community.

4. The sub has been doing the work for at least five years.

5. The sub is listed in the phone book.

6. The sub can be reached by phone and/or returns phone calls promptly.

7. The sub's workplace and truck is neat and well organized.

8. The sub wears appropriate work clothes, including safety shoes, hearing protection and glasses.

9. The sub is insured.

10. The sub's bid is written down and your questions are fully explained.

11. The sub's tools are in good working order.

12. The sub shows concern for safety and building to meet code.

13. The work is warranted with a written guarantee.

14. The sub is a member of a trade organization.

15. The sub is recognized by peers, suppliers and inspectors as competent.

16. Sub, if in a licensed trade, has a current license.

17. Stable life, solid citizen—many subs involve their families, especially their spouses in their business; if there is a problem there, it will affect their work.

18. Someone you know has used them and were pleased.

19. They stick to their bid.

(fly-by-night), there are some good reasons. One could be that they are new to the area. Being new is not necessarily bad. Some of the best subs I had in Charlotte recently came from Indiana. They were new but far superior to any sub in the city. Another reason is that they have more work than they can handle. In an industry that functions very well (for some) by word of mouth, being listed in the Yellow Pages would only be a nuisance. I also have seen subs with huge ads in the Yellow Pages that I knew to be crooks. Many people choose the sub with the largest ad thinking they are the best. These guys were the best crooks.

Another source is the local Home Builders Association. Most places have these at the town, city or county level. You can call or visit the office and get a list of contractors. You will probably be dealing with an answering machine because most of these offices are staffed part-time. You can ask for references, but the person you will be talking to will be circumspect about who is good or not. They do not want to get in the game of recommending one member over another, which is bad for business and the goals of the association. What you will have is a list of the predominant players. Like the phone book, not all subs will be listed and their absence is not necessarily a bad sign. I know of a number of good builders who are not members. They view the association as a social club for those who have already made it in the business and they do not have the time or the money to join. While this is a bit short sighted on their part, it should not be a reason to not consider nonmembers.

On the other hand, being a member shows that the sub has an interest in their profession and wants to associate with other capable builders. The association has instructional and informational sessions at each of their meetings that keeps them up to speed on the state of the art. They can compare notes and find solutions to similar problems. They also would normally have the respect of their peers or they would not go. Jealousy of good skills and success are just as common as ill feelings towards bad quality, reputation and ethics. Most members view the association as a club with like-minded members.

The next place to look is in active subdivisions or any place you see a house going up. Many builders put site-up signs that list their name and phone numbers. If the sub isn't there, you can call them later. You can at least look at the house they are building and make your own judgment of the quality and organization of the work. If they are there, talk to them and tell them of your interest. Obviously, someone thought they were good enough to hire for their job and that is usually a good sign. If you want to pursue the relationship but want to check further, you should try to find out whose house it is and speak with them. This can be especially useful and might be all you need to make a decision whether to use this sub or not.

Another place to check is with the building code office. While these

SIGNS OF A BAD SUB

1. You don't like them.

2. The sub is unemployed.

3. The sub lives far away or is new from out of state (not always bad, but something to think about).

4. The sub is new at the business (without an apprentice program).

5. The sub does no marketing, especially if he doesn't because he can't afford it.

6. Sub doesn't answer pages or phone messages, or people who answer his phone are rude, are incompetent children, have poor phone manners or "just don't know where he is or when he'll be back" after 9 p.m.

7. Workplace is a mess, including beer cans; truck is a mess with poor tool storage and beer cans.

8. Inappropriate work clothes, offensive T-shirts, tennis shoes rather than steel toed safety shoes.

9. No insurance. You have to see the paperwork and ensure that it is up to date. Call the insurance company and confirm it is not forged or due to run out before your job ends. If sub is uninsured, you are the one getting sued. Do not take their word for it. Insurance is expensive and might explain why their bid is so low.

10. Sub won't give you a written bid or is evasive to your questions about what they are providing regarding labor and materials.

11. Sub's tools are dirty, poorly repaired, old, show poor maintenance.

12. Sub's workplace and safety devices (i.e., scaffolding) look unsafe; offers to do work below/around the code.

13. No or vague warranty.

14. Sub is not a member of the local trade association, especially in an area where membership is high.

15. Referral checks show sub to have problems.

16. Sub is unlicensed (if in a licensed trade).

17. Unstable life, personal problems, i.e., recent or impending divorce, drug problem, brushes with the law.

18. Their bid changes dramatically from the initial estimate to a final one after they've looked at the job. In fact, throwing out a bid without first looking at the job is unprofessional. It is a common trick to bid low to stop you from looking elsewhere, then to reassess the job and push the bid up. Even if further checking shows their revised bid to be fair, you've been tricked, which is not a good way to start a job. You need to bite the bullet and look elsewhere.

19. You get a bid but can't get them to start the work. Once you've got your range of prices and other good feelings about the sub, you need for them to start the work. Some subs will agree to do the work when they can't possibly start it anytime soon. Their hedging is a bad sign. Keep looking, even if you have to start the process all over again.

folks are busy, you might be able to get an inspector to recommend someone, especially a sub-trade like an electrician or plumber. It is in the inspector's best interest that good subs keep getting work. This makes their job easier. You probably will have a hard time getting the inspector to give one or several names because they do not want to get into the referral business, either.

However, they do not have the pressure that the Home Builders Association has to be neutral. Often building inspectors are very opinionated and will tell you who is good. You might need to prompt them by giving them the names of several that you are considering and see if they'll bite. Usually, they will tell you all those are competent. If one is not, they will probably tell you and you can eliminate that one from your list.

Supply houses and lumberyards are also good sources of subs. While not an endorsement, you will probably find a bulletin board with business cards of subs. This will at least give you direction in your research. You can also ask one of the salesmen in these companies who they would suggest. They too will be hesitant to tell you one particular person, but you might get lucky. You can also use the elimination game where you give them a list and they hesitate at one of the names. Salesmen know not only who is busy, but also who has been in the business awhile. If they've been in trouble they probably know as well because it is a small world they live in. They also know who is competent by the questions the subs ask and the mistakes they make. They also know their demeanor and how well they handle problems and mistakes.

Finally, the most common way subs are found is by word of mouth and referral. As mentioned before, many subs advertise very little, if at all, because they have enough referral business to keep them busy. Just ask your friends and acquaintances–they will be glad to refer you to the good guys and away from the bad. The subs most likely live in your town, go to church, have kids in school and are visible in some manner. People know them in their workplace and in the community. A personal referral will often put you in touch with a good candidate.

Throughout this process, you have probably come up with a number of candidates for subcontract work. You should have several prospects rather than settle for one too early. Chances are that most on your list can do the work. However, you probably want the best house ever built and it would be worth it if you took a few extra steps to get the very best *for you*. The very best sub might not be what you need. You need one that meets your requirement and everyone has slightly different requirements.

What to Look For

You are looking for superman. Unless you really do live in Metropolis and the *Daily Planet* is your local paper, you are not going to find him. Clark Kent is the best you're going to do and he's just a fine fellow. While this section will give you a lot of things to look at and consider, it will most likely go back to a gut feeling about the sub.

It is not rocket science. The best sub last year might be on his butt this year. We are dealing with human beings here and they, like houses, are not perfect. However, there is enough criteria available to give you a reasonable chance of getting most of the subs right. Review the list of considerations highlighted on the previous page. No one consideration should be used to make or break the decision. ■

23

Contracts and Guarantees

Fixed Bid or Time and Materials (Cost Plus)

There are three general ways to contract for labor and materials on your house. These are: Fixed Bid, Time and Materials (cost plus), and a combination of these two. Each has advantages and disadvantages with none being better than the other. It depends on what you are looking for and what you can get.

Fixed bid is where you know exactly what it is going to cost for a specified amount of labor and materials. This labor and materials is also called "in place," which means that the work includes all the labor and material to do the job. The owner supplies nothing, the job is totally done by the contractor. It could be to build a house *as specified* for "X" dollars. In theory, there will be no surprises. You get what you want (and are expecting) and the contractor gets paid.

Fixed bid could cover the entire project or just one phase, for example, the wiring or plumbing. The more straight forward the project, the easier it is to contract for a fixed bid. Things that are easily measured are typically contracted with a fixed bid. Roofing, siding, drywall, painting, flooring, etc., come under this category. These items are easy to measure off the plans and fixed in price prior to building. Licensed trades typically sell their goods and services at a fixed bid rate. Typically, the spec is *per the plans*, *in place*, and *to code*. If this work passes code inspection and all the parts are there, the sub expects to be paid the agreed upon amount.

Items that are harder to determine prior to construction are typically not contracted with a fixed bid. Examples would include lot clearing, debris hauling, excavation, footings and foundation work. These items could be assigned an hourly or in-place rate, but the hours or number of pieces might not be known until the job is completed. For example, an in-place block might cost $2.75. Unless the lot is perfectly flat, the total blocks used would not be known until after the wall is erected. However, each block would have a fixed price. Clearing and excavating work would also be assigned an hourly rate, but it would not be known how much work is needed because it is often difficult to know what a wooded lot has hidden within it.

In This Chapter . . .

▲ What is the best possible contract?

▲ How to contract for unknowns

▲ How good are warranties?

Typically, bids for excavation are not fixed and also have what is known as a "rock" clause. What this means is that if underground rock (sometimes called "ledge") is found, all bets are off. Hourly rates go out the window and new elements come into play. This could include a bigger or different machine, or the use of dynamite, to remove the rock. You would get back on track once the rock is removed and then revert to the agreed upon hourly rate.[23]

Block and brick work was also typically done on a fixed, in place basis. Since it was easy to count block once it was in place, we paid for what it took to build the foundation. It was just that we did not know what that amount was until the hole was dug and the footings were in place. This is not a problem everywhere, especially in flat areas where most foundations are level. In these cases, a predetermined fixed bid might be the rule and not the exception. Rolling and hilly terrain often requires an in place bid.

Sometimes a sub would want to work on a time and materials basis (plus a mark-up). This occurs when the cost is harder to pin down. It is also a great gamble, but might be the only way the work can proceed. In other words, a sub expects the work to be a hornet's nest and they don't want to get caught losing money. In this case as well, you might feel that the fixed bids you obtained (if you got any) are out of balance and you believe the work can be done cheaper if you watched closely. This might be the case, but you have to have a lot of confidence that you are right. I have seen fortunes lost with this method.[24]

Time and materials can be a problem in two areas. Both have to do with incentive. First, there is no incentive to do the job with any speed. While professionals prides themselves with the speed they can work, it is awfully tempting to take a break on these jobs, especially if no other job is looming out in front of

War Stories

#23: When I was building houses in Charlotte, our excavators were on an hourly rate. It was difficult to estimate how much that phase would cost until after the work was done. Since our houses were sold at a fixed cost prior to construction, we were at risk of losing a lot of margin due to overages in excavation. By the way, excavation was the phase that had the least control because we never knew what was on the lot or concealed by the underbrush. The company decided to put all excavation on a fixed bid basis. A number of formulas were worked out and an average price derived. We presented this to our subs and they had a fit. They ranted and raved and the largest of the group quit. We needed cost controls and they wanted windfalls. The end result was that we had a fixed bid on each lot. Unusual situations were negotiated on a case-by-case basis. The subs that remained were happy and so were we. Nevertheless, this was an unusual situation.

#24: I once was watching the construction of a foam core panel house where the builder didn't want to give a fixed bid. Winter was fast approaching and he established an hourly rate for his crew of four. What I noticed (I was selling land nearby and, though not involved in the house, checked its progress daily) was that very little was being done each day. My feeling was that the crew had "settled in" for the winter when work was slow and found someone to keep them employed until spring arrived. It became a very expensive house. If you contract for time and materials, you need to know how much labor a crew can do in a day or they are going to "settle in" on you.

them. Second, there is also no incentive to purchase wisely because they are going to make a percentage of whatever they buy. With a fixed bid, you can be assured they will be careful shoppers looking for the best deal.

Why would you use a time and material bid? Primarily if the work is unusual and no one will give you a fixed bid. Unfortunately, people unfamiliar with building systems typically want this kind of bid because they are unsure of how much time the work will take. If this is the case, you have to be sure that you separate out everything except the system itself. For example, the footings, foundation and first-floor system should be the same as a regular site built house. It should be at a fixed bid or, at least, a fixed in place bid. Once the system is up, fixed bids should cover the rest of the house.

Sometimes you might want work done that is outside the original contract. Often your sub will want to do this as time and materials rather than as a fixed bid. They are either unsure of the work or just don't want to take the time to figure out a fixed bid. You might be tempted to do this to save time. You want it done now and are trapped. Tough call.

Subs make a lot of money on change orders. Change orders are items done outside of the original contract. Often they are done at rates much higher than the original contracted rate. I know one builder who says he likes modular building systems, but only builds stick because stick built houses are more prone to change orders and he can make thousands more in extra profit through change orders. Other builders hate change orders because they often involve tearing things out. These builders will charge three to four times as much to discourage it or to make it worth their while. Time and materials is often the only way they will do change orders, much to your detriment.

A combination of these methods is quite common. A certain percentage of the house is done on a fixed bid, some parts on a fixed in place or hourly rate bid, and other parts on a time and materials plus a percentage rate. While a fixed bid is typically desired, you can be assured that there is some fluff in the bid, especially if there is some unknowns or strange things going on. Time and materials can address these elements, but you have to be vigilant to what is happening.

Another element of a contract is what is known as "allowances." Allowances gets you to a final figure based on so many dollars assigned to variable items. Typical items in the allowances column are lighting and plumbing fixtures, appliances, grades of carpet, vinyl and wood flooring, and wall paper. Here a certain amount is assigned in each category and you, the owner, select exactly what you want. If you choose a less costly item than in the allowance, you save the difference. Of course, hell will freeze over first. If you choose a more costly item, you pay the difference, which is most often the case. While this is quite fair, often the difference from one bid to another might be the amount of allowances. Since allowances are under your control, you might be tricked, especially if the sub knows your bottom line and wants to meet it even though they know the allowances they put in the bid only covers the cheapest of all components. Sometimes the good guy gets hurt here because their typical and ordinary allowance figures are closer to reality than the guy who knows how to trick you.

Your contract is important and should clearly point out what is being supplied

Subs make a lot of money on change orders. Change orders are items done outside of the original contract. Often they are done at rates much higher than the original contracted rate.

regarding parts and labor. Warranties should also be addressed in a contract. The contract can be made even more clear by referring to plans, details or sketches. It should be clearly defined what takes precedence, the plans or the contract. Often they do not agree through oversight and a final "policy" should take over. For example, the contract might say that it is also based on a set of plans, dated and revised a certain date, and that the contract takes precedent over the plans in a dispute. Therefore, if the plans say the roofing materials are to be supplied by the contractor, but the contract doesn't have it listed, the buyer has to pay for the roofing. This problem often occurs as things are added and dropped out of a contract at the last moment, yet the plans are not changed to reflect this.

If the plans say the roofing materials are to be supplied by the contractor, but the contract doesn't have it listed, the buyer has to pay for the roofing.

You might want your lawyer to look over the contract for anything terribly out of balance. You can be assured that your lawyer will find something wrong with the contract. It absolutely is not in your favor. However, lawyers are paid to find fault and danger with all human endeavors. If we did everything lawyers told us to do, nothing would ever get done or built. The lawyer might find something that is totally wrong and give you good reason to not sign the contract. There might be something there that is quite unfair. Often the sub knows this and will back off. Clauses are often put into contracts for that one in a 100 client who was totally unfair in the past and the sub wants to avoid a similar problem in the future. Your lawyer will at least let you know what you are getting into. Typically, all contracts are requesting that you do your job (like pay on time or take delivery as promised). The bad stuff is there for when you don't.

Realize, too, that a sub might not allow changes to their contract. If they won't budge, it is for a very good reason. Most likely, they've been hurt badly in the past in that area. It does not mean you have to sign the contract. If you don't like the terms and can't negotiate relief, don't sign them. Find someone else.

What Happens When It Breaks

Guarantees are barely worth the paper they are written on. If you are dealing with ethical tradesmen or builders, they will honor their promises to you. If they are less than honest, the best warranty in the world won't help you. Should you just ignore warranties? No way. Just don't be lulled into a false sense of security because of a warranty. It is only as good as the company issuing the warranty. It is also only as good as what it really means. Some vinyl siding companies now have 50-year warranties. Sounds great. You can be assured that very little of what is covered is going to go bad. The chances that company being around 50 years from now is also pretty slim. Most things that are going to go wrong with a house go wrong in the first year and certainly within the first five years.

While I might be picking on the siding people, I do know of cases where they have warranted some earlier products that failed (the color faded) and these items were quickly replaced, including labor. This increased my confidence in them as well as future business. Roofing companies also have long warranties, from 10 to 20 years. These typically are pro-rated and since most shingles last at least 10 years under normal conditions, there is little warranty left over to mess with at the 14th or 19th year.

The best warranty you are going to find are with the licensed trades (plumbing, wiring and heating systems). These warranties are usually real, but typically last for only one year or no more than five. If you go with a jack leg company, you can usually forget about a warranty. However, most reputable companies have and will honor their warranties. Appliance and third-party warranties are often harder to enforce. It really is a case-by-case matter blurred by responsibility. The manufacturer might supply a 30 cent piece for free, but you have to pay $75 to have it installed.

Another common warranty is a structural warranty, usually 10 years. I have seen these work very well in favor of the homeowner. However, if your builder is a fly-by-night, you might need to kiss this goodbye. There is a trend in the business toward warranty companies that cover major damage. While these are worth having, their remedies usually don't go into effect until after your house falls down. Don't expect anyone to get too excited because you found a loose paint chip on the wall or a small crack in the drywall. The bad news is that these warranties don't cover these small items. The good news is that these are small items.

If you do have major structural problems, you need to be firm but fair. Some problems could force a company into bankruptcy. If you want to be a jerk about it, some business owners will go under just to get you out of their hair, especially if they are struggling anyway and you are just one more straw in a bundle of straws gone bad. If they go under, you're out of luck. Many builders or tradesmen work hand-to-mouth and lose interest in pursuing their trade if they have to put up with you and your annoying lawyer. A $10,000 problem could put many small companies out of business. A cooperative customer will give them encouragement to stay in business and address your problem. A jerk will send them out of state. They can reincorporate elsewhere, and your house is yours forever. Your friends will soon tire of your stories and probably secretly agree with your builder.[25] ■

Don't be lulled into a false sense of security because of a warranty. It is only as good as the company issuing it.

War Story

#25: Just a reminder of the earlier story in Chapter 18. Remember the house that the slab settled (Case Number 5)? It cost over $20,000 to fix. However, the goodwill earned from this paid off many fold because it showed that the company was good to their word. The story was used by all the salesmen and helped close many a deal. There is value in honoring warranties, even tough ones. However, it made it easier to honor that one because the customer cooperated and didn't throw lawyers into the pile. The company also acted responsibly and quickly so everyone's cool head helped solve this rather serious problem. A screaming customer would not have gotten the problem solved as amicably.

Notes and Sketches

24

How To Get Along With Your Subs

When Do You Pay?

You pay "as agreed." If your contract lays out a payment schedule, you must abide by it. This is why it is important to read contracts carefully. Failure to pay as agreed will subject you to more grief than you can imagine. Your very life might be in danger. If you do not like the terms, ask for an exception. If you cannot come to terms, get another sub. Don't wait until later and try to pull a fast one. Subs usually have had this experience before and will not be happy with any games. They often are working on such a tight cash flow that your failure to pay as agreed will often mean that they cannot meet their weekly payroll.

The best time to pay is after the work is completed and you are satisfied. The important part here is *after* the work is completed. The worst thing you can do is pay in full prior to the work being completed. All incentive to complete the work is gone. The very best of intentions go out the window. If the sub has been paid, they lose interest in the work. While most will come back and eventually finish the work, they will never come as quickly as when they are looking for a check.

There are a number of things you should be looking for when establishing a payment schedule. First is to clearly determine when the work is *done*. It can be after passing a code official's inspection (if it is work that requires inspection.) It can be after your inspection, in a joint meeting with you and the sub. If you schedule an inspection/payment meeting and know of a problem you want fixed before you pay, let the sub know so that he will have the proper tools and material to fix the problem on the spot. If it is a clearly seen and agreed upon problem, but cannot be fixed in a short period of time, do not schedule a meeting. Tell the sub that you will meet once it has been resolved. It is best to not be there during the repair because it is a tense moment. If you are there, you will be under pressure to accept the work and pay on the spot. What usually happens is that you see the work being done and figure that it will be done in an hour or two. You are tempted to pay and leave. Don't. If you do, what can (will) happen is that as soon as you drive off (expecting them to work several more hours to meet your requirements) they will be leaving shortly, too.

In This Chapter . . .

▲ When is the best time to pay?

▲ Is housing mythology real?

▲ What will make your subs do better work?

Some subs will want a deposit before the work begins. This is not uncommon, especially for small companies. They use this money for one of two things. First is to buy materials for your job, e.g., carpet or framing lumber. The second thing they might do is pay someone else's bill or make payroll that week with your money. There is nothing wrong with this. However, it is also not unheard of that this is the last you see of your money and that sub. It is almost never an intentional fraud. People don't pose as subs to rip you off. It is just not unheard of and usually is associated with a sub's last few weeks in business. This is why you need to carefully screen your subs and look at their real cost. Let's say that the sub you selected is the low bidder, but wants a 50% down payment on their work. The next low bidder will accept payment after the work is complete. The difference in the two bids is called peace of mind. It is a consideration.

Nevertheless, do realize that a deposit is a normal way of doing business. It is fair and things will turn out right 98 times out of 100. If those odds are not good enough for you, go with a sub who will do the work with full payment upon completion. The bottom line of all this is to pay as agreed and agree on a schedule that does not pay in full until you are totally satisfied with the work.

There are two very wrong things you can do in paying subs. First is paying too much up front or paying too early (before the work is done.) The second thing is to pay too late or play games with the sub. Unfortunately, I have seen too many cases where customers, for whatever reason, do not want to pay as agreed. Sometimes they are afraid that they will not see something and get stuck. Sometimes they just don't want to take the time to inspect the work. You have to realize that many subs need this money to run their business. Your insecurities or laziness is more harmful than you think. Leaving the country for a week might be fun for you, but might result in a very angry sub camped out on your front porch when you get back home (I've seen this more than once).

How Can You Keep Them Happy and Why You Should

All subs want is to do their work and get on to the next job. They want to be treated as professionals and as human beings. As remarkable as this sounds, it is unfortunate that many people treat subs as though they were third-class citizens. They are in the business because they are good at what they do, they like the work and they make a decent living at it. They work with their hands and with their minds. Many people think that since their jobs are dirty and often very manual, they are not as smart "as you and I." This attitude towards subs shows through and can destroy a house.

The first thing a sub wants is a clean, safe and, if possible, warm place to work. You can have some impact on this by either insisting that all subs keep their workplace clean and safe or cleaning it up yourself. You might feel this is beneath you or someone else's job. If so, you can hire someone else to do this. However, the person who would do this kind of work will require a lot of supervision.

The next thing you can do is bring small things to your subs. Things like cake and cookies or hot chocolate in the winter, or cold drinks in the summer. Maybe something from work if you have a job that makes products with universal appeal. I once built a house for someone who managed a Red Lobster restaurant. He gave me a few $5 off coupons. I love seafood and you can be assured that I went the extra mile for this person.

Subs do not expect small gifts or kindness, so doing something nice will be well received. If it is food, try to come during their normal break times, as many subs do not like to be interrupted during their work. They often get into a "flow" and your gifts might have a detrimental effect. Subs, like everyone else, want to be treated fairly. If there is a problem, tell them immediately exactly what you feel is wrong. They will not catch all mistakes.[26]

How to Jinx a House—Bad Vibes, Voodoo and Witchcraft

I truly believe that a house can be jinxed. It starts with it getting behind schedule and events mushrooming. It's not mentally hard to get the jinx off, but it does take considerable effort. What happens to a jinxed house is that every sub that comes to it develops a bad attitude towards the house. Their work becomes sub-par. They don't clean up and you hear the phases, "good enough for government work." Even building inspectors get into the act and become prone to turn inspections down.

I didn't realize the strong historical culture of building until I got into building systems. There is little ceremony with production building. However, with historic antique heavy timber structures, they have a small ceremony when they get the roof on a building. They nail a small tree at the very peak of the rafters. You will see this especially with hand-crafted homes and those built by the Amish.

Another example of witchcraft and voodoo in housing is seen with modular houses. Modular houses are built of the same materials as a stick built house. Exactly the same. However, some people will not live in a factory built modular house. Simply will not do it. You can go over the house point by point, board for board and get nowhere. There is witchcraft loose in that house and they simply won't have it. While I can almost understand this for a customer, I've seen this attitude from professional people like building inspectors and bankers.

War Story

#26: I once was building a house that was a week from completion. One day the owner came up and told me that he saw a broken truss when they were delivered two months earlier. I asked him where it was and he said it was on the roof somewhere. Since the house was almost completed, I asked him why he didn't tell me earlier. He said he wanted to see if I would catch it. Of the many thousands of things that happen in the building of a house, I had not. I asked the carpenter if they had. Luckily, they said they did and fixed it the first day of framing. The point is that if you see something obviously wrong with your house, tell the builder immediately so that they can fix it. This incident fits under the category of not playing games with your subs. I wanted to tell the customer that he needed counseling and that I didn't appreciate his "game." I didn't, however, and, surprisingly, never had a problem from this guy again.

These very unscientific feelings and attitudes about building spill over into a house that has gotten into trouble. It reminds me of thinning the herd, of social Darwinism. If a house is visibly out of phase or out of control, people react to the building like it has a disease. If it has a particularly good beginning, it is blessed with good luck and a good attitude.[27]

The best way to keep a house from getting jinxed is to keep it in phase and clean as possible. Subs do not want to work in a messy house. On the outside, they also want clear and clean access to the house. Bales of straw in the winter mud will do wonders.

If something does go wrong with your house, you have to be doubly careful and not let others develop a bad attitude about working there. Even though the subs get paid by the hour or the job, they can develop a bad attitude towards your

War Story

#27: I have worked on at least two jinxed houses. Both houses cost the original superintendents their jobs. I took over the mess in each case and eventually "unjinxed" the houses and got them finished. Both were spec houses, which might explain why they became jinxed to begin with. Spec houses are prone to be "orphans." The first house was one where the trusses came in wrong. The house was supposed to have a cathedral ceiling, but came with a flat ceiling. It was already sheathed when the mistake was found. While a serious mistake, it was a reasonable one from the fired superintendent's point of view. In this case, he did not order the trusses and just missed the fact that they were wrong. My first exposure to the house was when I walked into it and saw one of our "not so good, Harley-driving" subs up in the trusses cutting out the bottom chord. I wasn't aware of the problem yet and about had a fit. This solution was approved (and engineered) earlier, but scared me to death. Normally, you would never cut a truss because each piece of the truss depends on the other pieces to make the truss work. Cutting any part causes the whole truss to fail.

The next thing I noticed was that, while the house was still in rough framing, it had been "stocked" with drywall. In addition, all the finish trim was there as were the appliances. The subs were using the drywall, trim and appliances for scaffolding. The other thing I noticed was the absolute filth in the house. Beer cans, the smell of urine, and cans and buckets full of things that I don't want to describe. Yes, this house was out of phase, out of control and truly jinxed.

The first thing I did was stop the framing crew and got them to help me to move the trim and the appliances out of the house into a nearby storage area. Next I told them to get their own scaffolding and stay off the drywall. I later had to move some of the drywall from the outside walls as it interfered with the insulating of the house.

While production building is often just sticking your head in the door of a house "under control," I stayed with this one until I got it "back in phase" and past the hanging of the drywall. Fortunately, subs after this phase had not heard of the house's previous problems and thus had a good attitude about the house when they came in. The jinx was released and the house finished up smoothly

The second jinxed house was built in the rain. It was a basement house that, every time it was dug, it rained, requiring the hole to be pumped out. It was just bad luck. However, the superintendent and the subs developed a bad attitude about the house. The result was the firing of a superintendent, a house six weeks behind schedule and a gray framing package. The gray framing package was especially disheartening. Wood, when it is new, is a bright yellowish white. Once it sits in the weather for awhile, it discolors and turns gray. While not a bad color for shingles, it is unexpected in framing lumber. Structurally, it is sound. Psychologically, it just looks bad. Guess when I finally got the jinx off of this house? After the gray frame was covered up with drywall.

house and not want to go back to it. They get especially upset if they have to work around someone's mistake. I've heard subs tell me dozens of time that they don't want to work at a particular house because of problems there. I usually get them back through special effort and personal involvement. It pays to keep a house out of trouble and if it gets in trouble, to get it back in phase as soon as possible. Otherwise, the jinx, with accompanying voodoo and witchcraft, will make your life miserable and cost you many times the norm.

How To Negotiate With Subs

Most negotiations are done at contract time. That period is often a discussion of terms and a matter of confidence in getting the job done. While price is an issue, you would be making a major mistake if price was your only criteria. You truly get what you pay for. Once a deal has been struck, you should be beyond negotiations.

If you need to negotiate again in the future, it will probably not be pleasant. The two most likely scenarios are a mistake was made and you have to get something else done or you've changed your mind. The first instance has to do with unforeseen circumstances. Something is clearly outside the scope of the contract or something just happened and needs to be fixed immediately. It very well could be that you told the sub to do something and it didn't work. You are unhappy and they are unhappy. You can let them correct the problem and worry about the details later or you can come to terms now. Guess what is the right answer? Don't leave anything for later. Ever.

You need to get a price and an understanding of what is being done for that price. Then you have to be sure that the price is fair. One good way to judge a fair price is to determine how long it will take and the hourly rate. If two men are going to work for two hours to fix something, it shouldn't be $400. That's $100 an hour per man. If you get that rate, remind the sub of the hourly rate and see if you can shame him into being more reasonable. Realize that subs just want to "get in and get out." They appreciate the work, probably really like you and possibly just love the wonderful design of your house. However, they want to do the job and move on. If extra work is now required, they are not going to be happy and will have a tendency to jack up the price to pay for their inconvenience.

If it truly is an unforeseen mistake or a misestimation, most subs will be reasonable about the extra work. Often, if you are nice about it, they won't charge at all. It is a different story if you are changing your mind. You have just crossed the line. No more Mr. Nice Guy. To put it nicely, subs hate for you to make changes. They just put their heart and soul into doing the best job they could for you and now you want it taken apart. Sure, they get paid for it, but it goes beyond being paid for it. Remember the tree they nailed to the rafters once the roof was completed? You are getting into their ritual, their Karma, if you change your mind or ask them to redo something. Things should be done one time and last forever. If you interfere with the "wholeness" of a house, you have destroyed the magic.

The first thing you hear after the groans is an outlandish price to do the work. Typically, it is three times as much, sometimes more. You paid for the work

Subs hate for you to make changes. They just put their heart and soul into doing the best job they could for you and now you want it taken apart.

initially. You will pay to take it apart. Then you will pay a third time to put it back together. Often the materials cannot be reused in the repair. These repairs often involve return trips from other tradesmen. They don't want to come back either. Time is lost, sometimes with a few day's layoff of the workers. They might start another job and have trouble getting back to yours. Here again, you will need to break the price back down into hours. Two men, three hours, $30 an hour per man plus materials. Even if some of the materials can be reused, most subs do not want to use "used" materials. You're in a pickle and need to realize that all your "people" skills need to be used to negotiate your way out of your "little changes."[28]

The bottom line of negotiating with subs is to maintain a good attitude, understand where they are coming from and don't make changes. If you think you are being overcharged, break the work done into hourly rates and negotiate from there. ■

War Story

#28: I was once working with a custom builder who was remodeling a house in Blowing Rock, North Carolina. It was a spectacular home originally built on a rock precipice in the 1920s. The remodel budget was over $900,000. The customer was filthy rich and, as is common with wealthy people, wanted what they wanted and were going to have it. The builder had problems with the customer making up their mind and doing proper planning. The house had two major cost overruns, neither of which were mistakes on the part of the builder. The first was the tile in the master bath. The original "new" tile was hand-painted Mexican tile that cost more than $5 a tile. The customer traveled the globe and came to the house occasionally. Their last visit witnessed the completion of the bath tile. While exactly what they selected, they didn't like it and wanted it replaced. When I came to the house, I saw this very beautiful tile thrown in a heap in the corner. It could not be salvaged. Imagine that you are a worker bee on a building crew. Your net hourly wage might be equal to each of those tiles. Do you think your attitude towards that house and the owners might change after they seeing that kind of waste? The customer could afford it but, the workers only saw arrogance and waste.

The same thing happened to the fireplace, which had a stone face. I noticed that it had an inner and outer layer. I asked the builder why he was covering up such beautiful (and expensive) stonework. He told me that the owner didn't like the original work so he was covering it up with a new veneer. I asked him what the stone mason thought about that since I knew that they took great pride in their work. He said the first mason quit rather than cover up his "work of art." The second mason was from outside the county because no one from that county would cover up another mason's work.

The builder eventually got "thrown off" the job because of cost overruns. He was a very good builder.

25

Exactly How Much Justice Can You Afford?

What Does a Three-Bedroom House Cost?

This is probably the most maddening question a builder ever gets. It is not only a trick question but could have answers hundreds of thousands of dollars apart. It is maddening on the part of the home buyer because they too want an answer to make sure they can afford to buy or build a new house. The short answer is that "it depends on what you want." Often builders put it in relationship to automobiles. You can have a Geo or a Mercedes. How much car (house) do you want? Most people then break it down into square footage cost, thinking they have solved the mystery of cost. The short answer, again, is, "Do you buy your cars by the pound?"

Many builders have given up and throw out square footage prices. One of two things will happen. Either you will be offended by the high price given or you will be lied to. Most people do not really want to know the truth because they think it is too high and thus will strike that builder off their list. They usually wind up with a builder who tells them what they want to hear. In the end, they will build the house closer to what the truthful builder told them than the one who lied to them.

This does not necessarily mean that all builders are liars. In fact, most are exceptionally honest. The problem is that most customers do not want to pay what houses really cost and therefore are often tricked into a contract they do not understand.

They are fixated by square footage price and totally miss the rest of the house. The obvious question is, "What is included in that square footage price?" Great question. Seldom asked. Each builder will give you a different answer because each one includes different things in their square footage price. Chances are that they will tell you verbally or in a contract, what is included. As I mentioned, they are rarely dishonest. The problem is "not in your stars, but in you, dear Brutus." Most people don't understand or don't ask. They want to hear a low square footage price and hope for the best.

This game is as old as the hills. Builders who don't play it have trouble getting business. Customers who don't play it don't get their projects built. The trick is to not be the first person to give an honest answer. That guy usually never sees the customer again, even if the customer eventually figures out that the builder's answer was correct. Most builders do not get caught because they leave a good paper trail. When the true cost of building raises its ugly head, they can (and have to) prove to you that they told the truth. You didn't ask the right question or didn't ask the question in the right way. The builder will either refresh your memory of a previous conversation or show you in the contract exactly what you were purchasing.

So how do you get to the truth? First, you have to be willing to seek it. You'd be surprised the number of people who build with no end in sight. While this is common, the bank does a pretty good job of keeping them in check. They cannot get too far off course if a bank is involved. The correct answer is buried somewhere in all that paperwork. One of the problems is that the loan does not cover everything. It is based on things that are easy to count. Things like fixed bids on licensed work like plumbing and wiring. These items rarely change from the original bid. You might get up to the full 80 percent of the supposed cost of your house totally under fixed bid. Pretty safe bet. The other 20 percent might not be 20 at all, because most of it is not a fixed bid. Another way you can get off track is through changes, allowances and mistakes. While banks are irritating to work with and often slow you down, they can help keep you on your budget.

Where people are unwilling to seek the truth, they find themselves short at the end. This is why landscapers have a hard time keeping contracts on new construction. It is usually at landscaping time that the customer is out of money. The main reason houses get landscaped at all is because the landscaping is usually part of the loan and has to be installed before the loan can be converted into a permanent mortgage. At best, landscaping plans are sharply scaled back to the minimal level acceptable to the bank and nowhere near the initial contract.

If you are willing to seek the truth, you must next be willing to do some work.

Entering the project in search of short, pat answers is perilous. If you tricked or cajoled a builder into a square footage answer, you must next see what is included in that bid. This requires work. My experience is that most people do not care to do this work or get so confused that they give up. While the bank often does most of this work for them, there are areas that the bank cannot unsurface. The hard parts are often left out of the loan. They come out of your pocket. Hopefully, you still have pockets left when the project is over.

The best way to get to the right answer is to compare apples to apples. This simple marketing technique is a favorite of builders who know enough about their market and competition to give them a leg up. You, however, have to be willing to not only listen, but also commit the mental energy to understand what you are getting. While a number of techniques would work, I would suggest that you compare contracts and bids side-by-side. What you will find is that they are not selling you the same goods. Items will either not be there or their quality level will be quite different. Some phases might have components included and some might not. Often allowances are made, as in the case of lighting and plumbing fixtures. Since you can pay $20 or $2,000 for one light fixture, you can start to see why the bids are all over the place.

Another aspect of the work involved has to do with specifications. The real cost difference of one house to another is not square footage but specifications. The number of the parts and the quality of the parts. You have to understand every single part in your house and that will take a lot of effort. One major decision you will make with your house is the brand of your windows. You will have about 50 choices of manufacturers that will range from "X" to five times *X*. This could translate into thousands of dollars of difference in the cost of your house. You will find this same difference in the cabinets, floor coverings, siding material, roofing, plumbing and lighting fixtures. This also explains why it is so hard to give an answer to the question, "How much does a three-bedroom house cost?"

Nevertheless, you can still get an answer to this question. You just can't get it at a party or a ballgame in casual conversation. The real answer can be arrived only after a few events and factors are reviewed. First, you need a complete set of plans. These plans are the ones you intend to build off of and not something you are planning to change. Second, you need to already have land and know where the house will go on that land. Third, you should have already made your specification selections on the components where you have choices, like windows, fixtures, flooring, etc. With this information and work out of the way, you can get your answer. With caveats.

Caveats. The savior of most builders. These are the things that are not known or are purposefully left out. A common item left out is called "site conditions." Site conditions include the suitability of the land and encompasses the slope of the land, the ability of the land to support your house and whether there is rock that has to be removed to build your house. Site conditions can cost you next to nothing on a very flat lot to over $100,000 (as was the case earlier on a lot in San Francisco).

Some builders will present very light allowances or leave them out entirely. This helps their "cost per square foot" price, but can give them an unfair advantage if you are not paying attention. Permit cost and other fees might be left out. While these fees are usually under $500 in many areas, they can be thousands of dollars in metropolitan areas. Engineering costs can also be left out of a bid because they are site and house plan specific. However, these fees can also be several thousand dollars. Some builders might include site requirements, like wind and earthquake loads, but leave out structural loads. Others might leave it all out, making it hard to compare apples to apples.

The bottom line of determining the price of a house is that you have to do a considerable amount of work before you can arrive at a solid number. You can play (and be tricked by) the game or you can approach the project maturely and with earnest. You can find an answer, but it won't be as the result of one question.

The bottom line of determining the price of a house is that you have to do a considerable amount of work before you can arrive at a solid number.

The Cadillac of Houses Should Match

In pricing a house, you should try to keep the components at the same quality level. If you have chosen the "Cadillac" of windows, the carpet and the cabinets should be at a similar level. If you get too many components out of whack, the total value will not be what you want. For example, let's say you're building a modest house, but want to put on a heavy tile roof. Everything else in the house is average. What will happen is that you will not get full credit for the more expensive roof. While there is nothing wrong in indulging yourself in certain areas, do not expect that one component's higher level will bring up the rest of the house. It won't. Determining the value of a house is an art requiring many subtle distinctions. The most important aspect of the value of your house is, as the realtors say, "Location, location, location."[29]

If you have chosen the "Cadillac" of windows, the carpet and the cabinets should be at a similar level. If you get too many components out of whack, the total value will not be what you want.

Why Do Houses Cost So Much?

I'd like to say government interference, but I would only be half right. This is because the government is only a reflection of what people want. While the government can get away with all kinds of evil, it is really doing what the people want. If most people wanted less government, they would get it. It is a democracy and occasionally you do see it working. It is not easy, but it is possible. However, people also want their cake and eat it too. Much of the rising cost of housing has to do with meeting government requirements in manufacturing and assembly. These requirements, though, are rooted mostly in safety issues and protecting the environment. You can go to Third World countries to see lower cost housing, but will also see hazardous waste dumps, unsafe building products and dangerous work practices. There are no free lunches.

Insurance has had a major impact on the cost of housing in the past 20 years. Construction is one of the most dangerous livelihoods today. In the old days, if a worker was hurt or killed on the job, that was too bad. The guys passed the hat and got on with their day. Insurance has changed all that. While a constant cry, I don't believe many people would want to return to the bad old days.

War Story

#29: I lived in the nicer part of Charlotte off of Carmel Road, where mansion after mansion was built in exclusive neighborhoods. However, my house and neighborhood was modest in comparison. My thought in buying there was that my house's value would go up with the neighborhoods around me. Directly across the street was a neighborhood whose homes were valued at $20 more per square foot. My house, however, remained at the lower level because it would not get credit for the higher values across the street. My value was based on only the houses in my neighborhood. My value was fixed by neighborhood (and my builder's specs) and not by square footage of houses surrounding me. No breaks for proximity, just like no breaks for getting some components into the luxury league when the predominance of the house is in the modest league.

I do not believe people in the industry are getting any richer than in days gone by. Housing is still a cottage industry and builders go bust every day. So do manufacturers. The main difference is that the environment is protected, workers have a safer workplace and the materials used in housing are healthier, more durable and protect your investment. The thrust of product innovation in housing is to increase quality while reducing costs. New products do both, but the cost overall continues to creep upwards.

Another aspect of housing cost is what is minimally acceptable to a customer now was a luxury 30 years ago. The automobile analogy works well here, since the cost of a car is much more now. However, cars now have air bags, automatic everything and increased fuel economy. Houses now have better insulation and windows, not to mention an average of two-and-a-half baths and designer kitchens. Comparing a 1950 three-bedroom, one-bath ranch to a 1998 typical starter house doesn't look bad in constant dollars and apples for apples. Add in the cost of safety and inflation and you are not far apart. Houses cost more because you get a lot more house. Safer, better equipped, larger and built on increasingly scarcer land. Speaking of land, do not leave that factor out. Land costs are a matter of supply and demand and the good land was bought by your parents and grandparents who didn't care or know about the effect of their homes on the environment. ■

Notes and Sketches

26

Where To Spend, Where To Cut (and Spend Later)

What's Important To You?

Compromise is the essence of building. While there is no such thing as a perfect house, there is also no such thing as an unlimited budget. One common aspect of homes from shacks to mansions is an upper limit on what is spent. It often doesn't mean that you do not have the money to spend but rather that you don't want to put too much money into a house. On the other hand, you want what you want. The reason you are building this house is because you want certain things in it. Since your budget is limited and you have certain needs to satisfy, you must decide where best to spend the money you have available for the house.

Obviously, you would never try to cut short the cost of a solid, structurally sound foundation. A savings you might want to explore though, is the cost of the veneer of the foundation. Veneers range from nothing (uncovered block) to stone. In between is painted block, stucco and brick. Whatever you choose, it is forever. You will not be coming back to this unless it is uncovered block that can be painted or stuccoed later. If you choose to stucco later, you should realize that stucco has a depth to it (about ¼") and this might create a problem when matching up to the siding.

The next thing to consider is the structural soundness of the house framing. Most homes are built to meet minimum code. This will satisfy most needs, but you can stiffen up the floor of a particular room if you know of a load problem. This is also something that you cannot easily do later. An example would be to add a few floor joists in a room with a heavy china cabinet, pool table or waterbed. While current code might carry the weight of these items adequately, you might be more satisfied with a stiffer floor. This need is seen in a dining room where the china cabinet rattles every time you walk through because of minimal stiffness in the floor.

Another part of the structure that cannot be changed later is the steepness of the roof. You will probably get pressure to lower the roof pitch if you get into budget problems. It is not the end of the world to reduce a roof pitch and there are some savings to be had (hundreds to a few thousand dollars depending on the size and design of the house). Here again is where your tastes play a role. A lower roof pitch is the first sign of a cheap house, however. It cannot be fixed later. You can also assign a cost to this change. You need to get to that exact cost before you give up on a steep roof. The costs will be in more materials and labor, especially roofing labor, which, while based on square feet of roofing material, is also based on the steepness of the roof.

A drastic cut in the house that can be fixed later is in the size and number of rooms. You can always leave a room off and build it later. If you have a cape cod or basement house, you can leave part of the house unfinished until later. You can create a design that will accommodate a room addition later, such as a family room. If your house has a garage, you can increase the roof pitch to allow for usable space in the garage attic in the future. The key is to plan for this expansion while building the house. Have the plumbing, HVAC and wiring "roughed in" for future rooms or additions. This is especially critical in a basement where the floor is concrete. Rough plumbing for a future bath is relatively inexpensive now rather than having to break up the slab later. If you know that you are going to go through a wall to add a room, reroute the wiring so that it does not have to be spliced later. Let the HVAC company know about future expansions so that they can size their unit and stub out for supply lines and a return. Many of these changes will have little or no cost now.

A large expense in most houses is the windows. Selecting the brand of windows is a major decision. The window industry is well developed with many excellent brands and superbly trained salesmen. Ranges in price are extraordinary, although many brands track together. Window quality does range between brands and especially from one level of window to another. The decision on which level of window to use is more important than which brand.[30]

This war story illustrates that you need to be very careful with the windows you select. It is not an area that you should plan to upgrade when you become

War Story

#30: I once was associated with a $500,000 house that had numerous problems. While the owner had $500,000 to spend on the house, it was a disaster in many respects. Visually it was a stunning house. Most of the components were first class. However, while they were selecting windows, they felt that the bids for exceptional windows were too high. They decided to go with lumberyard supplied wood windows. They probably saved $10,000 buying windows that belonged in a house that cost six times less. The problem was best seen during the first winter. The windows, though double paned, were so sloppily assembled that the air that leaked through could put out a candle. The house was freezing and the energy bills were out of sight. The house was already built when I arrived on the scene, but I had to help remedy the problem. My first suggestion was to get storm windows. The price of these almost exceeded the price of the original windows (but their combined price was more than a decent branded window that would have done the trick). The owner rejected the storm window solution and was looking for others. We used a combination of a plastic film that was heat stretched over the inside of the window frame and a rope caulk. This helped some, but looked horrible. Again, more appropriate for a house that cost six times less.

rich and famous. While you do not need to get designer windows, you do need to pay attention to the window salesmen and listen for common features. Once educated, go for the best deal with the appropriate features. While windows are highlighted here, this also applies to doors. However, doors usually are pretty good across the line insulation wise, with the major difference dealing with quality of materials and finish. Your doors are going to be fine relative to function. Appearance is another issue, which becomes a matter of personal taste.

Another area that is hard to fix later is insulation, especially in the side walls. Most houses are built to minimum code, but you can exceed that with a reasonable expectation of pay back. Some insulation companies can show you the relative cost/benefit ratio of insulation. If they cannot, check with your local power company. If you are planning to beef up the insulation, you might have to change the framing to accept the thicker insulation. It is a decision that has to be made prior to building. The only insulation decision that can wait for later is in the ceiling, provided you are using a blown or loose insulation in an attic that can be easily accessed.

Most everything else in your home is going to wear out at some time in the future. Obviously, the better quality items will last longer, but they too will wear out. Here you have to decide what is important to you. Many items are also not going to wear out anytime soon, but might go out of fashion. The most obvious example of this is the kitchen appliances that came in harvest gold, avocado and bronze colors during the 1960s and '70s. These very much date a house, but many of these appliances still work fine. If you are selecting colors or finishes for your house, be careful to not get too far out on the fashion ledge.

The strongest, longest lasting components of your house are the foundation and the structural framing system. The foundation can last from 75 to 300 years if it is sitting on solid ground to begin with.

What's Going to Wear Out First (After Your Wallet)

Some parts of your house will probably never wear out under normal conditions. At least not in your lifetime. Everything will wear out eventually. The strongest, longest lasting components of your house are the foundation and the structural framing system. The foundation can last from 75 to 300 years if it is sitting on solid ground to begin with. The frame can last 50 to 150 years if it can be protected from rot, mildew, insects and decay. If not, these normally long-lasting parts of your house can fail within one to 10 years, especially if there was a structural problem to begin with.

For example, if your footings are improperly installed or on unengineered fill, you will see the problem well within the first year. Insects can get into your house in tropical areas within the five years if not protected. Rot and mildew can destroy your house in the same period. All of these problems, however, are rare and not usually subject to wear out.

The first thing most likely to wear out in your new home will be the paint. Obviously, the interior paint will get chipped, scratched and dirty first. The exterior paint will start to wear out sometime within the first two to five years. This problem can be lessened somewhat by the grade and type of paint you use initially. There will be a direct relationship to the cost of paint and how long it lasts. Whether you choose to buy a less costly paint initially to save money should be tempered with your feelings about repainting in the future. Choosing a less costly paint is not necessarily a bad decision since you are going to have to repaint at some time in the future anyway. No paint or stain lasts forever. However, the savings in using a lower cost paint or stain is relatively small.

The next thing to wear out will be the carpet. Actual wear on the carpet will affect how long it lasts. Lots of foot traffic means lots of wear. Quality level of the carpet will have some effect on how well carpet lasts relative to wear. Wear can start to show in the first few years in the life of carpet. Carpet, however, can last for 10 or more years, depending on the initial quality and the amount of wear. Carpet can also go out of style as seen with the shag carpet of the 1960s. Berber carpet is in style now but can go out in the future. When selecting carpet, you might want to see the trend in carpet and ask the salesperson if something is a fad or has been around awhile and looks like it will remain in style.

Carpet is an area you can save some money on if your budget is tight. It is an item that costs in the several thousand dollar range, with a range in quality of one to six times ($10 to $60 a yard).

Carpet is an area you can save some money on if your budget is tight. It is an item that costs in the several thousand dollar range, with a range in quality of one to six times ($10 to $60 a yard). A typical room would cost from several hundred to over a $1,000. A consideration is to go less expensive in rooms with little use, i.e., bedrooms and look for a long wearing carpet in rooms with a lot of use. Of particular interest would be a room with a normal foot traffic pattern. The pattern will start showing up in the first year. A way to avoid this is to use another type of flooring in high traffic areas, i.e., entryways and hallways. The worse case I've seen is homes with the front door opening into a large carpeted room with no foyer. The 3x3 square feet of carpet at the door wears out almost immediately and ruins the entire piece of carpet.

The next thing to wear out is the resilient, also known as vinyl or linoleum. This is usually used in kitchens, baths, utility rooms, foyers and hallways. It is great stuff and is quite durable. It has a fairly tight price range (one to three times) and should last at least five years if properly cared for. However, since it is vinyl, it is subject to damage, most commonly cuts and tears. The finish also is prone to wear off after many cleanings, giving it a dull look. It too is expensive, often three times more than carpet. Vinyl is typically sold by the square foot while carpet is sold by the yard. Still, it is an area to save money if you think you might want to change it in the next five years. A typical kitchen's floor might be a $1,000, but you could spend twice that according to the grade you choose initially.

Door locks, especially interior door locks, will wear out in five to 10 years, depending on the initial quality. The savings between brands and quality levels could be in the several hundred dollar range. Again, this is an area to save now and deal with later. A suitable front door lock could cost less than $20 or be well over $200. Somewhere in the middle is a suitable door lock, even though the higher priced one might be more appealing. Chances are that the higher priced models are no better mechanically than a modestly priced lock. The difference in price is usually in the material it is made of, typically solid brass.

Appliances will start to wear out in about 8–15 years. While the price of appliances can be one to four times, the durability is about the same. The price difference has more to do with features than durability. Even so, you might find some durability improvement in twice the cost, but certainly not four times the cost. Realize, too, that there are a lot fewer manufacturers of appliances than there are brands. Some brands are identical to others, sharing the same manufacturer. Salespeople will know the difference. Watch for fads in appliances, especially in colors. Dishwashers today typically have a variety of interchangeable and reversible front panels to address the fad color changes.

Roofing can range greatly in price, although the vast majority of roofs are asphalt/fiberglass and not the more expensive roofs, such as cedar shake, tile, slate and metal. These more expensive roofs will certainly last longer, but need to be in line with the cost of the rest of the house. As mentioned before, quality levels should match throughout the house. An exception to this is found in Florida, California and the Southwest where tile roofs are common on modestly priced houses. This is because the sun is brutal on asphalt/fiberglass roofs and the more expensive tile roofs are actually a more economical choice because of wear.

Areas that you should not try to save money on include windows, doors, cabinets and trim. These items need to track with the other parts of the home, but you should be able to find a quality, modestly priced window, door, etc., to meet your needs. Do not go with the least costly window just to save money. You will regret it the entire time. Make up the extra cost by going down in grade in the carpet, vinyl, paint or siding.

Careful shopping, especially on key items like windows, doors, cabinets and flooring, will give you an education on the various aspects that are important to the components of your home. You will eventually hear the same features to look for. Once you are comfortable with the features and have found some common ground among the choices, look for price advantages with the same features.

While careful shopping and tradeoffs will help get your home back into your budget, the overall design of the home is still a key figure in costs. While you might not have used a professional designer or architect in developing your house plan, you can still use one to help you out of budget trouble. Ask them for an overall review, explaining that you need to cut the plan to meet your budget. A pinch here and a tuck there can save thousands while costing only a few hundred. Beyond the savings, you will have a better designed, less costly house that will still meet your needs. ■

Do not go with the least costly window just to save money. You will regret it the entire time. Make up the extra cost by going down in grade in the carpet, vinyl, paint or siding.

27

What Are The Choices?

A Shopper's Paradise

Another title for this chapter is "specifications." Specifications is the word used to determine exactly what is going into your home. It deals with items from how thick the footings are to how far apart the studs are to the color and model number of your stove. Every house has specifications for every component. As a homeowner, you are supposed to select every single component in your home by its specification. There are literally hundreds of choices within a range of thousands of available possibilities. Specifications are the most important part of determining the final cost of your home and can have a far greater affect on the price of your home than its' simple square footage.

Specification selection can be the most enjoyable part of building your house or the most frustrating. You can get terribly confused and consumed with the time it takes to select from so many choices. You can (and will) make bad choices. You certainly can blow your budget with the choices you make. You can also be assured that if you don't make the selections, someone else will. Since it is time consuming and confusing, many builders will make most of the choices for you, leaving you with color and model selections from a reduced list of options.

Many choices will be made for you without your knowledge of alternate choices. The reason is that builders, suppliers and tradesmen are either unfamiliar with all the choices or just don't want to waste their time showing you the many hundreds of options within one aspect of a house.

Some suggestions of the choices available to you in determining the specifications for your home are listed on the following page. This list is not all inclusive, but most likely will show you more options than you will be presented with by the trades. Some of these suggestions will not be available to you for a variety of reasons. The lack of these choices should not be considered as the makings of a bad house, but more due to limited availability of products or trained local tradesmen. This list is made in order of how houses are put together and what is done first and then next.

In This Chapter . . .

▲ Who determines the quality level of your house?

▲ Who can help you?

▲ Who will spec your house if you don't?

Specifications are the most important part of determining the final cost of your home and can have a far greater affect on the price of your home than its' simple square footage.

1. **Footings** — Build to code.

2. **Foundation** — Block or poured wall, build to code.

3. **Veneer** — Painted or stuccoed block, brick, stone. Veneer can stop at framing or cover entire building; another choice is to cover only the front of the house. In the case of brick and stone, you will have a number of color and masonry style choices.

4. **Framing** — Build to code or exceed code in a number of areas, i.e., more sturdy floors to accommodate heavy furniture or extra insulation. Also the use of trusses to save money or, in the case of floor trusses, to give a flat ceiling in the basement. You can also specify that floor decking be "screwed and glued" rather than nailed to reduce squeaks. Thicker plywood can also be requested for a more sturdy floor.

5. **Mechanicals (HVAC, Electrical and Plumbing)** — Here the choices are endless. Self education is helpful, but can be confusing. You must build to code. Considerations would be a larger than normal panel box, a larger or two separate water heaters, dual zone heat/AC systems, special fixtures in both plumbing and wiring, i.e., a super hot water tap for instant coffee/tea, spotlights or light sensors. You will most likely get lots of help in these areas since there are so many choices, plus these trades are better than average in presenting these choices.

6. **Millwork** — Lots of choices for windows and doors. Professional salesmen are helpful but can be confusing. I would recommend you look at a wood, vinyl clad window by a major manufacturer and compare various brands from there. You should consider the various choices of doors, including solid wood, insulated steel and fiberglass/hybrid. You usually cannot go wrong with a middle of the road choice here.

7. **Insulation** — To minimum code. However, consider the cost ratio of extra insulation. If you plan to be in the house for awhile, you should consider boosting it to the next level. Consider also insulating around baths for soundproofing.

8. **Drywall** — Consider screwing the drywall rather than nailing; which will reduce nail pops and other problems. Nailing is normal, screwing will cost a little more.

9. **Drywall ceiling finish** — Choices typically are: (A) Blown or "popcorn" finish; (B) A textured finish, usually in a swirl pattern; and (C) Smooth finish. I would suggest a blown or textured finished because it is so difficult to get a smooth finish right. There are inconsistencies in drywall that are quite obvious in a smooth finish. The other finishes hide these normal problems easier. Many installers charge extra for a smooth finish because it is so hard to get it right.

10. **Interior paint** — Flat latex on walls, semi-gloss latex on trim. Discuss with your supplier or painter the various grade levels. Labor should be the same regardless of the grade of paint. Oil base will cost considerably more, if at all available. Not a good choice. Suppliers and painters will tell you the details.

11. **Interior trim** — Moldings can be "finger jointed" if painted, should be solid if stained. Colonial baseboard and door casing is by far the most common, but should match the design and style of the house and doors. Baseboard should be taller than average if ceilings are taller than eight feet. You are not going to get a lot of help in selecting trim as it is usually not sold through a trained sales force. Your trim carpenter will have some ideas, although an architect will be the expert here. Specialty trim such as railings, balusters, oak treads and stair parts and shelving are typically pre-manufactured in "kits." These usually are quite acceptable and often far superior to what could be produced locally or on the job.

12. **Interior doors** — Personal taste will rule here, with choices from hollow core to solid wood doors. Hollow doors are usually adequate for a modest or low budget. A quality giveaway is the number of hinges. Better quality interior doors have three hinges rather than two.

13. **Cabinets and vanities** — Solid wood doors are a good choice, although sides made of vinyl coated pressed or hard board might be acceptable in most modest homes. Usually vanities are a grade lower than the kitchen cabinets. Quality giveaways are hinges and door glides. There are plenty of choices and trained salespeople to show you the many differences. Concentrate on hardware more than wood and finishes.

14. **Fixtures** — (A) **Plumbing:** Again, you have hundreds of choices, almost all of which should be satisfactory. Check on tub stoppers as there are a lot of choices and some work better than others. Installing outside faucets (called hose bibs) are relatively inexpensive and should be located in strategic places. Two is a typical number of hose bibs. Low flush, energy saver toilets are a good choice. Toilets can range in price from under $100 to over $500. There is little to no difference in function.

    (B) **Electrical:** Hundreds of choices. Like hose bibs, consider outside receptacles. One at each exit is normal. However, most garages only have one receptacle. If you have a wood shop, consider more outlets there. Consider also extra outlets in the kitchen or a specialty room for appliances, hobbies and computers. Remember also to pre-wire for phones. Consider wiring for a security system, stereo, cable TV, phones, computers and intercom.

15. **Flooring** — Consider durable flooring in high-traffic areas, hardwood in rooms you want to show off, i.e., a foyer or formal dining room and carpet elsewhere. Vinyl in kitchens and baths are normal. Hardwood in foyers and halls are typical. Carpet and vinyl sales people will be very knowledgeable about their product and will be quite helpful.

Remember the Architect's Skills and Taste

A helpful ally in determining specifications is an architect. Specifications or, more accurately, specifying jobs (houses, commercials structures, restaurants, etc.) is a big part of their job. Determining the specifications of a home can be part of the entire project or, as is sometimes the case, left for the owner to decide. The architect provides at least two services in specifying a job. First, they are very knowledgeable about what is available in the market. Architects maintain extensive libraries and catalogs of building products. A major catalog is *Sweets,* which has as many pages and volumes as many encyclopedias. The second thing architects provide is the knowledge to get the components in the right scale and within the correct architectural style. Their sense of proportion and knowledge of appropriate periods of architecture is vitally important to a home. It could be something as simple as the baseboard moldings. As mentioned before, these need to be sized relative to not only the ceiling height but also speced to match the other moldings, doors and bi-folds in the house.

War Stories

#31: When I started in housing in 1982, it was at the bottom of an industry disaster. Interest rates were just coming down from about 20 percent. I joined a national production builder who specialized in entry-level housing. They knew every trick in the trade. Their credo was a dollar saved was actually $4,000 saved, because that was their volume nationwide. To meet the demand for affordable housing in a period of unreasonable interest rates, they "down speced" their houses. They reduced overhangs, eliminating them entirely on the gables. They reverted to eight-foot wide gravel driveways. Foundations were all slab, with exposed block painted to match the siding. However, one thing they did not take out was a wood, vinyl clad sliding door. Aluminum doors were plentiful and about $200 cheaper. I asked my boss what the deal was. He said that before they switched to these doors several years earlier, it was their number one customer complaint. The aluminum doors leaked, came off track and were generally a real problem. From a marketing point of view, a wooden sliding door was a definite step up from an apartment. Since many of our customers were stepping up from apartments (which typically had aluminum sliding doors), this wooden door represented a real house. The doors would remain.

#32: While my first company had the right idea on the wooden sliding door, it took a while longer to get smarter on its bi-fold doors. Their spec was a metal bi-fold, with every house having several. The problem was multifaceted. First was that the door was prone to denting. We replaced an average of one door per house because it got dented before the house was turned over to the customer. The second problem was that the hardware of the door kept slipping, causing the door to drag on the track. This required constant adjusting, which was difficult to do because of the location of the adjusting device and the small size of the closets. We complained enough to the company that they eventually switched brands with supposedly better hardware. We found that the adjusting device was better. However, one day a door fell off its hinges as it was being opened. The doors bent like butter. The tradeoff was a slightly better adjusting device but a much thinner gauge door. The factory sent out their rep to defend their door. He was almost killed. Superintendents hated to adjust or replace bi-fold doors for a variety of reasons, including the awkwardness of the door. No improvements were forthcoming and, with a number of superintendents threatening to quit, the door was eventually replaced with a better door. The new door worked fine, even though it cost about $10 more. It was well worth it.

If you are not using an architect in your project, you might find it difficult to find one to help you with specifications. You will have to check with several to find if they will do the work and what they will charge. Among the items you might want them to become involved in is the cabinet and vanity selection, the baseboards and door and window casings, the stair parts, and possibly the outside trim and decorative moldings. These items should be easy for them to determine. Proper selection of these parts can make a significant difference in the appearance of your home and add greatly to its perceived value at very little expense. Proper selection of components could also pay for the design service entirely, especially if the components selected costs less than you would have chosen without their help.

You Get What You Pay For

Nowhere is this statement truer than in housing. The ultimate quest in housing is for a more affordable house. It is elusive. Savings and innovation hold back the floodgates. You can have lower cost housing, but compromises in quality or quantity will have to be made. You can shop wiser and reduce the cost upfront or long-term. You can find a commodity that is cheaper "on the vine." However, if any service, like a warranty or intelligent answers to question about the product, is needed, the lower price goes out the window.[31]

The point is that some items are not worth going cheap on. If it costs less, it probably has a problem that you don't see. This doesn't mean that you should buy the most expensive components on the market. Rather, it means that you should understand why it costs less and what compromises were made. Sometimes the change is a product improvement. Sometimes it is a serious mistake that someone who speced it at the factory doesn't know what they are doing.[32]

The point of my war stories is to realize that you get what you pay for. You must discover the reasons for the lower costs and determine if you can live with them. Every price is justified, whether through design, craftsmanship, materials or warranty. You will be the one who determines which of these elements are important to you and pay the appropriate price. There are no free lunches. ■

Every price is justified, whether through design, craftsmanship, materials or warranty. You will be the one who determines which of these elements are important to you and pay the appropriate price. There are no free lunches.

Notes and Sketches

28

Remember That Math You Forgot About in High School? It's Back!

Finally, After All Those Years, You've Found a Use For Geometry

It's been said that all every crew needs is one smart guy. Everyone else is a worker bee. That one smart guy needs to know the math of construction. Math is a part of most jobs in construction. It is used for estimating materials and to determine that things are used correctly. Some of the math can be used to cover a number of different phases. Most of the formulas are quite simple yet incorporate algebraic, geometric and trigonometric calculations. The following is a chart of phases and formulas most commonly used in calculating materials.

PHASE	FORMULA
Footing material	Length x Width x Depth ÷ 27 = Yards
Concrete in a slab or wall	Same as above
Block	Length x number of rows (courses) ÷ 1.33
Roofing	$a^2 + b^2 = c^2$
Siding, sheet rock, sheathing, etc.	Length x height ÷ coverage of material

> **In This Chapter . . .**
>
> ▲ The formulas you need to estimate materials
>
> ▲ Where to find the numbers you need
>
> ▲ What the formulas are used for

Another aspect of building is to get the structure plumb, level and square. Plumb and square is determined through the use of a level. Plumb measures vertically, level measures horizontally. Usually a four-foot level is used to determined plumb and level, although a dumpy level or transit can be used to determine level as well. Determining if a structure is square is determined mathematically using the "$a^2 + b^2 = c^2$" formula. In any square or rectangle, either horizontal (a slab or deck) or vertical (a wall), the diagonal measure of the structure will determine if the structure is square. No math is required if it is in square because the diagonal measurement from one side to the other is identical. If both are the same, the structure is square. However, using the formula, you can determine the exact measurement before "pulling the diagonals," which means to measure the building. Diagonal measures are typically provided on the foundation plan so that calculations need not be made in the field.

Simple Stuff, Using a Scale or a Tape Measure

The numbers you need to estimate materials are located on the plans. Sometimes the plans give you the actual numbers you need, as in the case of the size of a foundation plan. Here the actual diagonal numbers are spelled out. Other times you might need to look at a number of pages to find the information. For example, to determine the thickness of footings, you most likely will see this information on a section that shows a slice of the building from the footing to the roof. This information might also be on a separate foundation detail sheet or written on the footing or foundation page. Many times standard details will be given that state that the thickness of the footing needs to be confirmed by local codes and soil conditions. Wherever found, this information is vital to not only estimating materials, but also to properly construct the building.

Other times, you have to scale off the plans, as in the case of determining roofing. You can use an architect's scale or simply a tape measure. This works well if the plans are drawn at quarter-inch scale since a tape measure has quarter-inch "hash" marks on it.

While details within the plan might show the builder exactly what they need, they often use their tape measure to do estimating rather than hunt down the correct page.

While details within the plan might show the builder exactly what they need, they often use their tape measure to do estimating rather than hunt down the correct page. They might also double check the data provided in a detail or section because sometimes draftsmen make mistakes. The builder is ultimately responsible for shortages or overages due to faulty calculations. While they might want to go back to the draftsman, its better to double check first than to sort out "who shot John" while the job is stopped because of a shortage. We'll look at examples that use these basic formulas in the next chapter. ■

29

Simple Trig, Yards and Squares

Cementing With Square Yards

We will use the house we designed in Chapter 8 as an example of these formulas. One of the first calculations you make for a house is the amount of concrete you need to use in the footings. Concrete is purchased by the square yard. The formula is: Length x Width x Depth ÷ 27. In the case of our sample house, we know that the main building is 40'x28'. We also know that an adequate footing for a two-story building is 8" thick and 16" wide. These figures are dictated by code, but are most likely also shown on the plans.

To use the formulas, you must first convert all the numbers to feet. For example, 8" is also .66' (8÷12). Sixteen inches is 1.33' (16÷12). The building has a perimeter or length of 136' (40+40+28+28). The formula is: Length (136) x Width (1.33) x Depth (.66) ÷ 27. The answer is 4.4 yards.

There is one more element to the equation that is not evident yet, but would be with a complete set of foundation plans. That is the piers necessary to carry the main girder of the house. These piers are typically 8" thick by 2' square. While these figures are fairly precise, concrete is not exactly rocket science and materials are rounded up to usually within ¼ or ½ a yard. This building is designed to have seven piers. The number of piers is determined by local building codes and the weight being carried by the floor system. Therefore, one state might require the piers to be closer together than another state.

The math calculation here would be as follows: Length is: 2' x width (2') x depth (.66) x 7 (the number of piers) ÷ 27. The answer is .68. Adding the perimeter figure of 4.4 yards to the pier figure of .68 gives a total of 5.08 yards. One important aspect here is to ensure that the width of the footing is correct. While code requires a 16" footing, sometimes backhoes will dig a 24" wide hole, throwing your numbers off. The reason for this is that backhoes (a machine commonly used to dig footings) have both 16" and 24" buckets. If you are not paying attention, you might order concrete for a 16" wide footing yet have it dug at 24". Most likely, you will run out. It is always best to order to the high side.

Another consideration is to have any other footings pre-dug and ready for any excess concrete. You are paying for whatever you ordered, whether you use it or

In This Chapter . . .

▲ Using the math to estimate materials

▲ Things often missed in estimating

▲ How to square things away

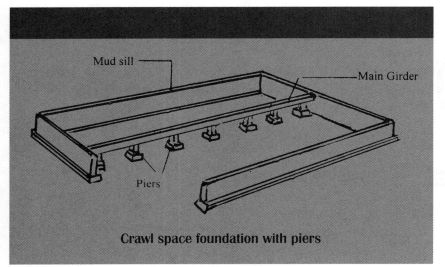

Crawl space foundation with piers

Mud sill

Main Girder

Piers

not. Often, footings for decks and porches are not poured at the same time as the main house for a variety of reasons. However, if you have excess concrete, you can install these at the same time. Also, you can pre-form some other concrete projects, such as a place for garbage cans or an animal pen, in case you have excess concrete as well.

Other considerations with ordering and installing concrete is the code requirement that a footing be poured all at the same time rather than incrementally. This is another reason to ensure that you have ordered enough concrete to at least do the perimeter. That is also why you should always start with the perimeter rather than the piers. If you run out while pouring the piers, you can save the next pier for later. Another consideration is to remember to count all the places you need a footing. Beyond the perimeter and piers, you will need (if it is part of the house) to remember the footing for the fireplace and front porch slab. Sometimes, these are forgotten in doing a takeoff (another word for estimation).

Block for Blockheads

Using the same foundation figures, we can simply determine how many blocks it would take to build this foundation. A typical minimum block foundation is 3 "courses" or rows high. In this example, the perimeter of the building is 136'. A concrete block is 16" long or 1.33'. Dividing 136 by 1.33 gives us 102.25. This is the number of blocks it would take to go around the foundation one time. Multiplying this by 3 gives us a figure of 307. With seven piers, each 3-block high and 2-block wide pier adds 42 blocks, for a total of 349 blocks. Since 8"x16" block normally comes in 90-unit cubes, ordering four cubes (360 blocks) should be adequate for this job. The extra amount is as an allowance for breakage. You might order more if the footing hasn't been installed yet or is not perfectly level (stepped). You would also need 12 corner blocks.

The foundation, footings and piers of this house would look like the illustration above.

If our house was a slab, the calculations would be: length (28) x width (40) x depth (.33, which is 4" ÷ 12) ÷ 27. The answer is 13.7 yards. You would most likely be safe by ordering 14 yards, but should have some projects prepared for the excess. However, there might also be places in the slab where it needs to be thickened to carry an extraordinary load like a porch or fireplace.

Roofing with Trig

Trigonometry ($a^2 + b^2 = c^2$) is used primarily in construction to determine the amount of materials used on a roof or gable. In our example, the house is 28' deep. The roof pitch is 9/12. We can measure off the plans to determine that the peak of the roof is about 10' above the top of the second-floor ceiling. With this we have two of the three figures we need to determine how much surface the roof has. The bottom of the triangle is 14'. The vertical side is 10'. We want to use our formula to determine the third side. Using the formula we take 14x14 (a or 14^2) + 10x10 (b or 10^2) = 196 + 100, or 296. Using a calculator, we determine the square root of 296 to be 17.2, giving us our c side of the triangle.

While we arrived at an answer, there are some details to consider. First is the overhangs of the building. We have two overhangs that have not yet been considered in our calculations. These are at the eaves and the gables. The gable overhangs are easy to figure. In our case, they are one-foot wide. The overhangs at the eaves are a bit different. In our case, they are also one foot on the a side by .75 foot on the b side (at a 9/12 pitch or 9 ÷ 12 = .75). The answer is the square root of 1.56 or .75.

Putting this together, we have a building that is 40' long plus 1'+1' (including the gable overhangs on each side) or a total of 42' wide. The roof surface is 17.2' x 42' x 2 or 1,445 square feet for the roof. While we have included the gable overhangs, we also have to add the eave overhangs. Their calculations are: 42 x .75 x 2 (sides) or 63 square feet. The total of the roof is 1,508. The figures are multiplied by 2 because our formula only calculates one side of the roof.

Three things are typically put on a roof. One is roofing, another is roofing paper or felt and the third is plywood. Roofing is sold by the "square," which is actually 100 square feet. Typically asphalt shingles come 3 bundles to the square. This building would require 15.08 squares of shingles. This figure would probably be rounded up to 16 or more squares to cover waste and other factors, such as using a double row at the eaves. A plywood estimate would be: 1,508 ÷ 32, which is the size of a sheet of plywood (4'x8'). The number of sheets is 47.12, rounded up to 48 sheets. Rolls of felt vary somewhat but would tell you how many rolls are needed to cover so many square feet of roof.

One of the most common mistakes made in determining how much roofing and plywood is needed to cover a roof is to forget the overhangs. We know that the eaves had an additional 63 square feet or about 2 bundles of shingles. The gable overhangs also had an additional 69 square feet. Combined, the overhangs had 129 square feet or an additional four bundles. This also represents 5 sheets of plywood. While this is not the end of the world, it could cause the job to stop and either idle workmen while someone goes to get the extra materials or cause a return trip and further delays. Additionally, roofing materials come in dye lots and the shorted materials could be replaced with a different dye lot that might be noticeable.

Squaring with the Greeks

The "$a^2 + b^2 = c^2$" formula is also helpful in determining if a building is built "in square." A building not built in square is sometimes called "racked." It is a serious problem. Serious. The most common things that can be out of square or racked in a building are the foundation and the roof. If this occurs, everything else in the building is going to be out of whack. Things just won't fit right. Materials like plywood will not join properly. Adjustments will be made in the field, most likely long triangular shaped slivers that are cut off to put the building back in square. Often builders just do the best they can. The problems are most likely not noticed to the casual observer. One place that it is noticed is in vinyl floors with a square pattern. The lines should run parallel to the walls. If the structure is out of square, the lines will not remain the same distant apart from the walls. If you know you have this problem ahead of time, you might want to use a floor pattern that does not have lines but rather an irregular shape.

To determine if a building is in square we would use our formula to "pull diagonals." The structure is 28'x40'. The short answer is: 784 + 1,600 = the square root of 2,384 or 48.82'. You would use the figure of 48'10" (converting it from tenths to twelfths) to measure a diagonal. The diagonal is measured from one corner, diagonally across the building to the opposite corner. In this case, you should measure 48'10". Measuring the other diagonal should be exactly the same. You can also just measure any rectangle without knowing the exact number. If the measurements are exactly the same, the building is in square. You will find these exact figures on every foundation plan or can determine it yourself using the formula.

While there is no such thing as a perfect house, the diagonal measurements should be within ½" to ¾" of each other. For example, if one diagonal measured 48'9½" and the other was 48'10¼" you should have no problem with the structure. The carpenter would most likely split the difference in the framing to make his life easier. He would most likely pull the structure in slightly over the foundation or extend it out slightly to make it work. If it is off too much, a solution might be to take off part of the top course of block and relay it or take other measures to get the structure back in square.

An experienced framing crew would know what they can live with. A superintendent would also know how to fix the problem if the carpenter is reluctant to build the structure. The answer usually is to adjust the foundation or the deck somehow.[33] ■

War Story

#33: I had hired a new masonry crew once to build a foundation. After the second day, they failed to show up. It took awhile to catch up with them and they made up some excuses but did said they would not be coming back. They said they also expected no pay because they could not finish the job. I hired another crew to finish the job. After a half hour on the job, the crew leader called me over and told me he knew why the first crew left. The building was 8" out of square. He also told me that probably what had happened was that someone pulled the strings they use to level the house with on the wrong side of the block. This accounted for the 8" difference, since 8" is the width of a block. I had the mason take the top 5 courses of block off and start over with the house built back in square. Eight inches out of square was unworkable.

30

What Are All These Parts Called?

The Major Parts

Footings, Foundations and Slabs

Footings are made of poured concrete, rest underground and are what the foundation rests on. These are either formed by framing members or rest inside a trench cut into the earth. They are always wider than the foundation and must sit on solid earth. They are underground to protect them from freezing, which can cause a foundation to break.

Foundations are what the wooden members of a house sits on. Part of every foundation is above ground, while part is buried underground. Foundations sit directly on top and centered on footings. Most foundations are made of individual block or are solid concrete, called a poured concrete foundation. Other types of foundations include an all-weather wood foundation, made of treated wood and plywood and foundations where Styrofoam blocks are used as forms for a poured concrete foundation. All wood foundations are typically installed by carpenters rather than masons. Styrofoam block foundations provide extra insulation in basement space. These two systems, however, represent a small percentage of all foundation types used. While there are cost differentials between poured and concrete block foundations, they are used interchangeably and typically limited regionally by the availability of materials and tradesmen.

Piers are small towers of foundation material, usually block, that support framing within the foundation. They are usually free standing and about 2x2 feet square. Since wood can only span so far (and usually is no more than 16' long), piers are located inside a foundation to carry the framing where it must be spliced or supported. Girders and posts typically rest on piers.

Slabs are foundations that incorporate the floor of the structure as well, with the floor being concrete rather than plywood. Slabs typically rest directly on the ground and are within a foot of the finished grade. The concrete is typically four inches thick. Slabs are typically seen in commercial structures, lower cost homes

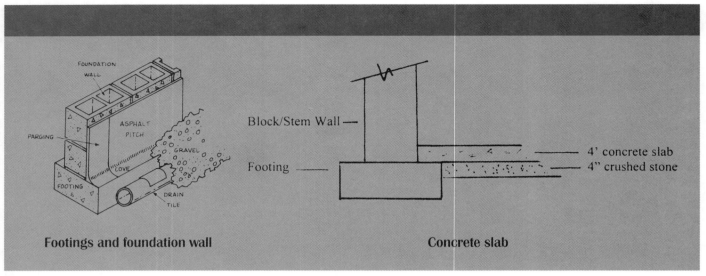

Footings and foundation wall

Concrete slab

COURTESY OF AMERICAN FOREST & PAPER
ASSOCIATION, WASHINGTON, DC

and in basements. Slabs are also prevalent is areas where the terrain is relatively flat. Usually the perimeter foundation wall of a slab is made of concrete block. Slabs are also called *slab on grade*, which means that the foundation is resting on top of the ground (or grade).

Framing

Dimensional lumber is a common term for pre-cut lumber used in framing a house. Usually the lumber is nominally 2" thick by 4", 6", 8", 10" or 12" thick. This lumber is actually about ½" smaller than its nominal size, i.e., a 2x4 is actually 1½" x 3½".

Mud sill is typically a 2x4 or 2x6 that rests directly on top of the foundation. It is often nailed, strapped, or bolted to the foundation. Since it is the first piece of wood to touch the foundation, it is pressured treated to protect it against decay. The mud sill is seldom exposed to the outside of the house and is usually covered by the siding or brick or rock veneer.

Girder is a heavy piece of wood, either solid or made of three nailed together pieces of wood that floor joists rest on. One end of the girder rests on the perimeter foundation wall and the other end on intermediate piers within the center of the house. Solid girders are rarely seen except in the West where Douglas Fir is typically seen. Most girders are called built-up girders because they consist of three 2x10s or 2x12s nailed together. Most homes will have at least one girder, though some may have more than one, depending on the size of the house.

Joists are the framing members that make up the floor system. They typically are 2x8s, 2x10s or 2 x12s. Their size is determined by how far they span, how far apart they are and how much load is placed upon them. They rest directly on top of the mud sill on the perimeter wall and usually end at a girder. Joists are typically joined at a girder in one of three ways. They can rest on top of the girder, passing it slightly. They can also butt into a girder and are notched to rest on a ledger board, usually a 2x2. The third connection method is also butted to the girder, but uses a metal connector called a joist hanger. All three methods are satisfactory, although resting the joists on top of the girder actually lowers the girder (called a dropped girder) which could interfere with head height in a basement situation.

Band Board is essentially a floor joist that is stood on its 2x side and perpendicular to the floor joist at the perimeter of the house. It closes the foundation framing and is flush to the outside foundation wall and the mud sill. Floor joists are recessed to allow the band board to be flush to the wall. Siding or veneer covers the band board.

Floor decking (or sheathing) is typically plywood or oriented strand board (OSB) that forms the floor of a house. It is applied directly on top of the floor joists. Typically, it is glued and either nailed or screwed into the joists. If nailed, a special nail called a ring shanked nail is often used. This nail, usually an 8 penny nail, has a spiral pattern on its shaft that prevents the nail from coming back out of the wood. This nail has the disadvantage of being very brittle and susceptible to breaking rather than bending.

Bottom plate is the first wall framing member to rest on the floor decking/ slab. It can be either on the perimeter or on an inside wall. It can be on any floor. It is the same size as the wall studs, typically a 2x4 or a 2x6. It is nailed directly to the plywood or slab and flush to the outside. The bottom plate on a slab foundation is pressure treated, as required by code.

Studs are 2x4s used to frame the outside walls and interior walls or partitions. They come in standard lengths, usually 93 inches. The 2x4s in longer lengths, used in bottom and top plates, are not called "studs." The 2x6s are sometimes used in place of studs for framing. They are typically used for framing plumbing walls as well as perimeter walls in houses that are speced to have R-19 side wall insulation. Plumbing walls are thicker because pipes have to run through them. The 2x4s are too narrow to run most pipes through.

Top plates are the same as bottom plates but at the top of a wall. Usually they are doubled, with the upper top plate being spliced at a different place than the lower top plate to add rigidity to the structure.

Cripples are shorter pieces of wood in a framed wall that are either above or below a horizontal member. Cripples are typically seen above interior door headers or below window sub-sills.

Headers are solid pieces of wood, usually 2x6s and larger that give additional strength over a window or door on the perimeter wall. They usually attach directly below the top plate and serve as the top framing of a window or door opening. If an interior door is in a non-load bearing place, headers are often not solid wood and use a horizontal 2x4 and cripples to fill the space up to the

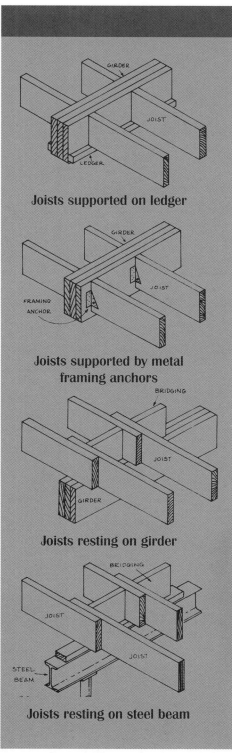

Joists supported on ledger

Joists supported by metal framing anchors

Joists resting on girder

Joists resting on steel beam

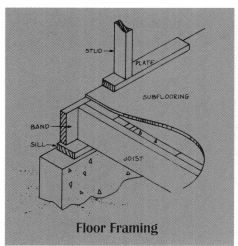

Floor Framing

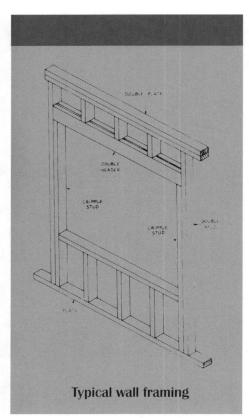

Typical wall framing

COURTESY OF AMERICAN FOREST & PAPER
ASSOCIATION, WASHINGTON, DC

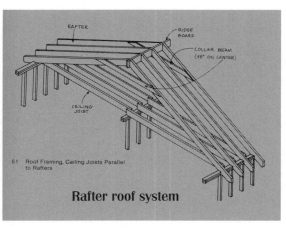

Rafter roof system

COURTESY OF AMERICAN FOREST & PAPER
ASSOCIATION, WASHINGTON, DC

top plate. Headers are typically made of two pieces of 2x material with a ½" piece of plywood between them to fill out the wall. This is because the typical wall is 3½" thick and two pieces of 2x material is only 3" thick (1½" + 1½"). The ½" plywood fills out the wall plus adds greater strength to the header.

Sub or rough sill is a horizontal member that frames the bottom of a window. Cripples usually fill in the void below down to the bottom plate. It is called a sub-sill because the finished *window sill* usually is attached directly on top of the sub sill.

Jacks are the vertical framing member that form the outside framing of a window and have the header resting directly on top of them. This makes window framing actually two studs thick on the sides. They are also called trimmer studs.

Ceiling joist are horizontal members, usually 2x6s, that frame the ceiling of a house. They rest directly on top of the upper top plate. They are typically used when a rafter roofing system is used. While load bearing, they often are not strong enough to support an attic room other than for light storage. If attic space is used as living space, the ceiling joists have to be sized and spaced to carry the proper floor load.

Rafters are the main element of roof framing. They usually range from 2x6s to 2x10s and rest directly on top of the top plate. They join with the opposite rafter at a ridge board at the peak of the roof.

Ridge Boards are the horizontal framing member at the peak of the roof that rafters tie into. They usually range from 2x8s to 2x12s.

Ridge Posts are vertical members that support ridge boards. They are typically in the gables and intermittently through the attic space where ridge boards break or need additional support. They are typically 2x6s.

Collar ties are the horizontal member that tie rafters together about ⅓ the way down from the ridge. They prevent the natural downward and outward thrust of a roof system from happening. In a typical rafter system, they are usually at least 8' from the floor, thus allowing the use of the attic space for storage or living.

Trusses are engineered structural pieces, usually used in floors or roof systems. They are typically supported only on the perimeter walls. Trusses used in place of rafters usually are cheaper, but the bottom *chord* (the horizontal piece that forms the bottom of the truss and thus the ceiling below) is not load bearing and thus cannot be used for attic storage or living. However, there are some specially designed trusses that do allow for attic living space. Floor trusses are used to span longer distances than normal floor joist systems. They also do not require a girder system, thus providing a flat ceiling with no interior posts. Roof trusses typically cost less than a rafter system but have limitation in steepness and length. Floor trusses typically cost more than joists/girder systems and are used in situations where special spans and flat ceilings are desired in the space below, i.e., the basement.

Sheathing is another word for the plywood or OSB. It is used to cover the outside walls and roof of a building. It usually comes about

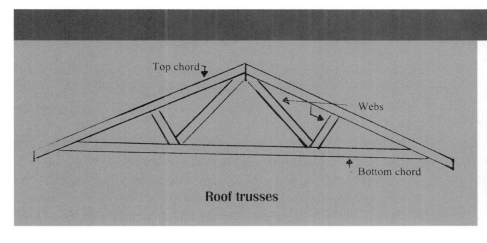

Roof trusses

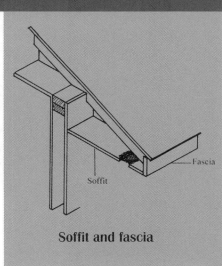

Soffit and fascia

½" thick, but ranges from ⅜" to ⅝" thick. Often plywood/OSB sheathing is only required on the outside corners of a structure with fiberboard or insulation board used to close the rest of the perimeter walls of a house. Plywood/OSB sheathing is used throughout the house where there are hurricane loads, such as at the beach.

Eaves are the horizontal overhangs of the house, usually on the longer/wider side of the house, which typically is the front and rear of the house.

Gables are typically the ends of a house where the steepness of the roof is seen.

Fascia is the board that covers the end of the rafters or roof trusses. They are typically 1x6 or 1x8 and covered with the guttering.

Soffits are the material that cover the bottom of the rafters/roof trusses that protrude from the face of the building and end at the bottom of the fascia. Soffits are usually made of plywood or vinyl and are often vented. They typically are at least one foot wide.

The Minor Parts

There are a lot of minor parts of the house that you might not be aware of or ever hear about. They are listed here for general interest, but your subs will be well aware of them, though you may never hear them talk about these minor parts.

Bridging is short pieces of wood placed between floor joists to stiffen them up. They can solid bridging, which is the same size as the joists or they could be 1"x2" pieces cut at an angle and criss-crossed. Bridging also prevents the joists from twisting, cupping or turning. Some bridging is made of metal straps that criss-cross like 1x2s.

Stringers are the side pieces of wood in a stair system. They are typically 2x10s or 2x12s and are either notched to accept the stair step or the steps are routed out or simply nailed between the stringers.

Treads are another word for stair steps.

Trimmer boards are usually doubled floor joists that frame the opening the stairs go through.

Deadwood is small pieces of wood that are not structural, but placed in a wall to serve as a nail base for a future part. Deadwood is used extensively in corners

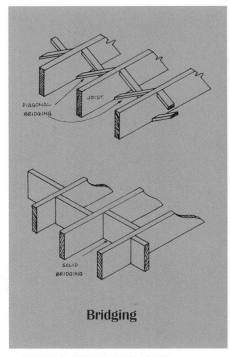

Bridging

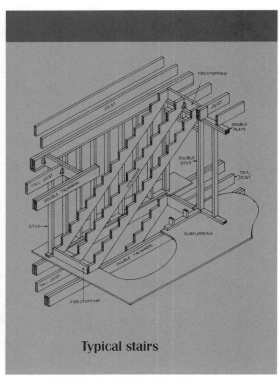

Typical stairs

to provide framing (sometimes called blocking) for drywall, cabinets, medicine cabinets, towel bars, heavy pictures, etc.

Parging is a thin coating of masonry cement that is applied over a block wall, usually as an undercoating for a waterproofing membrane. Parging is the name of the material as well as the act of applying the material. Walls are parged to help keep water from coming through the wall.

Rafter tail is the bottom piece of a rafter (or roof truss) that extends beyond the face of the house. Usually a fascia board is nailed directly onto the rafter tail or it is left exposed, as is common in the Craftsman era of house design.

Pickets are vertical pieces of trim framing that are part of a rail. If made of wood, pickets are typically 2x2s.

The A.K.A. Parts

Many parts of a house have more than one name. Some of the parts use brand names in lieu of technical names. Some of these names are regional. Examples are as follows:

Footers is another word for footings. No known reason. Regional.

Stem wall is another word for foundation wall.

Plywood is used in lieu of *OSB, particle board* and *flake board*. While these pieces serve the same function, they are manufactured differently and have different engineered qualities.

Sill is another word for a bottom plate of wood. It is sometimes also called a "shoe."

Ring joist is another word for band joist or *band board*. This is the piece of wood that is the same size as a floor joist that "rings" the house at the floor system.

Grade is another word for dirt, such as brick to *grade*. *Grade* also is a verb meaning to move or shape dirt as in the case of *grading* a lot in preparation for building. The yard of a house is first rough *graded* to shape it at the beginning of construction while it is finish *graded* to prepare it for landscaping at the end of the building cycle. ■

31

Building From the Ground Up—Footings to Carpet

What Do You Have To Do?

The primary steps of building a home are listed on the following page. They are listed in an order that is typically called "Critical Path." Some people also call this "Critical Path Method (CPM)." Critical Path means the order you do things, with the preceding item having to be accomplished prior to undertaking the next item. While housing has a definitive Critical Path, many items are done in an order that does not necessarily have to be done that way. For example, the mechanical items in a house are typically done in the order of HVAC first, plumbing second and then electrical. These could be done in a different order, i.e., plumbing first, then HVAC. However, some items, especially those that will be covered up later by sheathing or drywall, must be done in a critical path manner. For example, you would waterproof a wall before you back fill. The chart that follows shows a typical critical path for the construction of a house.

Another part of the chart is which items are typically inspected and when they are inspected. As we have discussed in the past, each area is different and not all items listed here are inspected. Also, a local area might have an inspection not listed here as well. If you are building the house yourself, you must find out which inspections are required and at what point the inspector wants to look at the work. These inspections become part of the Critical Path because the next step cannot be taken until that phase has been approved. Waiting on inspections will stop the forward progress of your house. For example, you typically cannot insulate the walls of a house until the wiring has been inspected. This is because the insulation covers up the wiring in the walls.

A third part of this chart is the approximate time each phase should take to complete. This is based on a typical house less than 2,000 square feet in size. The time is also based on a full-sized professional crew doing the work. Obviously, if you are doing the work, it could take longer. This chart does give you a benchmark to check your progress against. The chart also assumes that all the parts are available and that nothing goes wrong on the job.

PHASE	INSPECTIONS	DAYS
Stake the lot		1
Rough clear		1-3
Re-stake		1
Grub		1
Dig foundation		1-2
Dig/form footings		1
Pour footings	Yes	1
Pin foundation (optional)		1
Build block/stem wall		1-3
Waterproof walls		1
Back fill walls		1
Frame structure		1-9
Rough Heat	Yes	1-2
Rough Plumbing	Yes	1-2
Rough electric	Yes	1-2
Frame check	Yes	1
Install wall insulation	Yes	1
Install drywall		1-2
Finish drywall		4-8
Prime paint		1-2
Install trim		1-5
Paint trim		1-2
Install vinyl flooring		1
Install cabinets/vanities/ countertops		1-3
Finish heat	Yes	1
Finish plumbing	Yes	1-2
Finish electric	Yes	1-2
Install carpet		1-2
Clean		1

How Can You Go (What Can Be Done Concurrently)?

There are a number of phases in home building that can be done at a number of different times. All phases eventually become part of the critical path. A missing screw that causes you to fail a final inspection is right smack dab in the middle of your critical path. That darned screw might have been missing for six months and passed on as unimportant. When you flunk an inspection, whatever it is, it becomes important.

Some items should only be done after a particular phase has been completed. They can be done anytime after that, but should not be done prior. An example is anything that might be damaged by rain.

The chart on the opposite page is a list of items that can be done concurrently and are typically not part of a critical path (though it will eventually become part of that path if not done).

Where Can You Fudge?

A number of phases can be combined to increase the speed of construction or to make up for lost time. However, combining these phases is not recommended because it causes more intense management and might result in a job that is less than satisfactory. It is typically done on jobs where the house has gotten seriously behind schedule. One aspect of building is that tradesmen want the house totally to themselves. They do not want to share and for very many, very good reasons.

First is that there is usually limited parking at a job site. Having too many trucks out front makes it unpleasant for everyone. Second, there often is limited access to power and water. Tradesmen don't like to wait in line for water or risk tripping breakers by overloading power sources. Third is that tradesmen need room to spread out their materials. If more than one sub is in the house, they physically get in each other's way. Fourth, if something goes wrong, it is hard to assign blame. Typical problems include breaking some part, i.e., a window, getting mud on carpet or tearing a vinyl floor or just trash disposal. If two or more subs are in the house, they will point the finger at the other guy if something goes wrong.

Still, if you have to, some phases can be combined. These include mechanicals (HVAC, plumbing and electrical), which can be done at the same time, though usually it is two of the three rather than all three at once. If this is being done to speed up the house or to keep it on schedule, you must let each sub know that the other will be there at about the same time. You need to be there when they arrive and stay with them for awhile to make sure that they both will remain. Often, even though you scheduled both of them, one will want to leave (and will) if you are not there to keep them there. They often will have an excuse or reason to leave. You, however, might be able to solve their problem or

PHASE	AFTER	BEFORE	DAYS
Waterproof	Walls have cured	Back fill	1
Back fill	Walls have cured	*	1
Roofing	Rough mechanicals	Wall insulation	1–2
Siding	Rough mechanicals	Drywall	1–3
Masonry fireplace	Framing	Drywall	1–2
Blown attic insul.	Drywall	Final insp.	1
Sidewalks/Drives	Trim	Final insp.	1–2
Wood decks	Framing	Final insp.	1–2
Exterior paint	Siding	Final insp.	1–3
Landscaping**	Sidewalks/drive	Final insp.	1-5

Notes: * I always liked to back fill prior to framing because it made it easier to frame the house rather than reaching over a deep, dangerous hole. Some builders, however, waited until the house was framed, worried that back filling a foundation might push a wall over and that the weight of the frame would strengthen the foundation. I've heard both sides of this argument but never got a resolve. My suggestion is that if you have the time for the wall to become solid (a week?) and that you are very careful, go ahead and back fill. It is also helpful if the home has a basement floor to go ahead and pour the floor to give it additional strength.

**In many areas, landscaping cannot effectively be done in winter months and is thus "escrowed" until the spring. What happens is that the bank holds back a portion of the final payment to the builder (an escrow, which usually is the bid for doing the landscaping) until it is done. This allows the customer to move into the house while still protecting them and ensuring that the landscaping will be done when the weather allows.

convince them to work around a problem. Once it seems clear that they will both remain, you can leave, but should still check on them periodically to ensure that they will finish the work and not encounter other problems.

You might feel like a referee and that probably is not an inaccurate description of what it takes to work two subs at once. Remember that this practice is out of the norm and should be used rarely. Also, if you do "jam" the house, you are adding a greater burden on your time to ensure that the work gets done as planned.

You can also combine the trim carpenter with some of the finish mechanicals. You must ensure that he installs any cabinet with a sink or appliance first, so that the plumber and electrician can do their work.

Where Do You Invite Disaster?

There are a number of serious mistakes you can make in scheduling a house. Among these are bringing in parts before the house is weather proofed. On the road to danger is to insulate a house without a finished roof or siding to prevent rain from getting the insulation wet. Insulation should never get wet, as it totally defeats its' insulation value.

The next disaster is to drywall a house before the roof and siding is on.[34, 35]

Another disaster you can cause is to schedule on top of the painter. They need the house to themselves and obviously, with wet paint, anyone else in the house is going to make a mess. In addition, you do not want to get in the way of the carpet layer, who needs free and clear access to the house to install the carpet. Besides getting in the carpet layer's way, you could also leave debris (or tools and parts) that could get installed under the carpet. ■

War Stories

#34: I worked with a guy once who was hired as a warranty manager for the company. I did not think he was especially good at that job and found out later that he left my company to work for a competitor as a superintendent. I thought that I might have misjudged him because the competitor was a much larger company with an excellent reputation. I later heard that he had been fired from that company for drywalling a house before the finish roofing and siding was installed. He did this twice, and in both occasions, a rain storm came up and ruined the drywall. Most of it had to be pulled out at a loss of thousands.

There are exceptions to this story. I was amazed when I was living in Reno, Nevada, when I saw that drywall was stored in the front yard of a house during construction. However, since it rained so infrequently there, this was a common practice. I also know that you can proceed with a house prior to a finish roof or siding if you "waterproof" the house. This means ensuring the roof felt is installed properly. It also means that any place a house might leak be temporarily weather proofed.

#35: We had houses that we called "leakers." These were homes that had different levels, such as a tri-level where the roof was broken by a part of the house. These houses would leak until the siding was installed. However, if the siding contractors were behind, we would get them to waterproof these houses with flashing until they could get to the job. We then could continue with the job of insulation and drywall without the danger of the house being damaged by weather. Simple houses, like Colonials and single gabled ranches are not "leakers" and all we had to be concerned with was that the roofing felt was properly installed.

32

Are We There Yet?

How Long Is Each Phase?

Chapter 31 shows approximately how long each phase takes. This, of course, is in a perfect world. In theory, a house could be finished in a month. Sometimes in 24 hours, which is a typical publicity stunt. In reality, most homes take a minimum of 90–180 days to complete. This extra time and wide range allows for the real world of rain and snow, late subs and missing parts, and the inefficiencies of building houses in America today.

The quickest a home can typically be built is about 1-2 months for a modular home. Custom stick homes can exceed half a year. While you make a critical path that maps out the entire house with actual dates, it is rare to ever meet this schedule. Even the world's best production builder, with captive subs and world-class systems, rarely hits it on the nose. If they do, it is often done in a manner (jamming a house) that was not the way they originally intended to build the house.

When Is It Really Under Control?

A house isn't under control until it is dried in from the weather. Prior to that, it is subject to every disaster known to man. Once it is dried in, it is smooth(er) sailing. Bids usually come in on time and on schedule. Costs are known from that point on and you can usually see the light at the end of the tunnel. Everything from that point on should be on a fixed fee basis. Provided your subs come as scheduled, you should be able to hit target finish dates with reasonable accuracy. Once the house is dried in, the only thing that can hurt you is a storm that takes away access to your house. This is not uncommon, especially in remote areas with dirt roads.

What Can You Do To Help?

There are a number of things you can do to keep your house on schedule and within budget. First is to ensure that there is good access to the house. Often this involves an adequate temporary driveway into the property. Most people put in a gravel drive early on in the construction process. However, after a few rains and a few larger trucks getting stuck in the driveway, the drive is virtually gone. Every sub after that drives into a mud hole. Not only is their attitude changed, they also drag all that mud into your house. A solution is to plan for an few extra loads of gravel to be brought in as needed. You can never have too much gravel in a driveway.

Another part of this is the walkway to your house. Subs might be parking on hardtop or your gravel drive but still need to get to the house. Often they walk through the mud, again developing a bad attitude and getting your house muddy. A solution is to extend the gravel over to the front door or to use pallets or straw to keep the path less muddy. Straw is a common approach. While you might not have had a chance to do so, back filling the foundation will prevent a lot of the mud problems and eliminates the "gangplank" most houses have over a 10-foot-deep pit.

In line with keeping the path to the house neat, it is always helpful to keep the house itself neat. While your contract should require each sub to clean up after themselves, this does not always happen. Rather than curse the darkness, you should clean it up yourself. It will be hard for a sub to leave a mess in a house that was clean when they arrived. It also affects their attitude and makes for a safer work environment. You can bet that if a sub comes to a dirty job site, they will leave it even messier.

You can also help by being there to meet each sub and answering any questions they might have. For some reason, I have found that some subs seem to be looking for reasons to not finish (or start) the job. If you are there to meet them, you can prevent this from happening, usually by solving the problem for them. Since the problem is often a missing part, you should volunteer to go after the part. That is typically a large part of the job of a superintendent and if that is your title, you should fulfill that role. ■

33

Site and Set the House

What's the Difference and Which Can Save You Money?

One of the most important things a superintendent or builder does for a house is to site and set the structure. "Siting" the structure means placing it on the lot. Some lots allow for many options while other lots virtually site the building for you based on covenants, zoning and the relative small size of the lot. The most common siting of a building is to face the street square on and position the house in the middle of the lot. Most sub-division houses are "sited" like this.

If you are building on a larger lot with no road to center on, you have much more leeway. Obviously, you still need to stay within zoning and covenant conventions but can usually turn the house anyway you want. Typically, you might want to capture a view or take advantage of a group of unusual trees or some other feature of the lot. If the lot has some slope to it, you would want to minimize the cost of the foundation. Solar considerations should also be taken into account, following general design rules. The most common of these is to face the "morning" side of the house to the east and watch out for the colder north side of the house.

The next thing a builder does to the house is to "set" the house. What this means is how high out of the ground the foundation wall comes. The basic rule of thumb is that a house should come out of the ground 8" at the high corner. However, if your house is on a public sewer, the sewer depth will provide an absolute minimum height above the sewer. This is because sewers work by gravity, with a slope of at least one quarter inch per foot. If you set a house too low for the sewer to work using gravity, you will need to purchase a mechanical lift station (a pump) that is quite expensive and prone to failure. Setting a house below the sewer was grounds for dismissal in the company that I worked for.

The goal in setting a house is to get it as close to the ground or finish grade as possible. You still need to consider preventing flooding and allowing for the sewer (or septic system) to work using gravity. There are two main reasons to get

In This Chapter . . .

▲ Considerations for siting the house

▲ How to set the house

▲ How to build a walk-out basement

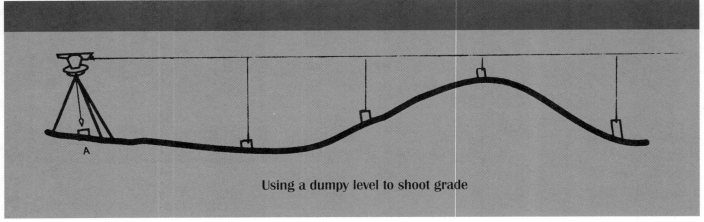

Using a dumpy level to shoot grade

A trick a lot of builders do

to decrease the amount of

foundation coming out of

the ground is to actually set

the top of the wall below the

current grade and then

come back and cut away 8

or more inches of the

current grade to get the

proper slope.

the foundation to come out of the ground as little as possible. First is to reduce the number of steps out of each door, primarily the front door. Two steps is optimum (one with a slab on grade). The second reason is to reduce the cost of the foundation. Since most houses with crawl spaces need only three blocks (24") above the footing to meet code and function properly, anything over that costs you money. If the foundation is brick or stone to grade, the less foundation exposed, the lower the cost. This is because you only use the more expensive brick or stone above grade and use the less costly concrete block below grade.

Houses are typically set using a leveling device to "shoot" or measure each corner of the house. This leveling device is typically called a "transit," but often is actually a "builder's" or "dumpy" level. In determining the relative "level" of the site, you will first establish the high or *control* corner. Normally, you want to come out of the ground 8" above that higher corner. This meets code and allows for the house to be out of the ground high enough for proper drainage around the house.

Codes will tell you the minimum thickness and depth of footings and the stem wall. For example, a footing might be 6" thick and the crawl space 24" high. With the frost line 12", you would dig the foundation 22" deep at the high corner. The total wall height is 30" (three 8" blocks plus a 6" footing). Digging down 22" allows the top of the wall to be 8" out of the ground. Since you are actually 22" down on the high side of the home site, you more than meet the needs of a typical 12" frost protection.

However, if the lot has some slope to it, you might need to dig below the current ground level on the low side of the lot. Here you would need to get below the frost line. For example, if the low side was 30" lower than the high side, you would need to dig the footings at least 12" below the current grade for frost protection. You would not, however, need to dig the crawl space any deeper on the low side since it would already be 24" below the top of the wall.

Another trick of setting a house is to ensure that water will flow away from the foundation. The rule of thumb is to have (like the sewer) a slope of a quarter inch a foot away from the foundation for a distance of 10'. In this example, the ground should slope away two and a half inches from finish grade (not the top of the wall, which is 8" higher than finish grade) at the high corner. A trick a lot of builders do to decrease the amount of foundation coming out of the ground is to actually set the top of the wall below the current grade and then come back and cut away 8 or more inches of the current grade to get the proper slope.

Another aspect of setting the house pertains to homes that have walk-out basements. These are homes where there is enough slope to the lot so that some portion of the house site is 8' (the typical height of a basement) below the top of the wall. In this case, you can walk directly out of the basement. The high side of the basement would be totally underground (except for 8"). This condition

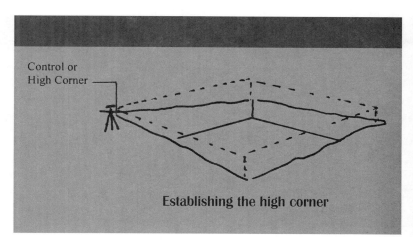

Establishing the high corner

is usually very much desired for a number of reasons. First is that a house that is totally underground is prone to dampness in the basement. Water typically has to be pumped out using a sump pump. These devices run on electric power, which often goes out during rainstorms, when they are needed most. A walkout basement also allows for an additional exit from the house that a totally submerged basement wouldn't have (unless it had a welled exit, which is prone to many problems including flooding).

The best part of a walkout basement is that some of the side or rear walls can be framed rather than constructed of masonry or concrete. This makes it easier (and cheaper) to build, insulate and to install windows and doors. Since a walkout basement does not have earth against one or more sides of the house, it reduces the common "dankness" of a basement.

In setting a house with a walkout basement, the goal is to have the highest corner 8' higher than the lowest corner, where the walkout basement is. If the low corner is more than 8', you will have to use extra block and do extra grading and possible retaining walls to have a level place to exit the house from. This sometimes is not possible due to the slope of the lot, but should always be a goal.

Another consideration in setting a house is how far finish grade is from the entrances and exits. Obviously, you would want to reduce the number of steps to the doors. As mentioned, you can shape the lot to lower the house so that it is closer to the ground or you can use fill dirt to fill in below an entrance. The optimum minimum is to have no more than three steps to the front door. More than that, you have to use a handrail and it just makes it harder to get into your house for the next 50 or so years. ■

34

Clear the Land,
Save (most of) the Trees

Why Would You Kill a Tree?

Joyce Kilmer aside, trees are a problem. You would kill a tree to keep it from falling on your house. You would kill a tree to make room for your house. You would kill a tree to make room for your lawn, your driveway and the drain field of your septic tank. However, it wouldn't be an act of wanton tree lust. Trees are hard to get rid of. Most times they have no value, either because they are "trash" trees like most pines or you have too few (less than 150 acres) to interest a logger to come take them. Notice I said take them, not buy them. Most people think their trees have value. One hundred and fifty acres of old growth trees along a state maintained hardtop road in an area that has never heard of the Sierra Club have value. Your one or two acres of 20-year-old pine trees are not an asset, they are a liability.

This is not to say that trees are not beautiful and can add value to your home and lot. They can. Trees can shelter you from harsh winds and sunlight. They can provide privacy and the building blocks for swings and tree-houses. They add value in the eyes of the beholder. Nevertheless, they have to be managed and sometimes killed to build your house.

A simple rule of thumb is to ensure that no roots from any tree comes within 10 feet of your house. If you cut a root, you might as well take out the entire tree. Tree limbs should not hang over your house. Those limbs *will* absolutely fall on your house, often as spears right through the ceiling. Disposing of trees is an expensive proposition. You have three basic choices. One is to haul them away to the dump. This is very expensive and often not an option.

Second is to bury them on the lot, usually in a far off corner. While not uncommon nor a bad choice, there are some things to think about. First, wherever you bury them, that piece of land can never be used again. Ever. Second, where

In This Chapter . . .

▲ When should you take out a tree?

▲ What should you do with the top soil?

▲ What precautions should you take when digging?

you buried them will settle eventually. You will have a small (or large) depression in your yard. Steam will come from the hole during the morning hours from the rotting of the wood. The hole itself could erupt and consume small domestic pets and children.

A third choice is to burn the trees. This, too, is common and also not a bad choice if allowed. Some areas won't allow burning. It could take a few days and usually a bulldozer or crawler is needed to keep the fire going.

The problems of getting rid of trees is what saves trees. No one wants to take the time or expense to get rid of any more trees than they have to. I have been accused of this by many a homeowner whose favorite tree I was accused of killing. I took them out primarily because they were in the middle of the home site or would have fallen on the house in the first year of occupancy. I took them out at great expense and as a favor to the owner. My reward was hatred. Never let a good deed go unpunished.

Grub the Lot, Save the Virgins

The first thing done in building a house is determining where the house goes and removing the trees that are in the way. What is left over is basically two things. These are underbrush and grass. To build a house, you must remove this underbrush and other ground cover, loosely called "grass." The removal of this grass is called "grubbing" the lot. You cannot build on grass. You must build on solid soil, without grass or underbrush.

You cannot build on fill.

You must build on solid,

undisturbed (in the last

500 years) virgin soil.

In fact, what you build on is called virgin or undisturbed soil. Soil comes in many layers. The first layer is called topsoil. It is usually only a few inches deep. Topsoil is very valuable. Once you have gotten the underbrush out of the way, you should try to remove the topsoil and save it. You would have to tell the loader operator that you want to save and stockpile the topsoil. Otherwise, he will just make a mess of your lot and mix all the dirt together. You should try to get him to remove the first few inches of topsoil and put it in a pile somewhere out of the way, but not too far away. Once you're ready to re-landscape your home, you can roll this rich soil back into the lot and use it to start your new lawn.

With the topsoil out of the way, you need to "site" and "set" your house. In *setting* your house, you will be digging only what you need to meet code and take best advantage of the lot. This minimum dig should get you into solid, virgin soil. Virgin soil is dirt that has never been built on. Nothing is in it or below it. If someone 50 or 100 or two years ago dug a hole and then filled it with dirt, you have a problem. You cannot build on fill. You must build on solid, undisturbed (in the last 500 years) virgin soil. If you don't, your house will settle and thus "break." You can tell if it is solid soil or not by looking at the layers of earth. Usually you will see a second topsoil "line," usually black from the color of decaying leaves and other material that used to be on the top of the earth. You will also see different colors of dirt, often red clay, that was used to fill a previously dug hole. You might also see other trash, like cars, refrigerators and tin cans. In days past, people often threw their garbage in deep ravines and eventually these ravines filled up and were covered with earth or the side caved in on top of the hole. You cannot build on this. It is not virgin, undisturbed soil. The solution is to dig through this until you find virgin soil. Sometimes there is no bottom to this hole. In this case, you need to find another home site. Often, though, you might just need to dig a few feet through the "trash" to get to solid ground.

In digging around on your lot, you must be careful that you don't cut any underground power, sewer or phone lines. If you are in the middle of nowhere, this is probably not a problem. If you are digging in a sub-division or near a city, you need to call all the utility companies and have them mark your lot. They usually need 48 hours advanced notice, so you need to plan ahead. Also, all they are going to do is to mark where the line should be. They are not going to tell you how deep the line is, which could range from one foot to at least six feet. You could still cut it if you are not careful. If so, you are liable. However, you will be in a lot less trouble if you called to have it marked and you can show due diligence.

While I was around a lot of cut lines, I never got in trouble when I called in to have it marked beforehand. My guess was that it was too much paperwork to come after someone who cut a simple line. Also, I had a sense that the utility company was often unsure of their markings and just didn't want to get into a big fight, especially if I did all I could and they might be in a weak position to blame me. Still, it is upsetting and sometimes dangerous to cut a utility line. You can also get a surprise by cutting a line that actually has been abandoned. This is quite common, but allows for some tense moments while you determine if the line is active or not. ■

35

Lien Release and Warranty

Are You Sure the Natives are Happy?

Most people who build a house think that they are in the driver's seat. Since they pay the bills, everyone else gets to jump when they say "Boo." Nice myth. Chances are that at least one of your sub-contractors is not going to be happy with you or the general contractor. Your first response is to not pay for the work. Your assumption might be that they will fade away into the sunset, buying into your assessment of their "shoddy" work. That line rarely works in the movies, why would you think it is like that in real life?

While most subs are "little guys," living from paycheck to paycheck, they are not without rights and protection from unfair practices. Chances are that if you have stiffed a sub (for whatever reason), you haven't seen the last of them. The reason is encompassed in a thing called a "mechanic's lien."

A mechanic's lien has nothing to do with auto mechanics. Technically, anyone who does work on your house is called a mechanic. What a mechanic's lien does is place an indebtedness on the title of your house. It "colors" the title of your house, making it not "free and clear." It doesn't mean that you are going to lose the fight and have to pay for shoddy work. It does mean, however, that you are going to have to come to terms with the problem to get clear title to your property.

This is not an uncommon occurrence. If a bank is involved with the financing and closing of your house, any mechanic's liens on your house have to be resolved before you can close. This is some pretty strong leverage. However, if no bank is involved, the "mechanic's" position is weak. They can still beat you up or kill you, but they've always had that option. They also have recourse with the law. However, legal fees often exceed the value of the lien and therefore make it difficult for a sub to get paid.

If that is the case, serious bodily harm becomes an option again. If the sub deems you "not worth killing," you might be off scot free, especially if you are a psychopath or have no conscience. If you live in the house until you die, only your heirs will have to deal with the problem. If your heirs keep the house, they too don't have a problem either. The lien only has to be cleared up when the house is resold and a mortgage is closed.

Another area where a mechanic's lien comes into play is where a builder's sub is not paid, but you paid the builder to do the work. The builder, unfortunately,

In This Chapter . . .

▲ Protections your subs have

▲ Protections you have

▲ What happens when your house is foreclosed

did not pay their subs. For example, let's say you hired a general contractor to do a number of things including painting your house. Once the work was done, you paid the builder and he took off for Florida. As far as you are concerned, you've paid your debt. You're happy with the work and everything is square. However, a month goes by and the painter who painted your house (under a sub-contract with your builder) tells you they haven't been paid. Your response is that you did pay, but you paid the builder. The painter should talk to the builder, not you. It's really not your problem, right?

It is very much your problem. The painter can put a mechanic's lien on your house and you have to resolve it. The paint is on *your* house, not the builder's, whose hotel bills in Florida are being covered by the money you paid him to pay the painter. Tough situation.

What can you do? Well, there is a thing called a "lien release," which certifies that all work has been paid for, including work done by sub-contractors. People have to sign that they have been paid. If they haven't been paid, they won't sign or they lose claim to being paid for the job. The way this usually works is that you exchange the lien release for the money you owe the builder or sub-contractor. While this is very common, it is not always done because it does take extra work. If a bank is involved in paying the builder, they usually do a better job of keeping track of this than most do-it-yourselfers. However, it is the only way you are going to know for sure that all the subs have been paid and are satisfied. If not, you could get that late night knock on the door. Usually the poor sub's entire family is in the car looking on, seeking relief from Daddy Warbucks (you).

Once the work was done, you paid the builder and he took off for Florida. As far as you are concerned, you've paid your debt and everything is square. However, a month goes by and the painter who actually painted your house (under a sub-contract with your builder) tells you they haven't been paid.

Who Owns Your House Anyway?

You and the bank, with the bank owning most of it. Never lose sight of that. Pay your bills and you'll never see those guys. Get behind in payments, and you'll be a popular guy. The bank can be your very best friend. They want you to have the house. Over 30 years they will receive three times what they lent you to buy the house. They are there to protect your investment from the start. They are slow to pay your builder or subs, making sure the work is done as promised. They have a huge stake in your property. If something goes wrong, they are going to take it back and then some. All or most of your equity will be consumed. They will eventually sell your house.[36] ■

War Story

#36: I was involved in the foreclosure and resale (not mine) of a house and was amazed at the bank's lack of interest in selling the house and settling the debt. While we got some bids, the bank wanted to hang tough for higher bids. They had not been paid for months and actually let more than a year go by before they finally accepted a low bid. Throughout this process, I brought bids for the house to the bank (and the bankruptcy judge), yet they did not seem interested or in any hurry to resolve the debt. My guess was that they wanted to eat up the equity with interest fees and penalties.

36

The Worst Is Saved For Last

The Final Days Can Be Deadly

The last few days in the building of your home are a flurry of activity. The hundreds of components and thousands of hours of labor that make up your house are being checked for fit and finish. It often is not a pretty scene. It is high tension. Parts are missing. Things get broken. Surprises loom under the dirt and grime. Your house enters a no man's land where it is hard to assign responsibility. Time steals from the debate. Things left for later now need attention because later is now.

Two important inspections need to take place before you can move into your house. These are the final inspection for the bank and the final inspection for the local code officials. Each inspection is different and looks for different things. Each can stop you dead in your tracks. The bank wants to ensure its investment. They lent you money to build a house according to plans and specifications. It is a house that should have been built to meet code and every part needs to be in place, fit properly and be in brand new condition. A missing, broken or dirty part will not be tolerated. It is show time and everything has got to be right.

The code officials are not as strict regarding all the parts. Some things can be missing. They care less about what should have been built than what was built. They don't care if the house is clean, if the flooring is in place, if it has been painted inside or if the landscaping is installed. Code doesn't address these items. Quality is also not a concern.

While the building final is certainly important, it is more critical because it often serves as a prelude to getting the power turned on to the house. Without power, you cannot live in the house. The building final allows the local officials to issue what is called a "certificate of occupancy" or "c of o." This means you can live in your house. The kicker is that there is usually a lag time from when the *c of o* is issued and when the power is turned on. It could be hours, it could be

231

days. While the bank cares about the *c of o* (it means the house is inhabitable), it doesn't care about the power. You do not need to have the power on to close the loan, only the certificate of occupancy.[37]

Another critical part of the last days is your satisfaction with the house. This is usually accomplished through a walk-through of the house, usually with the person who built it. If you built the house, this obviously won't happen, unless you like to talk to yourself. This moment is high tension because you are looking for flaws, missing pieces, damage, and an agreement on the state of the art.

Check, Check, Double Check

The final check of your house, if built by someone else, is typically called a "walk-through" or "pre-settlement inspection." It is often done the day of or the day prior to your closing at the bank. It is your chance to inspect the house and have things corrected to your satisfaction. It is also an opportunity to learn how your house functions. You will learn where to turn the water off in case of an emergency. You will learn where the filters are and how to change them. You will learn how to make routine adjustments. You will most likely be given a list of the major sub-contractors who built your house so that they can be called in an emergency or for warranty work. This part of the walk-through is very important, so you have to pay attention and keep a clear head.

Where you might not have a clear head is where you are inspecting the quality of the house. When your house was finished several days earlier, it had, on average, more than 25 things wrong with it. Often, a tradesman, typically called a "punch out carpenter" goes through your house looking for these minor problems. Usually the problems are very small, often relating to paint, caulk and drywall. The "punch out carpenter" touched up the nicks and scrapes in the walls and woodwork made after the painter left more than a week ago. These marks were most likely made by the carpet layers, cleaning people or any tradesman who was last in your house.

The final check of your house is often done the day of or the day prior to your closing at the bank. It is your chance to inspect the house and have things corrected to your satisfaction.

War Story

#37: I was building a house in the winter and got turned down for a final inspection because there was an inside corner on the outside of the house where it was not back filled. I had never been turned down for "landscaping" before because that is not normally a part of a final inspection. The ground was frozen and I couldn't get the dirt to break up to fill the hole. All I got was clumps of frozen dirt. Yards typically were not installed in the winter for this reason. However, the house had to be back filled to provide positive drainage away from the house. I was talking to another superintendent about the problem as we were looking out of the front window. We spotted a small pile of mason's sand. While the dirt was frozen in clumps, the sand was not frozen. Sand doesn't freeze because water drains from it. I back filled the offending corner with the sand and got the final inspection.

Other items the "punch out carpenter" checked and fixed included the adjustment of doors, bi-folds, shelving, moldings and locks. He also checked for missing or broken parts. If things are found to be deficient during the walk-through, this same "punch out carpenter" will make the corrections and adjustments.

The biggest complaint about new homes have to do with drywall, paint and caulk. These items are easy to fix and are the least important part of your house. Most of the flaws seen in the walk-through will never be seen again once you've moved in. They typically are the nature of the beast and the state of the art. However, many customers go nuts when they look at their naked house and see these natural flaws. This is not to say that some unacceptable flaws are there and should be corrected. It is to say that there are thousands of them and all of these do not need to be corrected or are outside the norm.[38]

When a house is new and naked, these normal flaws are much more obvious. However, when they move their furniture in and put up drapes, these flaws are not seen at all. Most times the customers will see their folly and give up, usually after they have moved in and can no longer see the flaws. There is a reality of building and that is as people move into their homes, they scrape, mark and sometimes punch holes in their walls. They could use the benevolence of a good "punch out carpenter" to help them here. In cases where the customer did not go nuts during their walk-through, they stood a good chance of some help. Those that nit-picked and complained blew their chance.

Beyond the superfluous things like drywall and paint, the walk-through should be an opportunity to check for broken, missing, chipped or torn parts. As mentioned, moving in is tough on a house. Things get broken and marred. A common occurrence is that the vinyl floor gets torn, often by the refrigerator. If it is not noticed during the walk-through or when moving in, who would know who was responsible? It pays to look at the vinyl floor carefully. It is easy to repair and seldom requires that it be replaced.

Another common, yet overlooked problem, is screens and grills for the windows. Often these are not installed or have damage that is not noticed. If they are installed, one or more might be missing but not noticed. Missing shelving is common as is poor adjustment of vanity, kitchen cabinet and interior doors. The culprit is often that darn "punch out carpenter" who replaces a broken or missing

War Story

#38: One of the most frustrating things about doing a walk-through as a superintendent is dealing with the flaws in the paint and drywall. It is not a perfect product, yet it often takes center stage to the detriment of things that are much more important. I have done numerous walk-throughs where I allowed customers to mark on the wall (with pencil) where they wanted a flaw touched up. However, some customers would want to make hundreds of marks and often tried to. I have had some get on their hands and knees and crawl along the floor and feel the walls, looking for irregularities. They just didn't understand.

part for a house that closed last week and never quite gets it back to where he took it (your house). The carpenter will most likely replace your part from a house closing next week, thus adding to a continuing chain of events. Usually the last house sold in a neighborhood becomes a "hanger queen" with many missing parts.

While you should be vigilant in your inspection, you should also maintain a good attitude towards whoever is walking you through the house. This is not the time to throw your weight around or bad mouth the builder or the quality. You are ultimately responsible for the quality of the components of the house because you chose them. If you feel that the doors feel flimsy, you can rest assured that you could have chosen more expensive ones. If something is wrong, the builder wants to fix it and make you happy. If you abuse them, they will have little interest in doing more than the minimum. A builder is a good guy to have as a friend. You absolutely could use them in the future. Abuse them and you ruined what should have been a long-term, useful relationship. ■

37

Common New House Problems

Why is the House So Wet?

There is a lot of water in a new house. As it dries out (usually it takes about six months), you will be hearing occasional "pops" and "moans" and see cracks and chips. What is wet? The wood, though kiln dried, still has some moisture in it. The concrete is also quite wet.

If you recall, concrete reaches its maximum hardness or curing time after 28 days. While most of the concrete in the house has been in place longer than that, many items, like the front porch stoop, sidewalks and driveways are often less than 28 days old when you move in. While the mortar in block and brick joints have been in place for quite awhile, these joints are still drying when the house is new. The drywall and the paint in the house is also very wet and it will take days and months for the moisture in them to stabilize.

Another item you might find wet will be the block walls in the basement. This will be more obvious if the house wasn't finish graded and landscaped until the end of the building cycle. Finish grading and landscaping sheds water away from a house. If this was one of the last things done, chances are that the basement walls will be wet for awhile.

One of the things you might see is movement in the drywall, usually slight cracking or bulges in the perimeter walls What is happening is that the nails are moving outward. This is a natural occurrence and easy to fix. It does not mean your house is falling down nor does it mean that your builder did a bad job. It mostly means that you built your house on planet earth with the normal technology of the day.

What's This Thing Called Gravity?

The greatest force on your house is gravity. You built your house on footings that aren't going anywhere. The concrete or block walls aren't going anywhere either. However, after that point, your house is made of soft woods which are

In This Chapter . . .

▲ What is naturally going to happen

▲ What to be concerned about

▲ Common causes of a wet basement

connected to each other with little pieces of wire (nails) that respond to the effects of gravity. The wood is rarely perfectly cut or the nails perfectly set. They are going to move on you, usually downward. After the house moves down, forces will occur on your house that will cause cracks, splits and outward thrusts. This movement is in fractions of an inch. If you are prone to worry, you might think your house is falling down. Chances are real good that this is not going to happen. If your house is really falling down, you'll know soon enough, usually within the first year.

The natural drying out of the materials and the effects of gravity, cause a number of things to happen in a new home. The most common occurrence is what is called a "nail pop." What you will see is a dimple in the drywall, often several in a vertical row. You might not make the connection, but they will be in a stud and often in an outside wall. What is happening is that the nail that was used to attach the drywall to the stud is coming out. Some force, whether gravity or the natural drying of the materials, is forcing it out. This is in no way cause for alarm. In fact, it if doesn't occur, you are in danger of losing your home to the national building museum for being the first perfect home. It is going to happen and it is normal.

The second common thing to occur in a new home is an audible noise or "popping". This you probably won't see. What is happening is that some part of your house, probably the piece that it was cut a quarter inch short and was held together with a nail, finally bought into the "gravity" thing and settled into its rightful place. This connection was unnatural from the start and was headed that way anyway. It signaled its final movement with a bang. This too is usually not a problem.

The third thing you are probably going to notice is cracks here and there. They too are usually not a problem, although cracks in concrete can be frustrating to you. As a rule of thumb, a crack in concrete that is less than one-quarter inch wide and/or one quarter-inch vertically are considered normal and often unavoidable. If this spec would bother you, use a different material as this cracking is possible in any home (although it does not occur in every case).

Another area you might see a crack is in anything that has been caulked. This too is common and is usually the result of the normal effects of gravity rather than defective caulk or poor workmanship. It could also be the result of a cheaper grade of caulk drying too fast. Usually the crack is self-limiting, which means it probably will not get any wider.

The fourth thing you will probably notice occurs only with homes with a basement. This is when you might notice that the block wall will get damp after a period of continuous rain. This usually does not mean that you have a cracked basement wall or that the builder did something wrong. What this probably means is one or both of two things. Either your gutters are stopped up or the dirt has settled around your house. Chances are that both have occurred, with one making the other worse. The reason the gutters have clogged up is most probably because you have leaves in them.

If you were always a renter, welcome to the world of a homeowner. This problem is never going away. Buy a ladder and clean them out. On the first go around you might also see where your roofer didn't do you any favors by leaving some of his debris, contributing to the clogs.

The second cause is that the dirt has settled around your house. This is a natural, gravity caused event and is quite normal. When your house was built, the excavation was probably at least two feet larger that the foundation. This was to give the mason room to build the walls. Good for him, bad for you because this over dig is going to settle, often several times until it stabilizes.

A Bop With a Hammer

So, you have a few problems. What do you do? Sometimes all you need is a bop with a hammer. Drywall nail pops are fixed this way. You simply knock the dimple with a hammer and then spackle over the dent with some "mud," let it dry, sand and touch it up with paint. A no-brainer. If you haven't built your house yet and know that this will still irritate you, specing the drywall to be "glued and screwed" will generally reduce this from happening. However, it is normal and easy to fix.

Sometimes a door comes out of square and doesn't close properly. The bolt might scrape the keeper or daylight shows through around the edges. Here again a bop with a hammer in the right place (at the hinge) will get the door back into square. Often another nail or screw is necessary to hold it in place as the "bop" might be a temporary fix.

If the concrete has a crack in it and it is within the one-quarter inch tolerance, you need to learn to live with in. There is no repair.

If the concrete has a crack in it and it is within the one-quarter inch tolerance, you need to learn to live with in. There is no repair. Filling the hole will not work as the concrete will still be moving and force the patch back out, which looks as bad as doing nothing. If you can't stand it, either don't use concrete in the first place or tear it out and hope for a better batch of concrete. You could get lucky, but it is an expensive fix.

If the caulk cracks, you can just re-caulk it. You might want to remove what is there first rather than caulk over it. If you know that you do not want to do this again anytime soon, get the best caulk you can find. They come in different grades, with the more expensive grade being longer lasting and more resilient. With many caulks, the better grades have added the ingredient silicone. Sometimes what was used to begin with might have been a lower quality grade. Here again, if you don't want to deal with this problem at all, make sure that the contract spells out the grade or type of caulk used. Talk to you painter. They will know what is best.

If the basement leaks, a gutter guard might be useful as part of the initial contract or as a retrofit. You can spec a gutter that has a gutter guard built in if you know that you don't want to deal with this at all. The solution to the ground settling around the foundation is to add more dirt every three to six months until it stops settling. You can stock pile the dirt in a non-conspicuous place in conjunction with landscaping or just buy some as you need it. This, again, is a common problem and common solution. You can solve over 90 percent of most problem basements by cleaning out the gutters and raising the grade around the basement. ■

SUGGESTED READING

Here's some books that you might find interesting:

The Visual Handbook of Building and Remodeling, Charles Wing, Rodale Press, Emmaus, PA.

Well illustrated with lots of pictures of good stuff — easy to understand.

A Field Guide to American Houses, Virginia and Lee McAlester, Alfred A. Knopf, New York, NY.

A well researched book if you are interested in a detailed account of architecture — I use it to determine styles and time periods of homes and to get the details right. It's not just a textbook, but also a wonderful read. You can also use this book to conduct an architectural tour of your own home town.

House Styles at A Glance, Maurie Van Buren, Longstreet Press, Atlanta, GA.

Maurie is a historic preservation consultant and has done a wonderful job in her book of quickly and easily identifying the styles of homes. You can write her at 40 Clarendon Ave, Avondale Estates, GA 30002, or use e-mail at mvanb@mindspring.com.

Architectural Graphic Standards, Charles G. Ramsey and Harold R. Sleeper, John Wiley & Sons, New York, NY.

An amazing architect's standard reference — it shows everything you could ever imagine about architecture. I used it to design parking lots and to build an Olympic-sized soccer complex. New, it cost over $175 — best to look at in the library or buy an older/used edition from a college or at a yard sale (like I did for $10.00!). You'll treasure this book.

Your local residential building code book

Check with your local technical college book store or with your state office. These change every year but will help you verify how the codes apply to your home where you are building. It can be very dry reading but important to know if you're building your home yourself. If you do something wrong (and fail an inspection), you can look it up in the code book.

National Construction Estimator, Craftsman Book Company, Carlsbad, CA 92018. Call (800)-829-8123 to order direct from the publisher.

A great book that will tell you how much your home should cost to build — allows for variations in quality levels and regional cost differences. Updated annually, this book breaks down costs into materials and labor. Surprisingly accurate, it will put you in the ballpark for estimating the cost of your new home.

The Holy Bible, various authors.

Covers building codes, suggested building materials (especially foundations) and how to work with subcontractors and vendors (WWJD). Newer section written about a world famous carpenter. Chapters on Psalms, Proverbs, and the Gospels especially beneficial when things don't go right.

INDEX